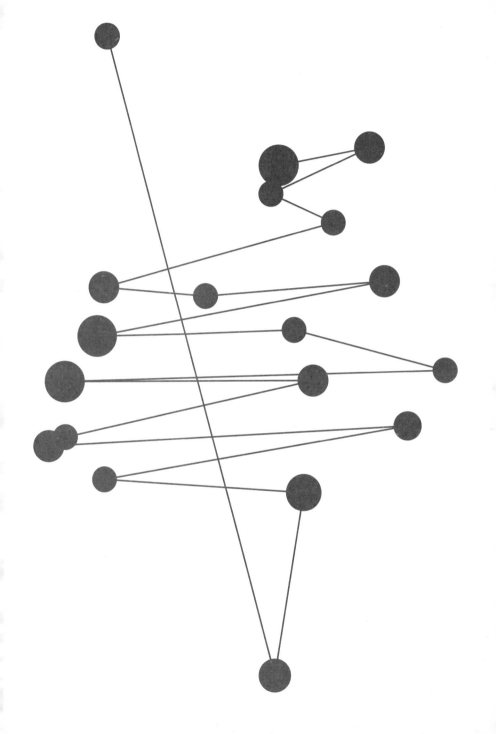

Edited by D&AD

The Copy Book.

How some of the best advertising writers in the world write their advertising.

TASCHEN

Bibliotheca Universalis

Contents

Preface

Welcome to the third edition of the *Copy Book* — D&AD's best-ever-selling publication — brought to you in a revised, more accessible size as part of TASCHEN's *Bibliotheca Universalis* collection, created to make great content more widely available.

Together we've updated it with the addition of five brilliant new writers, to inspire you to seek excellence in your own work.

Inspiration is what D&AD is about — stimulating, inspiring and enabling creative excellence in a world that, sadly, increasingly often defaults to the mediocre or worse. Why do we bother? Because the good stuff invariably creates better outcomes than the bad stuff — commercially, socially, culturally, environmentally, politically. And if a thing is worth doing, it is surely worth doing well.

The world has changed almost out of recognition in the 23 years since the first *Copy Book* saw the light of day. The design and advertising environment we inhabit is fractured, fragmented, automated, dominated by social media and other technologies. The new platforms available to us as designers and communicators devour content at an unprecedented volume. And sometimes the creators of that content seem not to care greatly about the quality of what they're writing and making.

But words — well-crafted, well-written, thoughtfully-composed words — that move, explain, sell, persuade, describe, have never been more important, nor at a greater premium. In a world of dross, the good stands out, jewel-like. It's how we make our work engaging, distinctive, successful. Great copy glitters.

D&AD's sees its role as 'stimulation not congratulation' and campaigns constantly for excellence. By buying this book — actually simply by *reading* it — you are joining us in a worthwhile fight — a war against mediocrity.

But perhaps most importantly enjoy it for what it is: the thoughts of 53 great writers and the secrets of their considerable craft. They have a lot to teach us; and it's never been so important that the lessons are learned and taken to heart.

Tim Lindsay
Chief Executive Officer, D&AD

David
Abbott

David Abbott started his career in 1960 as a copywriter in the advertising department of Kodak. In 1963, he moved to Mather & Crowther where he was made copy group head.

In 1965, he moved to DDB London as a copywriter. In 1966 he was transferred to DDB New York for nine months where he worked on Mobil and Volkswagen. In 1967, he became creative director of DDB London and just before his 30th birthday, managing director as well. In 1971, he left to start French Gold Abbott.

In 1977, he started Abbott Mead Vickers where he was chairman, and creative director. (And copywriter.) He retired from AMV in 1998.

He won many awards in his career and created many celebrated campaigns. In 2001, he was inducted into the One Show Creative Hall of Fame, the first Briton to receive this honour since David Ogilvy.

In 2010, he published his first novel, *The Upright Piano Player.*

I write with an Artline 200 Fine 0.4 Pentel — blue ink, never black. I generally work on A3 layout pads but will sometimes switch to an A4. Definitely low tech stuff.

I write with my office door open — more often than not I keep my jacket on and in defiance of my mother's instructions, my feet are usually on the table.

Whatever the size of the layout pad, I write body copy in column widths. This habit goes back to my days on the VW account in the Sixties. I knew how many words to the line were needed and how many lines to the ad. Writing in columns made it easier to get the word count right.

Alongside the column I jot down thoughts or phrases that come to mind before I need them. They stay there in the sidings until there's a place for them. I also write down in the margins all the clichés and purple bits that clutter my head. I find that only by writing them down do I exorcise them. If I simply try to forget them they keep coming back like spots on a teenage chin.

I rarely plan the shape of a piece of copy. By the time I come to write, the structure of the argument is somehow in my brain. I spend a lot of time fact-finding and I don't start writing until I have too much to say. I don't believe you can write fluent copy if you have to interrupt yourself with research. Dig first, then write.

Like many other copywriters, I read my copy out aloud as I write. It helps me check the rhythm of the line and ultimately the flow of the whole piece. I often adopt the appropriate accent or tone, though my general "reading-copy" voice is laughably mid-Atlantic (I read silently if there are other people in the room).

I am a fast writer and in a sense I am not interested in words. I don't own a Thesaurus, I don't do crosswords and my dictionary has pictures in it. Words, for me, are the servants of the argument and on the whole I like them to be plain, simple and familiar. I believe that I'm paid to be an advocate and though I get pleasure from the *bon mot*, the bon motivater thrills me more. Word-play is fine if it helps the cause but I use it sparingly, or not at all. This wasn't always the case; I used to pun for England.

When I'm working on concepts, I draw the shape of the ad space and write the headline (or scribble the picture) within its borders. It's odd but I can't judge an *Economist* headline until I've drawn a line around it. When I was younger I used big Pentels and large pads and swashbuckled my way to fertility. An ad a page. Now my would-be ads are much smaller and I might cover a page with six or seven thoughts — though sometimes when I'm stuck I go back to the big pad and the big pen. A change in procedure is often a good idea when you're not getting one. I've been writing copy since 1960 and by now I'm comfortable with the job. I don't panic and I know that the best thing for me to do when tired or thwarted is to walk away from the ad and do something else. The job still surprises me and for every easy problem, there's a stubborn sister. I might rework a headline 50 or 60 times to get the thought and balance exactly right. If I think there's an ad in there somewhere, I nag at it until it comes out. I'm often surprised how quickly time passes when I'm doing this. I look up and discover that I've been fiddling with the words for three hours.

Agency life rarely allows for this level of concentration so I also write copy at home, late at night, or I'll book a hotel room and work from there. (This piece, for example, is being written at the kitchen table.) I couldn't work in an open-plan creative department, but I'm sure there are brilliant copywriters who do. Great copy has been written in cafés, on trains, on beaches, on planes, in cars — even occasionally at a desk. How you do it is less important than what you do.

I've never been much of a theoriser about copywriting, but here are five things that I think are more or less true:

1. Put yourself into your work. Use your life to animate your copy. If something moves you, chances are, it will touch someone else, too.

2. Think visually. Ask someone to describe a spiral staircase and they'll use their hands as well as words. Sometimes the best copy is no copy.

3. If you believe that facts persuade (as I do), you'd better learn how to write a list so that it doesn't read like a list.

4. Confession is good for the soul and for copy, too. Bill Bernbach used to say "a small admission gains a large acceptance". I still think he was right.

5. Don't be boring.

Opposite
Client: Volkswagen
Agency: DDB London
Year: 1969

Next spread
Client: Chivas Regal
Agency: AMV
Year: 1980

This ad is about Chivas Regal but it's also about me and my father. (I really did have a red Rudge bicycle). It's a risky ad and, for some people, it's sentimental but I know others who say that it vividly echoes their own experience. Incidentally, if you try to write a headline for this ad, you'll discover why it doesn't have one.

If he can make it, so can Volkswagen.

No disrespect intended, Mr. Feldman.

But no-one would ever mistake you for Gregory Peck. Yet you've made it right to the top.

On talent.

And that's kind of reassuring when you make a car that looks like ours.

The Volkswagen isn't pretty, Mr. Feldman. But it's got talent.

It has an air-cooled engine that can't boil over in the summer.

Or freeze up in the winter.

It's the kind of engine that can go on and on and on.

We know one person who went right on for 248,000 miles.

And for a little car it's got a great talent for fitting people in.

There's more headroom than you'd expect. (Over 37½" from seat to roof.)

If you were 6' 7" Mr. Feldman you still wouldn't hit the roof.

And because there's no engine in the front, there's room to stretch your legs in the front.

We've even got a space behind the back seat where you can sleep a baby. In a carrycot.

So you see, Mr. Feldman, looks aren't everything are they?

VOLKSWAGEN MOTORS LIMITED VOLKSWAGEN HOUSE PURLEY SURREY TELEPHONE: 01-668 4100

Because I've known you all my life.

Because a red Rudge bicycle once made me the happiest boy on the street.

Because you let me play cricket on the lawn.

Because you used to dance in the kitchen with a tea-towel round your waist.

Because your cheque book was always busy on my behalf.

Because our house was always full of books and laughter.

Because of countless Saturday mornings you gave up to watch a small boy play rugby.

Because you never expected too much of me or let me get away with too little.

Because of all the nights you sat working at your desk while I lay sleeping in my bed.

Because you never embarrassed me by talking about the birds and the bees.

Because I know there's a faded newspaper clipping in your wallet about my scholarship.

Because you always made me polish the heels of my shoes as brightly as the toes.

Because you've remembered my birthday 38 times out of 38.

Because you still hug me when we meet.

Because you still buy my mother flowers.

Because you've more than your fair share of grey hairs and I know who helped put them there.

Because you're a marvellous grandfather.

Because you made my wife feel one of the family.

Because you wanted to go to McDonalds the last time I bought you lunch.

Because you've always been there when I've needed you.

Because you let me make my own mistakes and never once said "I told you so."

Because you still pretend you only need glasses for reading.

Because I don't say thank you as often as I should.

Because it's Father's Day.

Because if you don't deserve Chivas Regal, who does?

Client: Chivas Regal
Agency: AMV
Year: 1979

Nice words and a pack
shot. When the idea is this
strong, keep it simple.

Opposite
Client: DDB
Agency: DDB
Year: 1967

I'm a writer at Doyle Dane Bernbach.
We're looking for two new account men.
This is what I think they should know about the job.

When they asked me to write this recruitment ad I said I was too busy.

'Just say we need two account men and leave it at that.'

Then I got to thinking. Chances are it won't be long before I'm working with one of the new people.

It could make both our jobs a little easier if he understood the place before he came.

And it's not always easy for an account man to see how he'll fit in here.

Do creative people really run the show?

Is it true the account men are just messenger boys?

Yes. Creative people do run the show. But they're not all art directors and writers.

No. The account men aren't messenger boys.

At DDB, they represent the agency's philosophy much more closely than at other agencies.

So the first thing they have to do is understand it. And believe in it.

Roughly, it goes like this:

To be perfectly honest with the client. To give him the work we think he should have, provided it fits his goal.

To be the experts in how to present the product to the public. Not to wonder what the client's wife is going to say about the advertising.

To have an honest viewpoint.

Hardly the work of a messenger boy.

Inside the agency, the account man has to work very closely with the likes of me.

I'll expect him to know everything about the product, its competition and the client's aims.

I'll expect him to give me all the information I need. I think that's reasonable.

I'll expect him to give me all the time I need. Sometimes that's unreasonable.

I'll expect him to believe in Doyle Dane. And to sell my work with conviction.

In return, he can expect an awful lot of the creative people.

He shouldn't put up with dull, ordinary work. Ever.

He should expect an awareness of the client's problems.

Including those of timing.

He should demand involvement.

There's a lot more I can't think of right now. But the general picture is this - there's no rule book at DDB so the account man stands or falls on his own ability.

Just like the rest of us.

If you're still interested, there are a couple of things I've been asked to tell you.

The people we're looking for will have had account management responsibilities. We don't want trainees.

They'll probably be between 25 and 30 years of age.

And it would help if they'd had two-three years experience on food or toiletries brands.

We need them because we've put on a lot of new business in the last couple of months. And we'll pay very well.

Please send a full resumé to Bill Wardell our Director of Account Services. As soon as possible.

I look forward to working with you.

Doyle Dane Bernbach Ltd.,
62/64 Baker Street, London, W.1.

"I never read The Economist."

Management trainee. Aged 42.

Client: The Economist
Agency: AMV
Year: 1989

The Economist campaign not only has its own look, it has its own tone of voice. What is potentially a banal positioning ("read this and be successful") is made acceptable and convincing by wit and charm. Directness has its place in advertising but so do subtlety and obliqueness. Things you can't say literally can often be said laterally.

IF THE WELDING ISN'T STRONG ENOU

That's me, lying rather nervously under the new Volvo 740.

For years I've been writing in advertisements that each spot weld in a Volvo is strong enough to support the weight of the entire car.

Someone decided I should put my body where my mouth is. So we suspended the car and I crawled underneath.

Of course the Volvo lived up to its reputation and I lived to tell the tale.

But the real point of the story is this; the Volvo 740 may

NEW VOLVO 740 RANGE STARTS AT £9,249. 2·3 LITRE ENGINES. CARBURETTOR AND INJECTION VERSIONS AVAILABLE. PRICES INCLUDE CAR TAX AND VAT (DELIVERY AND NUMBER PLATES EXTRA). CORRE

, THE CAR WILL FALL ON THE WRITER.

ave a different body shape, a fast and frugal new engine, a
ew interior and a new suspension system, but in one respect
's just like the Volvos of yore.

It's so well built you can bet your life on it.

I know. I just did.

To: Volvo, Springfield House, Mill Ave, Bristol BS1 4SA. Please
send me details.

Mr/Mrs/Miss

Address

Postcode **THE NEW VOLVO 740. FROM £9249.**

Opposite
Client: Sainsbury's
Agency: AMV BBDO
Year: 1992

Next spread
Client: Sainsbury's
Agency: AMV
Year: 1990

Pages 024–025
Client: RSPCA
Agency: AMV
Year: 1989

Oh, the joy of it! On the afternoon before Budget Day, the *Evening Standard* prints a photograph of the Chancellor of the Exchequer in Downing Street. Some of his papers are stuffed into a Sainsbury's bag. Wonder of wonders, the slogan is clearly visible. I write a line and we move fast to produce an ad — the client says yes and we run the ad on Budget Day and I fall in love again with this crazy, wonderful business.

I like headlines that draw the reader into the ad — a question is an obvious way to do it. In this case the question is partly answered by a witty visual and the copy does the rest. I was tempted to use "uncannily like fresh fruit" as the headline but resisted. However, you'll often read ads where the body copy contains a better headline than the one the writer chose. Remember to check your copy for buried treasure.

No surprises so far.

Guess what Sainsbury's new

In its own little way our new canned
grapefruit is something of a milestone.

It's vacuum-packed. (As far as we know,
the first on sale in Britain.)

The outcome is grapefruit that tastes
uncannily like the fresh fruit.

But taste isn't the only advantage. With
vacuum-packing, we're able to put much more

canned grapefruit tastes like?

grapefruit into the can.

On average, 25% more fruit than with traditional canning methods.

You can buy our new 'flavour seal' grape-

fruit, unsweetened in pure juice or in a syrup.

Either way you get more flavour and more fruit.

Good food costs less at Sainsbury's.

When the Government killed the dog licence they left us to kill the dogs.

One thousand dogs are killed in Britain every day.

For the most part, healthy dogs and puppies with years of life left in them.

The killings take place at local vets, in RSPCA centres and other animal charities throughout the country.

The dogs are given an overdose of anaesthetic and die within seconds.

A van makes regular collections and the dead dogs are taken to the local incinerator.

It doesn't take long to turn a Jock, Spot or Sandy into a small pile of ashes.

This daily slaughter is strange work for a society founded to prevent cruelty to animals.

We hate the killing.

We are sick of doing the Government's dirty work behind closed doors.

We want you to help us force through a dog registration scheme.

The dogs we kill are homeless dogs. Unwanted, or strays left to roam the streets and parks, often in packs.

There are at least 500,000 of them out there right now.

Left to themselves, the figure would be close to 4 million in ten years' time.

Homeless dogs cause road accidents, attack livestock and foul our parks and pavements.

And yet we can't blame the dogs, for we live in a society that makes it more difficult to own a television than a living, breathing creature.

There is no licence required. The Government abolished the licence last year and we are now seeing the consequences.

The RSPCA want to see a dog registration scheme introduced.

And so it seems do most of you. In a recent poll, 92% of you said "yes" to registration.

If there was a registration fee it would encourage responsible dog-ownership.

Each dog could be identified with a number so that its owner could be traced and held responsible for the dog's actions.

The money raised would finance a national dog warden scheme, more efficient clean-up operations and more education for dog-owners.

These measures seem so sensible you wonder why they haven't been tried before.

Well, many of them have.

Sweden, America, Germany, Australia, Russia, France and Ireland all have a more enlightened policy than Britain.

Help us catch up.

Write to your MP and press for dog registration.

If you're not sure how to go about it, call free on 0800 400478 and we'll give you an action-pack and add your name to our petition.

Do it now, for every day that goes by sees another 1,000 dogs put down.

And what kind of society kills healthy dogs? **RSPCA**

Registration, not extermination.

Nick Asbury

Nick Asbury is a British writer for branding and design. Originally from Manchester, he started out selling ad space and got his first writing job at a recruitment advertising agency. For five years, he co-ran London creative agency Other.

Since 2002, Nick has been a roving writer for design companies and direct clients. In 2008, he became one half of Asbury & Asbury, whose projects include Pentone (the written equivalent of Pantone), Corpoetics (corporate copy rearranged into verse) and Realtime Notes (Instagram poems responding to current events).

Nick is co-author of *A Smile in the Mind* (Phaidon 2016) and has written for the *Guardian, McSweeney's* and *Creative Review*. After 15 years in London, he moved back north in 2009, mainly as a way to get out of meetings.

Copywriting isn't what it used to be.

Professionally speaking, I grew up in the shadow of the greats in this book — people trained in the tradition of classic long copy advertising. It's a tradition with roots in door-to-door salesmanship and direct mail — copy as an extended product sales pitch, weaving together features and benefits with wit and charm, and carrying readers skilfully towards the killer close.

I have one foot in that tradition too — starting out in telesales, then working for years in advertising and direct response charity copywriting, where every sentence has to earn its keep. For as long as companies want to sell things, it will always be a relevant tradition. Brands like Apple could learn a lot from old Volkswagen ads.

But my other foot has been in the less well-defined world of 'writing for design' — something that has always been around, but has become more visible in the last 20 years. People lament the passing of the great long copy era in advertising, but it's more of a migration. Long copy has shifted to packaging, websites, brand narratives, tone of voice guides and copy-led identity schemes.

There are downsides to that shift. Instead of sharply honed sales pitches, most packaging copy consists of loose screeds of chattiness, designed to convey a personality more than a message. I suspect David Abbott would not have approved.

The upside is that copywriters are getting to do more things. I've been involved in projects where the writing isn't marketing the thing — it is the thing. Sideways Dictionary was a project with Jigsaw and the *Washington Post*, creating an online tool that explains technology using analogies instead of straight definitions. Not because analogies do the whole job, but because they provide an entry point and a memorable hook that IT people can use in presentations and reports. Writing and lateral thinking as a public resource.

Another positive change — lower costs of production mean writers are more able to produce their own projects, instead of waiting for a brief. Perpetual Disappointments Diary started out as an idea to produce an appointments diary with a series of disappointing twists. It contains a series of demotivational proverbs, reminders of Notable Deaths, and a contacts section for People Who Never Call. As a copywriter, you're often taking familiar things and giving them a twist — this was born of the same habit of thinking.

Writers are routinely getting involved in the creation of brands. Most of my work is in collaboration with design companies, often at the stage when they're branding or rebranding a company. I get to write verbal blueprints — strategic thinking combined with the basis of a personality — that become the brief for the visual identity and the basis for the whole brand. That's an interesting thing to do, like tinkering under the bonnet of a brand.

Copywriters have always been a combination of the huckster and the poet. But the poet has been given more of a free rein in recent years. I get to write weird stuff — a cut-up poem for a paper company, a 1000-word text-only mailer for a photographer, a book of corporate poetry called *Corpoetics*. Some would say we're meant to be in the business of selling, not creating art. But art sells — ask Damien Hirst. Brands look to writers to bring the weirdness and writers should revel in that.

That will be even more the case as writers start giving voice to interfaces, turning brands into real characters rather than the notional, disembodied ones that have existed in the past. It's an interesting time to be a writer because things are shifting — there's new territory to explore and claim before anyone else does.

But most of the time writing is the same as it ever was. When I worked on a campaign for Cambridge University with design company Johnson Banks (a company led by a great verbal and visual thinker), it was based on the idea of an open letter from Cambridge to the world, which in turn sparked a series of imaginary letters from alumni — from Isaac Newton to Laura Bates. It's an idea that could have been done any time in the last century, relying on verbal wit more than any particular technology or trend.

There's good and bad in the way copy has developed. Sometimes it does feel like the great skills of the past have been lost. You look at all the vague chat and vapid brand lines and despair. But there has always been bad copy around — it's what makes the good stuff look good. If they were writing now, I suspect David Abbott and Margaret Fishback (look her up) would be having fun. They might even enjoy the fact that copywriting isn't what it used to be.

Opposite and next spread
Client: Cambridge
University Development
and Alumni Relations
Design: Johnson Banks
Writers: Nick Asbury,
Michael Johnson
Year: 2015

A major fundraising
campaign devised by
Johnson Banks to
celebrate Cambridge's
impact on the world, in
the form of an ongoing
open correspondence.

To: Humans
cc: Apes
So I've been thinking about these finches.

Yours, Darwin

Charles Darwin (Christ's College 1827), naturalist and author of *On the Origin of Species*
cam.ac.uk/YoursCambridge

Dear Sir/Madam,

Why do Sir and Madam always come in that order?

Yours,
Laura

Cookie—

It's like a dog relieving itself to mark its territory. And you're the lamppost.

Sideways Dictionary

One-Time Password—

It's like snowflakes. Each one unique and each lasting only a short time.

Sideways Dictionary

Clients: Jigsaw, Washington Post
Design: Google Creative Lab London, Hello Monday
Year: 2017

Sideways Dictionary is an online toolkit of over 300 analogies to shed light on technological terms, now open to public contributions. The analogies have been embedded into the *Washington Post* website and are available as a Chrome extension.

Dark Web—

It's like the dark side of the moon. The bright side (the internet) is visible to everyone – all you have to do is look up. To access the dark side, you need specialist software (a rocket).

Sideways Dictionary

Zero-day—

It's like realizing you've left your King exposed in chess. You stay quiet, hope your opponent hasn't noticed, and start working on a defense. In the worst case scenario, your opponent noticed five moves ago and has been toying with you ever since. Checkmate.

Sideways Dictionary

Useful Phrases
English, French, German, Spanish and Mandarin

I have lost my passport

F: J'ai perdu mon passeport

G: Ich habe meinen Pass verloren

S: He perdido el pasaporte

M: 我丢了护照

I am on the wrong plane

F: Je me suis trompé d'avion

G: Ich bin im falschen Flugzeug

S: Me he equivocado de avión

M: 我上错了飞机

I have destroyed my hire car

F: J'ai accidenté ma voiture de location

G: Ich habe mein Mietauto kaputt gefahren

S: He estrellado el coche de alquiler

M: 我毁掉了租来的车子

I do not have health insurance

F: Je n'ai pas d'assurance maladie

G: Ich habe keine Krankenversicherung

S: No tengo seguro médico

M: 我没有医疗保险

When will the construction work finish?

F: Quand est-ce que les travaux de construction seront-ils finis?

G: Wann sind die Bauarbeiten vorbei?

S: ¿Cuando acabarán las obras?

M: 这工程什么时候竣工?

Can I book an alarm call for midday?

F: Puis-je vous demander de me reveiller à midi?

G: Kann ich bitte einen Weckanruf für mittags buchen?

S: Necesito que me despierten a mediodía

M: 我想订一个中午叫起服务?

A table for one, please

F: Une table pour une personne, s'il vous plaît

G: Einen Tisch für eine Person, bitte

S: Mesa para uno, por favor

M: 一位

What meat is this?

F: Quel type de viande est-ce?

G: Was für ein Fleisch is das?

S: ¿De qué es esta carne?

M: 这是什么肉?

Do you have any very cheap wine?

F: Avez-vous un vin vraiment bon marché?

G: Haben Sie irgendeinen sehr billigen Wein?

S: ¿Tienen algún vino barato?

M: 有没有便宜的酒

Same again, please

F: La même chose, s'il vous plaît

G: Das Gleiche nochmal bitte

S: Más de lo mismo, por favor

M: 再来一样的，谢谢

I am sorry I spilt your drink

F: Excusez-moi d'avoir renversé votre boisson

G: Tut mir leid, dass ich Ihr Getränk verschüttet habe

S: Siento haberle tirado la bebida

M: 对不起我打翻了你的杯子

Anywhere. Just drive.

F: N'importe où. Vous n'avez qu'à conduire.

G: Egal wohin. Fahren Sie einfach.

S: A donde sea. Limítese a conducir.

M: 开车 - 去哪儿都好

If a tree falls in the woods and
no one is there to hear it, does
that remind you of your life?

If ignorance is bliss,
why are you so sad?

Client: Asbury & Asbury
Agency: Asbury & Asbury
Year: 2013–2017

An appointments diary
with a series of disappointing twists, including useful
travel phrases, weekly
demotivational proverbs,
and blank pages for point-
less doodles. Available
from Pan Macmillan and
Chronicle Books.

Tony Barry

Tony Barry has worked as a writer at some of the best agencies in the UK. Including Simons Palmer, Leagas Delaney, Wieden+ Kennedy and Lowe, where he was made joint creative director in 2005.

His work for clients such as Nike, Whiskas, Heineken, British Airways and Tesco has won many awards including One Show, D&AD Pencils, British Television Golds and two Cannes Gold Lions.

In 2008 Tony started directing through Academy Films. He is currently represented by Knucklehead.

I can only imagine D&AD got a bit desperate.

You know.

So-and-so was on holiday, what's-her-name was too busy or maybe thingamy jig had simply passed away.

Because, quite frankly, I have no idea what I'm doing here.

(A sentiment shared by my ex-wife who practically spat her coffee out when I told her.)

You see, like a lot of the other contributors in this book I've always hated writing copy.

But unlike the others I've actually gone out of my way to avoid doing it.

Often in quite weaselley and disingenuous ways.

"Oh… we don't need any copy."

"What? And spoil the simplicity of the layout?"

"My hands hurt. Can't someone else do it?"

A derisory approach plainly evident in my selection of ads.

(And here I do have some advice: always, always keep copies of your work. I've felt like JR Hartley trying to track this lot down.)

A few pithy headlines, some "interesting" visuals captioned with the odd line or two.

But a distinct lack of copy. So when it comes to pearls of wisdom on the art of copywriting, I'm at a slight disadvantage.

Hand on heart I can only suggest you turn instead to the proper writers in this book.

There's plenty of advice I wish I'd read when I was a writer.

Or failing that, offer up my solution to the blank page when all excuses fail.

Marry a writer and get them to write it for you.

It's like you
became invisible
and instead
of hanging around
changing rooms
giggling,
you sneaked into
one of our
top level meetings.

www.mlhsbc.co.uk

It's like
an online investing,
banking and
trading service that
gives you
unprecedented
access to the
financial intelligence
institutional
investors rely on.

It's like that
because it is that.

Merrill Lynch HSBC

invest with intelligence

SHOCKING ISN'T IT? YOU PROBABLY DO IT EVERY DAY.

IN THE AVERAGE BOTTLE OF SQUASH, THERE'S OVER ½LB OF SUGAR. LOOK AFTER THEIR TEETH. LOOK FOR SUGAR FREE.

DON'T LET THE ROT SET IN. CUT DOWN ON THE SUGAR.
FOR MORE INFORMATION CONTACT YOUR HEALTH VISITOR OR DENTIST.

MOST FIZZY DRINKS CONTAIN 6 TEASPOONS OF SUGAR.

THE FEWER SUGARY DRINKS YOUR KID HAS, THE LESS CHANCE OF THE ROT SETTING IN.
FOR MORE ADVICE CONTACT YOUR HEALTH VISITOR OR DENTIST.

Above and top
Client: Health Education
Authority
Agency: Leagas Shafron
Art Director: Graham
Cappi
Year: 1990

Opposite
Client: Merrill Lynch
Agency: Lowe
Art Director: Damon
Collins
Year: 2002

Next spread
Client: Olympus
Agency: Lowe
Art Director: Steve Dunn
Year: 1998

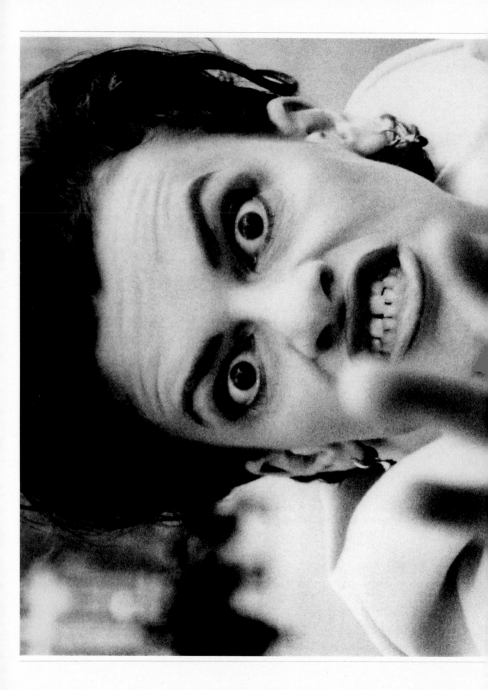

"Take one more shot of me and I'm going to cross that street, jump over that fence, run through that wood, swim that river, climb to the top of that mountain and ram that camera right down your throat."

Whoever said the camera never lies was, to put it bluntly, lying. And there's no bigger liar than the Olympus Superzoom.

Its 35-120mm lens tells the massive whopper that you're right in the thick of the action when you're actually a safe distance away.

And when, like the charming Ms Bernhard here, your subject is more likely to respond with something stronger than "cheese" you'll find the Superzoom's other features come in handy.

For instance, a high speed recording action captures any fast moves. And when that mouth starts, it really motors.

By re-distributing the camera's weight we have also improved its balance and minimised any camera-shake. So your hand

remains steady even if your pulse isn't.

But if you do get near enough to enjoy a filthy look, the flash makes sure it won't be coming from a pair of red eyes.

In fact, no less than four different flash modes adjust automatically as you get further and further away from your subject.

Throw in an ultra compact, light-weight and weatherproof design and we

think you'll agree it makes quite a neat little package. Which, to be frank, is more than you'll have if Ms Bernhard were ever to get hold of you.

OLYMPUS SUPERZOOM 120

Client: Nike
Agency: Simons Palmer
Denton Clemmow &
Johnson
Art Director: Andy McKay
Year: 1992

Client: Skol
Agency: Leagas Shafron
Art Director: Graham
Cappi
Year: 1992

John Bevins

John Bevins was eponymous creative director for 28 years of advertising agency John Bevins, which he founded in 1982. Independent to the end, the agency closed its doors while it still had major clients: "This way," the partners said, "the agency that has always been in control of its destiny can ensure that it does the right thing by everyone who works in the place (the newest employees started nearly ten years ago) — and ensure that each of us heads off with happy memories of working together and working with those great clients. To us, that's the ultimate success."

John has won many awards, and is in the Award Hall of Fame.

"If you don't enjoy writing it, no one will enjoy reading it" is one of my mantras. The very first ad I had published as a junior copywriter, I really enjoyed writing. Masterfully art-directed, it featured an overweight man plonked in an armchair with his cup of coffee beside him. Behind him was his wife — surreptitiously slipping a Sweetex artificial sweetener into his drink. LET HIM HAVE IT screamed the headline.

It appeared in the iconic *Australian Women's Weekly* around 1970. The copy chief, Arthur Hankin, came up to my desk beaming as he slapped down the magazine. Every ad in that ad-saturated tome had been ranked by the then-standard Starch research method.

Congratulations, Hank said, you've achieved the lowest scoring ad I've ever seen. It would be many years before I got the confidence to practise — properly — my risky mantra. But once I did, I started to learn a lot more things that supplemented that early, vital lesson on self-indulgence and relevance (and having bad ideas).

While I can't teach you to write copy, I can tell you what writing copy has taught me. You can have bad ideas but you don't, at least in my experience, "have" good ideas. You find good ideas. Maybe once in your career, a good idea will fall serendipitously into your lap. One did a long time ago for me with an ad for a strange new product called Microsoft Word. The encyclopaedia I was desperately grasping at fell open, revealing an idea that, once written up, got so much reaction it gave me the confidence to be a real copywriter.

To be that, I learned, you have to hunt down ideas. If I'd have tried to "have" an idea for New Zealand Tourism, slavishly following the flawed brief from the market researcher — "Australians think New Zealand is sickeningly wholesome, so make it a little bit wicked" — I'd never have gone to Queenstown and wandered aimlessly around the back streets looking for... what? I had no idea. But I found it, screwed to a gate. It inspired a campaign for a country you could never make even a tad wicked, a campaign that achieved in months the result the client had expected would take years.

On countless occasions, copywriting has taught me to respectfully ignore briefs — good and bad. Bankers Trust wanted a TV campaign but were intrigued by the suggestion of a long copy print campaign with no pictures at all. One that sought this response: Gee, even their advertising makes me richer, I wonder what would happen if I gave them some of my money.

I learned how important great clients are, individuals like BT's Sheenagh Stoke and Jan Mohr with open minds and open hearts, who would open their doors to a curious copywriter. Clients who would trust you to find their brand truth and then connect it in your own way to an essential human truth.

Copywriting has taught me that Theodore Levitt was right when he said work can enrich or impoverish. Especially so, our work — which enriches or impoverishes not just us, but society itself. When we borrow attention from total strangers or, worse, steal their precious time, we should strive to give something more valuable back. If we do that, wonderful things happen.

Copywriting has taught me that you don't write great ads, great ads write themselves. All you need to do is dig relentlessly for gems in the most unlikely of places. MBF had a screening mammogram clinic that they'd told no one about. It was worth investigating. Dr Joan Kroll, who ran the clinic, mentioned to me in passing a painting depicting breast cancer long before it was discovered by medicine. Professor Michael Baum, from the Rayne Institute in London, uses it in his lectures, she said. I called him up that night. Ah, *Bathsheba at her Toilet*, you know it of course, by Rembrandt? I didn't, but once I saw it, and learned its story, I knew we had an ad.

Copywriting has taught me that branding is nothing to do with a big logo, or the brand name in the headline, or even mentioning the brand early in the copy. What it's all about is there in the MBF ad. To my everlasting enlightenment that ad was also Starched. It too appeared in the ad-saturated *Women's Weekly*, some 20 years later after the shameful Sweetex ad (the publishers had brought back the research technique). 83% of all women noted the MBF ad. It got the second highest Read Most score and 69% correctly attributed it to the right brand. All without any conventional "branding techniques". Bookings to the clinic increased by over 800%.

Copywriting has taught me that data like that, as boring and baffling as data can be to copywriters, is priceless because our job is to get results for our clients.

It's taught me too these others mantras:

You never know what you're looking for until you find it, and you'll never find it if you know what you're looking for. (There's no process.)

Spell it out and it's out with the spell. (The reader's imagination is as important as yours.)

Product advertising explains the product to me. Brand advertising explains me to me. (Empathy.)

It's taught me that great clients and colleagues are crucial to great work, you never do it alone, and therefore you have to find the right agency.

Or start your own.

It has taught me that you have to be in the right mood to write.

(And that the way to get into the right mood to write is To Write.)

Opposite
Client: MBF
Agency: John Bevins
Year: 1993

800% increase in visits
to the clinic.

Next spread
Client: New Zealand
Tourism
Agency: John Bevins
Year: 1990

The campaign reversed
the decline in visitors from
New Zealand's primary
market — Australia.

Pages 052–053
Client: Bankers Trust
Australia Group
Agency: John Bevins
Year: 1994

"Even their advertising
makes me richer. I
wonder what would
happen if I gave them
some of my money."

Pages 054–055
Client: Microsoft Word
Agency: John Bevins
Year: 1985

Our fledgling agency did
the campaign for this
fledgling product. Wish
we'd taken a few shares
rather than a fee.

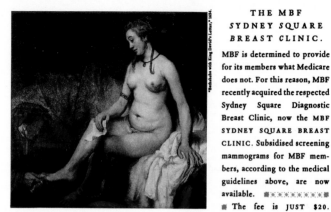
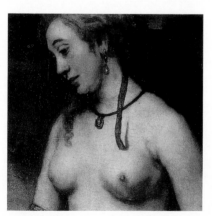

TRUST NEVER SLEEPS

A good example of this trust is honesty stalls.

Driving down the Central Otago Road to Queenstown, for instance, between Millers Flat and Roxburgh, you'll find lots of honesty stalls.

Indeed, one that's not so much an honesty stall as an honesty emporium. A huge shed packed with huge bags of walnuts, peaches, dried apricots, plums and apples — apples that still have their leaves on. *Leaves.* Instead of sticky, little labels. To buy something, you simply drop some money into a jar that's temptingly — nay, trustingly — full of notes and coins. You help yourself to the change, and then leave with your bounty. Feeling, well, enriched.

A RETREAT, NOT A RESORT.

Clearly, New Zealand is different.

A place where you can be reminded of what life should be

Cliff'll cook you dinner, but he expects you to catch it. (You'll never go hungry, mind you. The waters are rich with fish.)

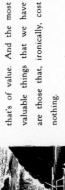

The islands of the sunset – Dusky Sound

OH, SOMETHING ELSE THAT WILL DAWN ON YOU IN NEW ZEALAND.

At last count, there were five thousand one hundred and twenty-eight million people on this little planet.

Most of them don't trust each other. A good place to ponder this peculiarity of "progress" is at Mt. Hikurangi, East Cape, as you watch the sun rise.

behind the rest of the world. It's actually ahead.

Not just several hours ahead. Several decades.

Real progress, it will dawn on you, is preserving what we have that's of value. And the most valuable things that we have are those that, ironically, cost nothing.

Until we lose them.

Trust. Clean air. Clean water. Stuff like that.

The North American Indians said that we don't inherit the earth from our parents, we borrow it from our children. It seems the only place anyone heard them was way down there in New Zealand.

Did you know, for instance, that the largest body of unpolluted water in the world is in New Zealand?

It's called Lake Taupo.

Lake Taupo is so unpolluted, the locals will encourage you to drink from its shores.

"Go on", they'll say, "have a sup."

at all – it's simple mathematics. But magic for most is more intriguing than maths, so let's think of it as magic.

Imagine you are 21 again. You decide, because someone explained this magic to you, to save $2,000 a year – until you turn just 30. Then you stop saving altogether and leave your nest egg alone until you turn 65. Let's say, for the sake of the exercise, that you earn an average return of 8% p.a. (after fees and taxes) which you always reinvest. Let's say, again for the sake of the exercise, that inflation is 0% (so your *real* return is a healthy 8%).

Now imagine an alternative scenario. Again, you are 21 but decide to do nothing about saving until you turn 31. At 31, you begin saving $2,000 a year and you continue to do so *every* year until you turn 65, again reinvesting the 8% p.a. average return. You figure you will more than make up for lost time by saving harder – i.e. for 35 years rather than 10 years.

Which is the better strategy?

The 10-year plan, in which you will have invested $20,000 will reap $428,378. The 35-year plan, in which you will have invested $70,000, will reap considerably

Age		
41 years old	$67,555	**$33,291**
42 years old	$72,959	**$37,954**
43 years old	$78,796	**$42,991**
44 years old	$85,100	**$48,430**
45 years old	$91,908	**$54,304**
46 years old	$99,260	**$60,649**
47 years old	$107,201	**$67,500**
48 years old	$115,777	**$74,900**
49 years old	$125,039	**$82,893**
50 years old	$135,042	**$91,524**
51 years old	$145,846	**$100,846**
52 years old	$157,514	**$110,914**
53 years old	$170,115	**$121,787**
54 years old	$183,724	**$133,530**
55 years old	$198,422	**$146,212**
56 years old	$214,295	**$159,909**
57 years old	$231,439	**$174,702**
58 years old	$249,954	**$190,678**
59 years old	$269,951	**$207,932**
60 years old	$291,547	**$226,566**
61 years old	$314,870	**$246,692**
62 years old	$340,060	**$268,427**
63 years old	$367,265	**$291,901**
64 years old	$396,646	**$317,253**
65 years old	$428,378	**$344,634**

The table shows the dramatic effect that compound interest can have on a

believes it's never too late to start saving yourself, you might like to investigate the BT Lifetime Trust.

BT will be happy to send you full details ...

Bankers Trust
Australia Group

For more information, see your financial adviser, call BT toll-free 008 022 555 or send this coupon to: Reply Paid No. 13, Bankers Trust Australia, PO Box H184 Australia Square, Sydney NSW 2000.

Mr/Mrs/Ms _____

Address _____

_____ P/code _____

122012PWA

Phone (BH) _____ (AH) _____

BT Financial Services Limited and member companies of the Bankers Trust Australia Group do not guarantee the repayment of capital or the future performance of the Trust.

A copy of the current BT Lifetime Trust Prospectus has been lodged and is dated 21 June 1993 and is available upon request from any BT office. Applications for investment may only be made on the form contained therein. BT Financial Services Limited is the Manager of the Trust. Performance returns are quoted in accordance with IFA Performance Standards.
John Bevins BT122012PWA

Nº 5 IN A SERIES 'INSIGHTS FOR INVESTORS', BROUGHT TO YOU BY BT FINANCIAL SERVICES.

Suspicious, critical or distrustful of people who invent words?

Suspicious, critical and distrustful were all invented by the one person. He also invented *lonely*, *assassination*, *baseless* and *bumps*. *Disgraceful?* He invented that, too.

The person's name: William Shakespeare.

In fact, as unbelievable as it may seem, *every* italicized word in this text was invented by Shakespeare.

There are some real surprises to come.

We owe *countless* (there's one already) words to the Wordsmith of Wordsmiths.

A Word Shakespeare Didn't Invent.

But there's one word we know for sure Shakespeare didn't invent, a word he would have loved to have worked with: Microsoft Word.

Had Microsoft Word been around in the you've written. Or create holes in text, insert thoughts, dig into other documents for facts, even access your own glossary – so instead of typing frequently-used words and phrases in their entirety, you do it with a couple of customized key strokes.

Of course, there is one potential problem. Just as a pneumatic drill requires a compressor to run it, Microsoft Word requires an equally-terrifying piece of equipment: A computer.

But please don't be intimidated.

The extraordinarily-popular IBM PC isn't extraordinarily-popular for nothing. And the remarkable Apple Macintosh is even easier to use (so easy, you can be writing within an hour).

Happily, there is a version of Microsoft Word for the IBM PC (and compatibles) and for the (like *denote*, which is another one of Shakespeare's words) it's easy. And you see it italicized on the screen. Similarly with **words in bold**. Or underlined. Or even superscripted and subscripted.

Significantly, with Microsoft Word you can store your information on tiny floppy disks instead of in tinny filing cabinets.

Nothing need ever again get *misplaced.*

Shakespeare could have stored all 38 plays and 154 sonnets on a few floppies. (With Microsoft Word he may well have increased his writing one hundred fold. But a handful of disks would still have stored his mountain of manuscripts.)

So, Microsoft Word not only facilitates better writing – it helps you organise your life's work.

We hope this brief *exposure* to word processing has enlightened you.

And the English language, even more richer.
(More richer? In Shakespeare's time "more richer" was a legitimate grammatical form.)

What is Microsoft Word? It's the word processor for those who love words.

You don't have to be a literary giant to use it.

And we certainly aren't suggesting that you try to out-Shakespeare Shakespeare† by becoming a *barefaced* inventor of words.

A *courtship* with Microsoft Word is best applied to the inspired arrangement of the 600,000 or so words already invented for the English language.

Microsoft Word simply allows you to write better. And write faster.

You can write, rapidly; inspired reports, crystal-clear correspondence, colourful memos, ads (this one was *drafted* and crafted with Microsoft Word – and when was the last time you read this far into an ad?). Even books and plays.

And if the term "word processor" turns you off, don't be *dishcartencd*. We hate "word processor" too. It's a misnomer.

Microsoft Word allows you to pro-duce anything-but processed words.

Think of Microsoft Word as a Pneumatic Drill.

Forget "word processor". Think of Microsoft Word as a tool.

A powerful pneumatic drill that rapidly gets you beneath the soft bitumen of superficiality and into deeper, harder, earthier communication. A tool with which you can instantly and effortlessly cut up and rearrange whatever

Why You Need a Computer.

Microsoft Word is the reason for anyone who works with words to "finally get a computer".

Not that you'll think of it as a computer.

With Microsoft Word, you can see your formatted work on the screen – basically as it will appear on the sheet of paper (this is especially so with the Macintosh).

You can forget complex formatting codes – which you'll forget anyway. With Microsoft Word, there is no need to *recall* anything.

If you want to *denote* something in italics

Program Disk   S-085
For IBM®
Personal Computers

034099. 200

† Shakespeare, incidentally, invented the expression "Out-Herod Herod" (Microsoft Word allows you to add interesting footnotes like this to your work – in type smaller than the main body of text).

threatening technology to some (thank goodness Shakespeare wasn't threatened by it).

We hope you are convinced that Microsoft Word could change your life – not, we admit, an entirely *impartial* suggestion. And we hope you have been as amazed by the possibilities as you were by the words Shakespeare invented.

For more information on Microsoft Word, send the Freepost coupon, call us on (02) 452 5088 or toll free on (008) 22 6850, or visit your nearest Microsoft store. But hurry. (Yes, Shakespeare invented that word too.)

Mike Boles

After graduating from Art College with a first in Graphic Design, Mike Boles walked into a job at Saatchi & Saatchi. It was the late '80s, a great time and place to learn.

With his partner Jerry Hollens, he picked up D&AD Silver Pencil and Campaign Gold for the NSPCC, and following a stint at the New York office, returned to become a group head. From there he moved to BMP DDB and helped win Sony. After winning awards on that, Volkswagen, and the Environmental Investigation Agency, he moved to Rainey Kelly Campbell Roalfe, later RKCR/Y&R.

There, he became creative partner, and won golds and silvers at the major awards shows on Land Rover, COI and the BBC, amongst others.

When my creative partner, Jerry Hollens and I left art school, we both wanted to be the writer. Maybe we'd both had our fill of the visual medium. After five years of art and design, copywriting seemed new and exciting.

I must have shouted louder, because I became the writer.

When we started at Saatchi & Saatchi in the late '80s, there was no shortage of great writers to learn from: Jeremy Sinclair, James Lowther, Simon Dicketts.

It was an inspiring place.

Back then puns were still in fashion, but from the looks on creative directors' faces when we tried it, I soon realised it wasn't the way forward.

For young copywriters today, there are new challenges. The world is becoming ever more visual and copywriting is being squashed into a corner. Many ad campaigns are global, so words won't always work.

And there are fewer and fewer copy craftsmen around, people who can teach you.

But perhaps crafting has become less relevant. Language and sentence structure are much more freestyle (check out books by Jonathan Safran Foer), more expressive of a feeling rather than a logical sentence. But in order to break those rules, you have to know them in the first place.

Your readers are way more tuned in to advertising, and more cynical than they used to be. They're simply not prepared to be manipulated by an ad.

On top of that, they have a short attention span. With technology, they're used to quick-fire information. Look at texting. Look at multi-channel TV.

The way we use words is changing, so our conversation with the reader is becoming shorter.

At Saatchi's, when I started, long copy was still part of the furniture. I wrote the NSPCC campaign there. I enjoyed writing it, but I've never had the need to write anything that long since.

The "Rape" ad was all in the preparation. I knew that writing about a man's childhood experience of rape by his own father had to be authentic. It would be unforgivable if it didn't come across that way.

Understandably, the NSPCC wouldn't let me have access to a victim of rape. The next best thing was an NSPCC psychologist, someone who knew the emotional journey of the victim.

Once I'd lived with and breathed in this experience for a few days, I was ready to put pen to paper (no laptop back then).

I waited until everyone at Saatchi's had gone home for the night. I wanted it to be dark in the corridors outside my office, and to feel lonely (like the victim).

And then I just wrote it in one go. It took less than an hour, and I made very few changes to that original outpouring.

It's based on emotion, not logic. The other ads in the campaign were more logical, and, in my opinion, not as good.

I saw the ad on cross tracks, heard two women talking about it, one asking the other if she'd read it yet. She hadn't. I stood behind them and watched as they both quietly read it. It was a real sense of achievement.

London Underground tried to get the ad taken down, as their station platforms were being dangerously clogged up by passengers reading it. That's the power words can have.

Back then I used a pen and A3 pad, lots of scribbles. Now I use a laptop and a pencil. I don't actually use the pencil, I just find it comforting to hold while I'm tapping away.

I love the freedom the laptop gives to chop and change, and see the words immediately in front of you in a font. You know straight off if it's right or wrong.

I also love being able to move whole paragraphs around, giving new meaning, and the satisfaction of highlighting and deleting a whole load of waffle into the ether.

Nowadays, I like to keep it short. Take the Land Rover ads. "Conditions" was the first ad Jerry and I did for Land Rover after winning the account. It's a simple tactical ad, playing on people's vulnerability in the winter weather.

The actual copy is super-short, as has become the way on most Land Rover work, where, being a global account, the international language of visuals rules supreme.

The knife crime ads were part of a campaign aimed at mothers. Like NSPCC, I had to make sure every word was authentic, I wanted to talk to them eye to eye.

These mothers were from tough backgrounds. Any whiff of being patronised and I knew they'd see right through it, and I'd lose them.

When it's about saving children's lives, you can't risk doing that.

For the Energy Saving Trust we wrote a TV campaign that uses humorous dialogue to try to charm the viewer into doing something for the environment. The thought was that if your boiler isn't energy efficient, it's behaving badly. The boiler hurled abuse at a poor, beaten-down family, calling the father "baldilocks and the three hairs" (YouTube: bad boiler).

Now, an important piece of advice for any up-and-coming copywriter — don't be afraid to use no words. Words are not always the best way to express what you're trying to get across to the reader.

If you think about it, most visual thoughts are verbal in origin. An idea has to be formulated into words. Whether it actually needs any words in its expression is another matter.

On Volkswagen, we were wrestling with how to express the feeling of camper-van nostalgia that the Sharan gave us. It came to us that the Sharan was part of the same family, from the same mould.

A long copy ad feeding off this nostalgia trip could have done the trick. But a far smarter trick was to condense that same feeling to its barest, simplest form.

And that thought, which started as a verbal notion, became a non-verbal ad. Sometimes, why use 200 words when none will do?

Below
Client: Volkswagen
Agency: RKCR/Y&R
Year: 1998

Opposite
Client: NSPCC
Agency: Saatchi & Saatchi
London
Year: 1992

Next spread left
Client: Land Rover
Agency: RKCR/Y&R
Year: 2001

Next spread right
Client: Home Office
Agency: RKCR/Y&R
Year: 2009

Perhaps "Copywriter" as a job description seems a bit outdated.

Jerry and I, like most good creative teams, are equally skilled both visually and verbally. I think you have to be. I know this book is dedicated to an art form called "Copywriting", but in ten years' time will the title itself even be around?

Whatever it's called, there'll always be a need for powerful verbal thoughts that perfectly capture emotions. But they just might not be beautifully crafted headlines or copy.

Sharan VW

What's it like to be raped as a 3 year old? A victim explains.

I FIRST remember being sexually abused by my father when I was about 3. It may have happened before, I don't know.

I can see it now, me lying in bed, with that big face coming towards me. He'd kiss me goodnight, but he didn't stop at kissing.

He used to tell me it was our secret. And if I ever told anyone about it I'd be sent away.

But even as a child I knew something wasn't right. It was those words, "I'll protect you." How could he be protecting me? He was bloody hurting me.

It's strange really, he was my enemy, but at the same time my only friend in the world. He made me depend on him. He controlled me. My body was his toy for more than 9 years.

At school I found it hard to mix. I felt different. I'd never let anyone get close to me. In the changing rooms after P.E. I hated people seeing my naked body. I was so ashamed, thought they might be able to tell what had been happening to me and call me a poofter.

Even when I managed to find a girlfriend I still wasn't sure if I was heterosexual. I was terribly rough with her. I suppose I wanted to be in control of someone, like my father was with me.

Sex terrified me. Having an orgasm just made me think of what my father did inside of me. And that big smiling face.

I met someone else eventually. We got married. After 2 years she left me. She said I was cold and didn't understand her.

But that's how I was. I just wasn't aware of causing or feeling mental or physical pain. Something inside me had been switched off long ago. There were times when I could actually cut myself with a knife and not feel a thing.

After the divorce, I turned to drink. It was a way of escaping. But I still suffered deep depressions.

Last year, my father finally died. I think that's what made me contact the NSPCC. I was 53 years old, and it was the first time I'd ever told anyone about my childhood.

Once a week for 6 months a Child Protection Officer worked with me. He got me to tell him everything about my experience. Talking about it was very painful. For over 40 years I guess I'd been trying not to think about it.

Eventually though, it started to work. He made me realise that what happened wasn't my fault.

For the first time I can ever remember I actually began to feel good about myself. It was just like being let out of a dark and lonely cell.

I'll never forget what happened to me. But at least I can start to live my life.

For further information on the work of the NSPCC, or to make a donation, please write to: NSPCC, 67 Saffron Hill, London, EC1N 8RS or call 071 242 1626.

To report a suspected case of child abuse, call the NSPCC Child Protection Helpline on 0800 800 500.

NSPCC
Act Now For Children.

THE DISCOVERY FROM £21,995.
FOR CONDITIONS SEE BELOW.

Don't be weather-beaten, test drive a Series II Discovery today.

THE BEST 4x4xFAR

Sure it's hard talking to your child about knives.

Not half as hard as never talking to him again.

If you went into your son's room right now, are you sure you wouldn't find a knife? Would you bet his life on it? Don't blame him. Instead, imagine being him. Every time he steps outside your front door, he feels scared. He could be getting pressure to join a gang. But once he's in, it's hard to get out. Your son doesn't have to be part of it. But why would he listen to you? Because he respects you more than you think. Reason with him calmly. Ask why he's putting his life in danger. Tell him it's braver to walk away. You're not alone. Other parents are worried too. Talk to them, or join a group. Talk to your son today. Tomorrow could be too late. Visit direct.gov.uk/talkaboutknives or call 0845 600 4171 for a leaflet.

Home Office

Tony Brignull

Tony Brignull spent most of his career at Collett Dickenson Pearce.

With his partner Neil Godfrey he won three D&AD Black and seventeen Yellow Pencils on such accounts as Parker Pen, Army Officer Recruitment, Birds Eye, Fiat, Clarks and the Great Ormond Street Wishing Well Appeal.

He also worked for DDB, AMV and for an exhilarating couple of years ran his own agency, Brignull Le Bas. On leaving advertising after 35 years he went to Oxford to read English then to King's College London to study Life Writing.

He lives in a house in the middle of a field in Buckinghamshire with his wife Voula, visited regularly by their three children and five grandchildren.

My own copy improved when it occurred to me that we relate to a company as we do to a person. Unless we're investors we don't ask how many employees a company has, what its financial gearing is, where it exports. We ask is it honest, reliable, modest, amusing, trustworthy. If it is, that company may eventually become our friend. I have come to think that helping companies turn into friends is the greatest thing we advertising people can do for our clients.

I start by asking if this company were already a friend what *wouldn't* it do? Well, it wouldn't lie, boast, shout, bore us or evade issues. It wouldn't change much over time, either. If a friend suddenly changes, develops a mid-Atlantic twang, for instance, we grow anxious. We like consistency, we feel comfortable with it.

This voice thing is very important. Copywriting can help establish a tone of voice which customers recognise just as we do our friends'. If you think about it, successful companies are recognisable. Volkswagen, IKEA, John Lewis, Sainsbury's, we sort of know how they sound. Even though they may say different things to different people — in sale time, in launch time, in good times and bad, we hear the same voice speaking. We don't want companies to get all matey when they talk to their peers in marketing or pompous when they speak to financial pundits. We want them to sound the same. Then we can trust them. I don't have to tell you how important trust is when you're buying something.

I realise this may sound dangerously idealistic. Hopelessly long-term. So let's get down and dirty. Wherever possible I get to know a client personally. I don't mean over lunch (though if you insist). I mean over the counter, in the office, on the forecourt. I visit the work place and talk to the engineers not the P.R. guys. I ask them what do you believe in? What would you do for money and what wouldn't you do? I talk to the chairman and the tea lady. Gradually I get to understand who this company — this person — is. Unless I know how can I tell the world?

I don't create a voice for a client. I try to express the voice that is already there but which may have been muted by expediency or distorted by poor advice. I believe that companies, like people, exist and grow by virtue of the *good* in them. And that if there is no goodness they will die. Sometimes their essential goodness is hard to find. Perhaps the client has neglected it or undervalued it or has been afraid to express it. But when you show them who they truly are and where their goodness resides, it rings a bell. Not infrequently you find the entire company lining up with a new sense of pride behind this revealed persona.

With Parker Pens, for instance, I expressed not merely their skill in making pens but their love of writing with a beautiful instrument, a far bigger idea. I sometimes quoted from great writers in their copy.

Before the Army Officer recruitment account came to us it offered young men a career of unalloyed adventure, sailing, skiing etc. John Salmon, creative director of CDP, offered them a challenge of a different sort: a role in world peace. He also gave them words with which they could explain their career decision to their peers. The tone of voice he created — thoughtful, mature, dutiful — was one I was grateful to continue.

But what if it's a wet cold day and you have to get an ad out by lunch-time and there's no tone of voice, no goodness you can detect and the brief is crap? Like you I try to be as original and creative as I can but then I go back to where I began, I speak for my client as a decent human being, good-humoured, friendly and, above all, an honest dealer.

If I'm in doubt I ask, would I walk up to a stranger at a drinks party and say these words to her? If she's interested, amused, engaged, I write on. If she starts looking over my shoulder or reaching for the peanuts I start again.

It's hard. But don't give up. It's worth doing.

Opposite
Client: Army Officer
Agency: Collett Dickenson
Pearce & Partners
Year: 1980

The account director,
Nigel Clark, presented this
for two years until it was
approved. In gratitude we
gave him a statue of a
bulldog inscribed "For
never giving up".

Next spread
Client: Parker Pen Co.
Agency: Collett Dickenson
Pearce & Partners
Year: 1979

Neil Godfrey found a real
plumber for this Parker ad.
The man said he'd never
done an easier day's work.

Russian armour entering Kabul.

Next?

Will Russian tanks roar across the plains of Germany?

Will crises erupt somewhere so remote we all have to scour maps to find out where it is?

Will one of our NATO allies call for moral support on its borders?

Will we be asked to join an international peace-keeping force to separate the sides in a civil war?

Frankly, your guess is as good as ours.

The world is so unstable it could go critical at any time without so much as a warning light.

This is why we have made the Army much more mobile.

And why we always try to recruit the type of young man who can add calmness and good humour to a tense situation.

Now we need another 900 young Officers whom these men will follow, if necessary, to the ends of the earth.

A job with no guarantee of success.

You may well argue that your joining the Army would not have saved one life in Afghanistan.

We would go further, it might not save anyone's life, including your own.

On the other hand, it might.

It might, if enough like-minded men join with you, help to prevent a nuclear war.

And it might, just might, hold the world together long enough for the powers of freedom and sweet reasonableness to prevail.

Some hopes?

Perhaps. But the alternative is no hope at all.

Hoping for the best, preparing for the worst.

Your part in this will be to prepare for a war everyone prays will never happen.

Depending on the job you choose, you will rehearse battle tactics in Germany.

Confront heat in Cyprus, Belize or Hong Kong.

And heat of a different sort in Northern Ireland.

You will practise, repair, train and try to forge links with your men that will withstand fire.

Occasionally, you may be asked to clamber into a VC10 on the way to, well, somewhere like monitoring a cease-fire in Rhodesia.

But more often, the worst enemy your men will face will be boredom, when it will take all your skills as a teacher and manager to motivate them.

Then it will be difficult to remember that you are still protecting your country and all you love most.

An easy question to dodge.

The question is, are you prepared to take the job on for three years or longer?

No one will accuse you if you don't.

Women won't send you white feathers and children won't ask what you did in the war.

All we ask is that every young man at least takes the question seriously and answers it to the satisfaction of his own conscience.

This way we are bound to get our 900 new Officers.

If you are undecided but want to take the matter a stage further without committing yourself in any way, write to Major John Floyd, Army Officer Entry, Department A 7, Lansdowne House, Berkeley Square, London W1X 6AA.

Tell him your date of birth, your educational qualifications and why you want to join us.

He will send you booklets to give you a far larger picture of the life and, if you like, put you in touch with people who can tell you more about the career.

 **Army Officer**

Redisc|over the l|

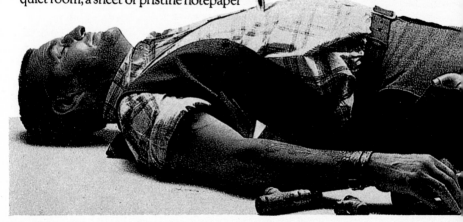

Do you know plumbers who never turn-up?

Hairdressers who missed their vocations as butchers?

Drycleaners who make your stains disappear—and your clothes with them?

Today, we at Parker give you the chance to get your own back.

Not only are we offering a beautiful new pen called the Laque which owes its deep lustre to a Chinese technique 2000 years old, but we are attempting to revive something that went out when the telephone came in:

The well-aimed, witty, malicious dart.

Imagine yourself, for example, in a quiet room, a sheet of pristine notepaper

before you and your Parker Laque poised like a javelin.

How about this to the dustman who keeps spilling litter down your steps:

May the curse of Mary Malone and her nine, blind, illegitimate children chase you so far over the hills of Damnation that the Lord himself can't find you with a telescope.

A good, old Irish curse and already you're feeling better. Now for the book club that won't stop sending you junk mail.

With gleaming wet words you see the Laque effortlessly transcribe your wrath into a death blow:

You louse in the locks of literature.

A nice bit of alliteration borrowed

Rediscover the lost art

st art of the insult.

m Tennyson but they won't know
at.

While you're at it, how about
post card to an airline that's lost
ur bags.

You have delusions of adequacy.

Or to a chef who nearly poison-
you:

Two partridges, ill trussed and
rse roasted . . . an old hare newly
led and poorly stuffed; celery and
me other trash; in short, a very poor
rformance. A.G.Hunter

You might say with some justi-
ation that you don't need a gold
bbed pen costing £34 to write a
cent insult, even if the nib is so sym-
etrical you can use both sides of it.

We can only answer that just as
beautifully made car tempts you

to drive so a perfectly engineered pen
tempts you to write.

Try this on the old bore who
keeps asking you your opinion of his
literary works:

Your manuscript is both good and
original; but the part that is good is not
original and the part that is original is
not good. Dr. Samuel Johnson

But you can knock spots off these
hacks, surely.

Come on, get yourself a Parker
Laque and let rip.

Someone, somewhere deserves a
real stinker from you.

✦ PARKER

An ABC of helpful words:				
Amateur.	Goatbrained.	Meat-head.	Oik.	Unprofessional.
Bodger.	Has-been.	Noisome.	Pusillanimous.	Verminous.
Cretin.	Idiot.		Quack.	Wally.
Dunderhead.	Jumped-up.		Rip-off.	Xantippe.
Egomaniac.	Know-nothing.		Sycophant.	Yes-man.
Feckless.	Lemming.		Toady.	Zombie.

THE PARKER LAQUE 180 SHOWN HERE.   RECOMMENDED PRICE £34.07 INC. V.A.T.

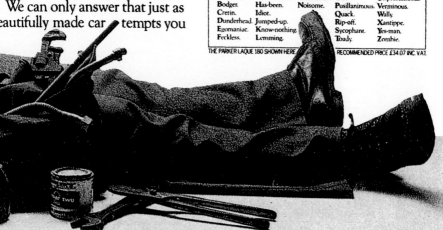

Answer these ten questions and work out the date of your own death.

Start with the age of 77 for a man and 81 for a woman (assuming you are over twenty years old now) and add or subtract according to your answers.

1. How old are you now?
Up to 50 no score.
51 – 55 add one year.
56 – 60 add two years.
61 – 65 add three years.
66 – 70 add four years.

2. Do you smoke?
Over 40 a day subtract 9 years.
Over 20 a day subtract 6 years.
Up to 20 a day no score.

3. Do you drink?
Heavily (more than 5 drinks a day) subtract 10 years.
Moderately, no score.
Teetotal, subtract 2 years.

4. Sex?
If you enjoy sex once a week, add 1 year.

5. Family History?
If any close relative has died of heart disease before 50, subtract 4 years.
Between ages 51–65, subtract 2 years.
If any close relative has suffered from diabetes or mental disorder, subtract 3 years.

6. Overweight?
If your problem is measured in stones rather than pounds, subtract 6 years.

7. Your job?
Professional, technical or management, add 1 year.
Semi-skilled, subtract 1 year.
Labourer, subtract 4 years.
But: active, add 2 years, desk-bound, subtract 2 years.

8. Exercise?
Proper exercise (heavy breathing) at least twice a week, add 3 years.

9. Life-Style?
Single, living alone, subtract 1 year.
Widow, or separated within past 2 years, subtract 4 years.

10. Health?
If you have an annual check-up, add 2 years.
Any serious illness or disease requiring hospital treatment in the last 5 years subtract 10 years.

These are the sort of questions actuaries ask before they insure you.

Answered honestly, they will give you a rough idea of your life expectancy, no more.

They won't tell you if you are going to plough your car into a lamp-post. Or jump out of a window. Or choke on a fishbone.

They are just statistics based on the lives and deaths of hundreds of thousands of people.

And we are raising this chilling topic on a Sunday morning for two reasons.

First, to make you think of providing for those you couldn't bear to leave unprovided for.

Secondly, and more unusually, to make you consider the last half of your life.

What are you going to do with it?

More than likely (according again to statistics) you are going to have a second career.

But whether it will be absorbing and challenging or boring and time-serving, is not just a question of your ability.

It will also depend on how much money you have to set up a business or supplement your salary.

And if after twenty years of screamingly high taxation you haven't a bean, don't worry, we can help you.

If you can put by something every month for the next ten years or so, we will invest it for you.

In this respect we are uniquely advised by no less than Warburg Investment Management Ltd., a subsidiary of S.G. Warburg & Co. Ltd.

We are also aided by the Inland Revenue. The taxman allows us to retrieve a certain amount of your income tax which we also invest on your behalf.

This way we can eventually give you a tax-free income or lump sum.

If you have read this far you are obviously of a fearless and enquiring mind. Let us tell you more about our savings plans.

This coupon will bring our brochures speeding to you.

For more about our plans please send this coupon to Peter Kelly, Albany Life, FREEPOST, Potters Bar EN6 1BR.

Name _____
Address _____
_____ Tel: _____
Name of your life assurance broker, if any.

Albany Life

Opposite
Client: Albany Life
Assurance
Agency: Advertising
and Marketing Services
Year: 1980

Next spread left
Client: Chivas Regal
Agency: DDB London
Year: 1969

Next spread right
Client: G A Dunn & Co.
Agency: Collett Dickenson
Pearce & Partners
Year: 1973

Pages 074–075
Client: Freedom Food
Agency: AMV BBDO
Year: 1994

I wanted to write an ad for
an insurance company that
would insist you read it.

One from a campaign
for Chivas Regal which
I had to present to Bill
Bernbach himself.

I threw this ad into the
waste bin. The account
man, Julian Seymour,
fished it out and sold it.

Treating animals respect-
fully, emphasised by
Stu Baker's strong art
direction.

"When."

When you're pouring Chivas Regal, it's unwise to let your guests draw the line.

So often they seem to find themselves with a mouthful of peanuts.

Or they decide to lose their voice.

The only consolation is that while they're drinking your Chivas, they're developing a taste for the 12 year old Glenlivet whiskies we blend.

(They're at least twice as old and smooth as most.)

So you shouldn't have long to wait before they buy themselves a bottle of Chivas.

And give you the chance to lose your own voice.

Success doesn't always go to your head.

When you're starting out you can probably wear our suits with flat-fronted trousers.

As you get desk bound you might need a couple of darts at the waist.

While business lunches usually mean you need two pleats.

A gentleman's waistline is nobody's business but his own.

For this reason we thought long and seriously about publishing the above photographs.

Are they indiscreet? we asked ourselves. Are we in the slightest way opening our customers to such smirking remarks as:

"You don't need a couple of darts at the waist, old man, you need a grapefruit diet."

But consider our predicament.

There are still some men who just won't believe a ready-to-wear suit will ever fit them.

Even though we have related countless times

that we have different fittings for slim, portly, short portly, stout and short stout men.

Not to mention how many times we've mentioned that we also cater for men with long arms or short arms, and men with long legs or short legs.

So we decided to release our waistband secrets and tell the world how we can soften the ravages of time and the business lunch.

Hoping that you will be persuaded to walk into Dunns and try on every suit in the shop.

Safe in the knowledge that even if you hate them all, it won't have cost you a penny.

Dunn & Co

Does it matter that cattle have fresh straw to lie on not bare concrete?

Does it matter that hens have room to forage and a quiet box to lay their eggs in?

Does it matter that sows should be able to root and explore instead of being tied to one spot?

We know it matters to the animals.

The question is, does it matter to you?

If it does, look for the 'Freedom Food' mark in your supermarket.

A new venture initiated by the RSPCA, it aims to give farm animals five basic freedoms:

1. Freedom from fear and distress.

2. Freedom from pain, injury and disease.

3. Freedom from hunger and thirst.

4. Freedom from discomfort.

5. The freedom to behave naturally.

With Freedom Food there'll be no battery hens. No tethered pigs. No overloaded cattle trucks.

The farmers, hauliers and abattoir owners have to agree to very strict conditions.

Freedom Food assessors visit them regularly and the RSPCA does unannounced spot checks to keep them up to the mark.

To begin with, you can find our stickers on a range of pork, bacon, ham and eggs in Tesco and the Co-op.

Soon we're extending the scheme to beef, lamb, poultry and meat products such as hamburgers and lasagne, in more shops.

Some may cost a little more, it's true. But any profits Freedom Food makes will help fund RSPCA farm animal welfare research.

And if you can find it in your heart to pay the extra, one day all animals raised for food will lead happier lives.

If you can't, they won't.

Sorry to leave the problem on your plate.

FREEDOM FOOD.
RSPCA MONITORED

They're dead.
So do does

it matter how they lived.

FOR FURTHER INFORMATION PLEASE CONTACT FREEDOM FOOD LTD. DEPARTMENT TG1. MANOR HOUSE, CAUSEWAY, HORSHAM, WEST SUSSEX RH12 1AG TELEPHONE 0403 223784.

Eugene Cheong

Eugene Cheong is Asia's most awarded copywriter and creative director. He was the first Asian to ever win a One Show Gold Pencil (33 years ago), and, 26 years ago, became the first Asian to ever have his work recognised by the D&AD Awards.

Eugene is one of a handful of creative pioneers who, in the mid-1980s, set in motion what is widely known in the industry as the "Asian Creative Revolution", which began in the iconic Ogilvy Singapore agency, before spreading north to Thailand and India.

Eugene's career with Ogilvy includes stints in London, Los Angeles and across Asia. He is now chief creative officer of Ogilvy & Mather Asia Pacific.

In his spare time, Eugene works for charity. He was the man behind the Hospice Council, East Timor and "God" campaigns.

This is how I write copy:

~~Let's get together this weekend.~~
God
~~Hahahahahahahahahahahhahahahahahahhahahaha.~~
God
~~If you can't hear me, maybe you're not listening.~~
God
~~If you think the Mona Lisa is stunning, you should look at my masterpiece in the mirror.~~
God
~~Why do you only talk to me when you're in trouble?~~
God
~~I have big plans for you.~~
God
~~Whenever I get bored sitting on my throne, I do a stand up.~~
God
~~If you think George Burns is funny, wait till you meet his producer?~~
God
~~If you think George Burns is funny, you should meet his producer?~~
God
~~If I take myself seriously, I'd have fried comedians for lunch every day.~~
God
~~Where do you think George Burns got his funny bone?~~
God
~~George Burns was a bad impersonator.~~
God
~~What do I have to do to get your attention? Take you out with a bolt of lightning?~~
God

What do I have to do to get your attention? Take out an ad
in the paper?
God
What do I have to do to get your attention? Run an ad on TV?
God
~~You might not agree with my sense of humour, but life is~~
~~my idea of a joke.~~
~~God~~
~~You might think life is a joke. I don't.~~
~~God~~
~~Is this the sign you've been waiting for?~~
~~God~~
~~I believe in you.~~
~~God~~
~~I have faith in you.~~
~~God~~
~~All my special effects are executed without the aid of a computer.~~
~~God~~
~~I have a sense of humour, I gave you Woody Allen.~~
~~God~~
~~Could you imagine the price of air, if it were brought to you~~
~~by another supplier?~~
~~God~~
~~Long before you were born, I planned that you would read this.~~
~~God~~
~~I let it rain today so that you can walk on water.~~
~~God~~
~~Earthlings, don't treat me like an alien.~~
~~God~~
~~It's not the end of the world. Not till I say so.~~
~~God~~
It's not the end of the world. Not until I say so, anyway.
God
~~All I want for Christmas is your presence.~~
~~God~~
~~Don't like the weather? Give me a few minutes and I'll change it.~~
~~God~~
~~Waaaaassuup?~~
~~God~~

~~If you have any doubt I have a sense of humour, just look at the hyena.~~
~~God~~
~~How can you call yourself a free thinker when you can't even accept that I exist?~~
~~God~~
~~How can you call yourself a free thinker when you can't even accept my existence?~~
~~God~~
How can you call yourself a free thinker when you can't even accept the possibility of my existence?
God
~~I like a good laugh, that's why I made the hyena.~~
~~God~~
~~Sure, I have a sense of humour, I gave you the hyena, didn't I?~~
~~God~~
~~Of course, I have a sense of humour, I gave you the hyena, didn't I?~~
~~God~~
~~Of course, I have a sense of humour. I gave you the giraffe, didn't I?~~
~~God~~
~~Of course, I have a sense of humour. I gave you the platypus, didn't I?~~
~~God~~
~~Of course, I have a sense of humour. I gave you baboons, didn't I?~~
~~God~~
~~Of course, I have a sense of humour. I gave you monkeys, didn't I?~~
~~God~~
Of course, I have a sense of humour. I gave you baboons with bright red asses, didn't I?
God

Opposite
Client: Anglican
Welfare Council
Agency: Ogilvy Singapore
Year: 2005

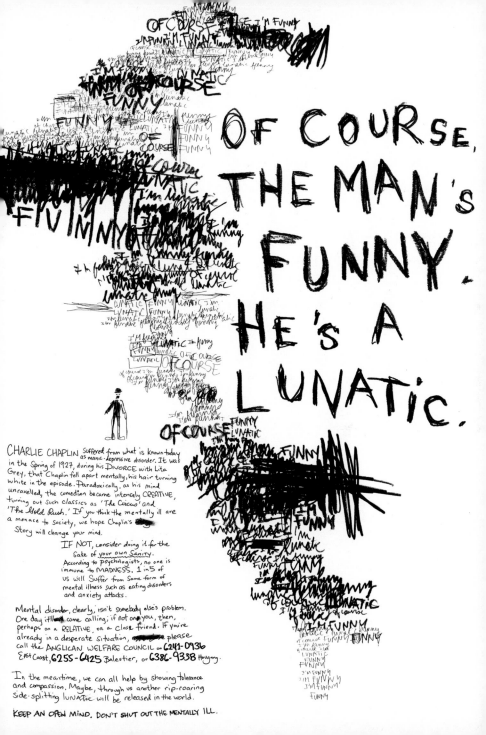

OF COURSE, THE MAN'S FUNNY. HE'S A LUNATIC.

CHARLIE CHAPLIN suffered from what is known today as manic-depressive disorder. It was in the Spring of 1927, during his DIVORCE with Lita Grey, that Chaplin fell apart mentally, his hair turning white in the episode. Paradoxically, as his mind unravelled, the comedian became intensely CREATIVE, turning out such classics as 'The Circus' and 'The Gold Rush.' If you think the mentally ill are a menace to society, we hope Chaplin's story will change your mind.

IF NOT, consider doing it for the sake of your own sanity. According to psychologists, no one is immune to MADNESS. 1 in 5 of us will suffer from some form of mental illness such as eating disorders and anxiety attacks.

Mental disorder, clearly, isn't somebody else's problem. One day it'll come calling; if not on you, then, perhaps on a RELATIVE, or a close friend. If you're already in a desperate situation, please call the ANGLICAN WELFARE COUNCIL on 6241-0936. East Coast, 6255-6425 Balestier, or 6386-9338 Hougang.

In the meantime, we can all help by showing tolerance and compassion. Maybe, through us another rip-roaring side-splitting lunatic will be released in the world.

KEEP AN OPEN MIND. DON'T SHUT OUT THE MENTALLY ILL.

Nietzsche is dead.
God

Client: Love Singapore   *Next spread*
Movement   Client: Lien Foundation
Agency: Ogilvy Singapore   Agency: Ogilvy Singapore
Years: 2001–2003   Year: 2007

Of course I have a sense of humour.
I gave you baboons with bright red asses, didn't I?
God

The End.

What if that is where your story begins?

Perhaps, your tale of woe began with a mole that changed colour and you've found out that the blemish on your skin has a terrifying scientific name. Fate, without your consent, has brought you to the final chapter of the book of life and it bids you to read on. Maybe, it's not you. But someone close like your wife, whose tummy ache has just been diagnosed as carcinoma of the stomach. The end, whoever the characters may be, is suddenly at hand. The Angel of Death stands at the door, and he's about to knock.

We are the Singapore Hospice Council and we are here to serve the dying and their families. The aim of this advertisement is to acquaint you with Elisabeth Kubler-Ross's five stages of dying. For those who have yet to experience the ebbing of life, all this talk about death might seem unnecessarily morbid. For those of us, however, who have recently been made aware of our mortality, this 'travel guide' will provide some light and comfort for the dark road ahead.

1. Denial. For as long as you can remember, you have never not existed. Since deep within our unconscious mind we are all immortal, it's almost inconceivable for any of us to acknowledge the possibility of our own demise. As a result, our first reaction to the news of terminal illness is a numbness that's replaced by the usual response of 'It can't be me; surely, they've made a mistake!' Which is followed by a ritual of shopping around for second opinions in the hope of dodging the inescapable. Numbness, denial, and withdrawal are all appropriate reactions to what is the most

we have to find the strength to say goodbye to all we have known and loved. If we are witnessing the end of a life, we have to find the strength to survive the pain of losing a dear one. However, we're stronger than we think, and we're never given more than we're able to handle.

5. Acceptance. If a sudden and unexpected death doesn't take us, we'd have enough time to work through the previously described stages and reach the point in which we are neither sad nor angry with our lot. We'd have given vent to our feelings of envy and anger for the living and

a mistake, rage, anger, and resentment will accompany the logical next question: 'Why me?' Doctors and nurses will be picked on, while the visiting family is received with little cheerfulness. Instead of responding with grief, tears and reduced visits, family members should try to put themselves in the shoes of the terminally ill. You, too, would be outraged if all your life's activities were prematurely and permanently interrupted. Given attention and some time, the ranting and raving will often melt away.

3. Bargaining. In this phase we will attempt to enter into some sort of an agreement with the Almighty, so that the inevitable may be postponed. The thinking goes, 'If the Almighty has decided to take us from the earth, and he did not respond to our angry pleas, perhaps, on the off chance, he will change his mind if we ask nicely.' The wish of the gravely ill is almost always an extension of life, followed by the request of quiet days without pain or physical discomfort.

4. Depression. There is no heartbreak worse than the pain of seemingly senseless and permanent separation from those we love dearly. While there are drugs for physical pain, there is, so far, no medicine to treat sorrow. The only way out of pain is *through* pain. The terminally ill will be grateful to those who can sit with them while they contemplate their approaching death. Visitors who try to cheer them up actually hinder rather than help their emotional preparation to leave the world. In this period of grief, there is little or no need for words. A touch of the hand, a stroke of the hair or just a silent sitting together will suffice. If we are dying,

happy stage. It is almost void of feelings. It is as if the pain has gone, the struggle is over, and there comes a time for, as a dying man phrased it, 'the final rest before the long journey.' We will be tired and, in most cases, quite weak. We will have a need to doze off or to sleep often and in brief intervals, just like a newborn child. While by now we have found some peace and acceptance, our circle of interest diminishes. And so it is at the end of our days, when we have worked and given, rejoiced and suffered, we go back to the place that we started out from and the circle of life is closed.

The power of hope. It is important to note that these five stages can exist next to each other and overlap at times. In some cases, whole stages are skipped. However, no matter the stage of illness, there's always hope for the dying. To have something to look forward to is a basic need of man. Hope should always be cultivated, regardless of whether we think that hope is valid or not. Whilst hope should never go away, what we hope for can change. First, we may hope to recover, or for a miracle; then, we may hope for a peaceful death. We may hope that the children will be alright, and we may hope to see them again. We may hope that there is a heaven, and we may hope for a new beginning there.

Should you need help or advice on end-of-life care, visit www.lifebeforedeath.org.sg or call 1800 333 6666. As hospice is a philosophy of care rather than a specific place of care, we can provide palliative care in a day care centre, a hospital ward, an in-patient hospice or even at home. Whichever part of our service you use, you can be assured we'll be with you till the end.

Marty Cooke

Marty Cooke was born in Columbia, Tennessee. He says his jobs worth mentioning are US chief creative officer, RAPP; chief creative officer, SS+K/New York; executive creative director of three Chiat\Day offices (New York, London and Toronto); and the New York office of M&C Saatchi. Earlier in his career, Marty was a copywriter and creative director at Doyle Dane Bernbach and Scali, McCabe, Sloves.

He describes his toughest boss as a tie between Ed McCabe and Jay Chiat, and his toughest partner Helmut Krone. Marty is most apologetic for being the first to take over an entire New York City subway car with one brand (Fruitopia), and most proud of being part of the media team that helped put Barack Obama in the White House.

Writing Is Thinking
or, Fishing Where The Fish Are.

Good copywriting has always been good thinking. When the first edition of this book came out, that thinking was usually visible as well-crafted words. Often paired with a brilliant visual to complete the thought. Always communicating a big idea.

Copywriters are still in the business of big ideas. And writing is still thinking.

But the final result may no longer contain any words at all. The thinking is as rigorous and inspired as ever. But the result might be a rubber wristband or a Big Urban Game.

Our job is, and always will be, to forge an emotional connection with people that motivates them to engage with a brand. Print, television, radio and outdoor are still powerful ways to do that. But as people migrate online, offline or avoid media altogether, copywriters have to go with them.

We have to fish where the fish are.

Microsites, games, viral videos, mobile apps and social media are the latest lures in the copywriter's tackle box. The copywriter must be as adept at creating stunts and movements as headlines and taglines. Sometimes the job of perfecting a piece of copy (now often pretentiously called "content") is replaced with figuring out how to get consumers to create the content for you. It takes a secure ego and a damned good idea to relinquish control to the masses.

Below
Client: Coca-Cola
Company
Agency: Chiat\Day
Year: 1995

Next spread
Client: Reebok
Agency: Chiat\Day
Year: 1988

Pages 088–089
Client: Lance Armstrong
Foundation
Agency: SS+K
Year: 2006

The Livestrong Manifesto,
read by Lance Armstrong
at every Livestrong ride
and event, was promi-
nently featured on the
website and made into a
popular video on YouTube.

Pages 090–091
Client: Nikon
Agency: Scali, McCabe,
Sloves
Year: 1985

My generation of copywriters grew up glued to the tube.
Writing TV scripts came naturally. Now, the first generation
to grow up with computers and the Internet is populating
creative departments. The wired culture is their native
habitat. Just as we mined TV Land, today's young copywriters
translate online culture into engaging ideas. Instead of
headlines and scripts, they're more often than not writing
descriptions of ideas that will be turned into pixels or events.

I think they're lucky. The best of them are protagonists in
the Second Creative Revolution. They're changing advertising
as profoundly as Bill Bernbach & Company did when they
upended the business fifty years ago. Perhaps more so. The
First Creative Revolution changed the content of advertising.
The Second is changing not just the content but the form
of advertising. No, it's even greater than that. It's changing the
very definition of advertising.

Is it still writing if no one sees your words? Is it still writing
if you didn't even write the words? Does it even matter?

As long as there's creative thinking to be done, there'll be
copywriters around to do it.

"WE FORFEIT 3/4 OF OURSELVES N ORDER 2 B LIKE OTHER PEOPLE" -ARTHUR SCHOPENHAUER

REEBOKS LET U.B.U.

LIVE**STRONG**™

We believe in life.

Your life.

We believe in living every minute of it with every ounce of your being.

And that you must not let cancer take control of it.

We believe in energy: channeled and fierce.

We believe in focus: getting smart and living strong.

Unity is strength. Knowledge is power. Attitude is everything.

This is livestrong.

Pete Turner on
why he always shoots
with Nikon lenses:

66

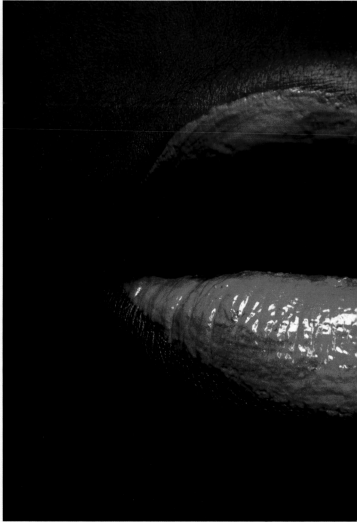

Pete Turner. "Hot Lips." 1967 Lens: 55mm f3.5 Micro-Nikkor.

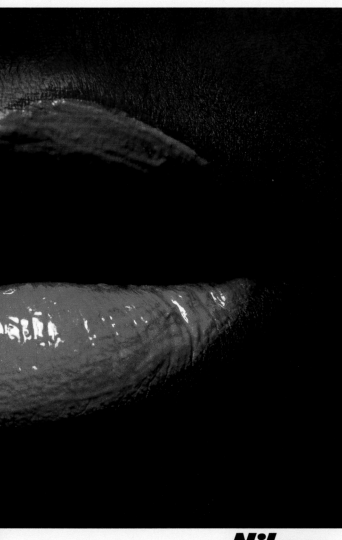

Nikon
We take the world's
greatest pictures.

Tony
Cox

Tony Cox studied for a Master's Degree at Edinburgh University where he worked in the Department of Educational Studies and helped organise a teaching programme for local prisons. Then, after a stint as a secondary-school teacher, he drifted into advertising, first at Hall's in Edinburgh, then at CDP/Marr and Davidson Pearce.

He joined DDB as creative director in 1985 and, two years later, the agency won the Grand Prix at Cannes. Tony was then instrumental in engineering a merger with BMP, an agency that, during his 13 years at the helm, won more creative awards than any other in the world.

He moved to AMV BBDO in 1998 and retired in 2004, having won D&AD Yellow Pencils for radio, poster and television, the Gold Award for Campaign Press, and the Creative Circle President's Award.

"Christ!" said the Duchess, "I'm pregnant. Who dunnit?"

The best stories usually hook you with their intro. They start as they mean to go on rather than clearing their throat before they get down to business. As the Editor in *The Front Page* asks, with more realism than sensitivity to a hack's vanity: "Who the hell ever reads the second paragraph?" When it comes to an attention-grabbing form of scribbling like advertising the copywriter had better let the reader know what's going on early. Or he may be left with no reader.

But the copywriter doesn't work alone. He works with an art director whose job it is to come up with the picture. And one picture, they say, is worth a thousand words. That sentence is ten words long. I still have 990 words left over. Think how much I can say with a few of them: "I love you." "Form follows function." "Less is more."

But however succinct and powerful, words like these seldom make a good press ad because the thoughts are, in themselves, complete. And a good advertisement requires the reader to complete the communication on his own behalf.

It stands to reason, doesn't it? An advertisement is made up of two elements. The words and the picture. Together, they make a whole. In isolation, they don't. Take the headlines on the press ad for the Advertising Standards Authority. The picture doesn't make complete sense without the words. And the words don't make complete sense without the picture. The reader has to decipher both to work out what the ad is saying. Only when the penny has dropped is communication complete.

What this implies, of course, is that the copywriter has to think visually. He has to "see" what goes into the space occupied by the picture because otherwise the words he writes will be misconstrued. Which brings us to the one unalterable thing that differentiates copywriting from all other forms of writing. An ad is never an end in itself. It always refers to something beyond it, the product. And just as there are only half a dozen stories of any kind, there are only half a dozen car stories.

Speed. Economy. Engineering. Style. Safety. Handling.

These stories have been told countless times before and left a legacy of advertising that has built a resevoir of goodwill towards Volkswagen. Most people, after all, have chuckled over a Volkswagen ad. At the very least they have appreciated its wit and style. Or enjoyed the honesty that treats the reader as an intelligent friend. The copy is self-deprecating rather than self-congratulatory, the tone irreverent and disarming. Disciplined, too, since the copywriter has only about 180 words of body copy with which to tell his story.

And now I'll let you into a secret. I don't drive. And neither do I fly-fish. On the face of it then, I'm as poorly qualified to write ads for Volkswagen as I am for Hardy's. To make up for my deficiencies, however, I do lots of research. Lots and lots and lots of research. In fact, I do so much research an art director once told me I should have been a librarian.

Be that as it may, I find research pays off. In fact, I can't lay pen to paper (and it's always pen to paper) until I know everything there is to know about the subject I'm writing about. Then I edit. And edit. And edit. Until I end up with the nub of the thing. Sometimes this can be a very big nub. As in the ad for Hardy Brothers: "Give us ten minutes of your time and we'll give you a hundred years of ours." Yes, it's a long copy ad. But with illustrations to help the eye through the text, and an audience that can never get enough of fishing, it didn't tax the patience of the hundreds who filled in the coupon.

Ah, the coupon! The ration-book! The powdered egg! Sorry, where was I? Yes, that little square in the bottom right-hand corner we were always being asked to "make bigger" so that even really stupid people with no interest whatsoever in the product would fill it in, and the agency claim "a huge response". Well, guess what? It really doesn't matter what size the coupon is provided the ad itself persuades enough people it's in their own best selfish interests to fill it in.

First, though, they have to read the advertisement, and they won't do that unless they're tempted to do so by an irresistible combination of headline and picture. And that, I seem to remember, is where I came in.

Opposite
Client: Volkswagen
Agency: BMP/DDB
Year: 1996

Has there ever been a better client than Johnny Meszaros? Or a better art director than Mark Reddy? If push came to shove, I'd have to choose "Mechanic" as my favourite all-time ad.

Next spread left
Client: Volkswagen
Agency: DDB London
Year: 1990

Next spread right
Client: Volkswagen
Agency: DDB London
Year: 1988

Do we drive our mechanics too hard?

For most people, going under a car is the end of their career.

For a Volkswagen mechanic, it's just the beginning.

He starts with the humble spark plug.

And works his way up to the digifant electronic system.

He takes every part apart. And puts it back together again.

Over and over and over again.

Until he can show us where every bolt, every washer and every nut goes.

What every part does.

And how to service every single one of them.

Then we really turn the screws on him.

Because, when he's not working on a Volkswagen, Volkswagen are working on him.

At one of our training schools.

There he spends seven hours a day study-ing the mechanics of the car.

So, by the end of his apprenticeship, he knows his Volkswagen bumper to bumper and sill to sill.

All this is part of the quaint Volkswagen notion that the service has to be as good as the car itself.

It's the kind of madness that makes us make our cars the way we do.

The sanest things on wheels.

The only squeaks and rattles you'll ever hear in a Volkswagen.

Who objects to decibels of delight coming from the back of their car?

Or to being able to actually hear a conversation, or the radio?

What is objectionable, is listening to the irritating results of shoddy workmanship and lazy engineering.

Which is why we at Volkswagen are so dedicated to building the soundest cars on the road.

To Volkswagen, silence isn't golden, it's dull grey, high tensile steel that we form into a rigid safety cell.

Inside, underneath, and around that rigid cell our engineers, robots and computers quietly set to work.

We make sure 10,000 times over, that a door shuts with a reassuring thud, not a hollow slam.

We torture bodywork.

We torment axles and wheel mountings.

And if something squeals in less than 300 hours of merciless testing, we dispose of it.

Why go to such great lengths?

Because there's something that's very important you ought to know when you buy a family car.

That it's a lot more than just sound. **Golf** Ⓥ

We put people in front of cars.

At Volkswagen, we've always worried our little heads about even littler heads.

We were among the first major car manufacturers to make all our models capable of running on unleaded fuel.

The first to produce a range of small cars, the Polo, with a catalytic converter as standard.

The first to produce the world's cleanest production car, the Umwelt Diesel. And one of the first to replace toxic paints with water-based paints.

That said, we can hardly expect you to buy a Volkswagen out of the goodness of your heart.

Nor, heaven forbid, should you buy one simply because we've been named Environmental Manufacturer of the Year.

We were, after all, among the first to intro-duce a reinforced safety cell with crumple zones front and rear.

The first to include rear seat belts as standard across the range.

And one of the first to make self-stabilising steering a standard feature.

When it comes to protecting your family, it seems, we rarely let anything get in our way.

Opposite
Client: The Advertising
Standards Authority
Agency: Davidson Pearce
Year: 1985

Next spread
Client: House of Hardy
Agency: CDP/Marr
Year: 1984

Colin Marr is the most
meticulous art director
I've ever worked with,
and clients like Hardy's
are the perfect showcase
for his skills.

DO ADVERTISEMENTS SOMETIMES DISTORT THE TRUTH?

The short answer is yes, some do.

Every week hundreds of thousands of advertisements appear for the very first time.

Nearly all of them play fair with the people they are addressed to.

A handful do not. They misrepresent the products they are advertising.

As the Advertising Standards Authority it is our job to make sure these ads are identified, and stopped.

WHAT MAKES AN ADVERTISEMENT MISLEADING?

If a training course had turned a 7 stone weakling into Mr Universe the fact could be advertised because it can be proved.

But a promise to build 'you' into a 15 stone he-man would have us flexing our muscles because the promise could not always be kept.

'Makes you look younger' might be a reasonable claim for a cosmetic.

But pledging to 'take years off your life' would be an overclaim akin to a promise of eternal youth.

A garden centre's claim that its seedlings would produce 'a riot of colour in just a few days' might be quite contrary to the reality.

Such flowery prose would deserve to be pulled out by the roots.

If a brochure advertised a hotel as being '5 minutes walk to the beach', it must not require an Olympic athlete to do it in the time.

As for estate agents, if the phrase 'overlooking the river' translated to 'backing onto a ditch', there would be nothing for it but to show their ad the door.

HOW DO WE JUDGE THE ADS WE LOOK INTO?

Our yardstick is The British Code of Advertising Practice.

Its 500 rules give advertisers precise practical guidance on what they can and cannot say. The rules are also a gauge for media owners to assess the acceptability of any advertising they are asked to publish.

The Code covers magazines, newspapers, cinema commercials, brochures, leaflets, posters, circulars posted to you, and now commercials on video tapes.

The ASA is not responsible for TV and radio advertising. Though the rules are very similar they are administered by

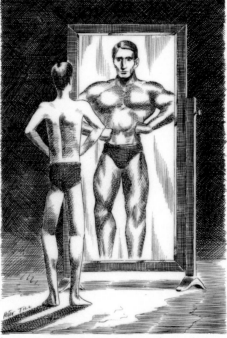

the Independent Broadcasting Authority.

WHY IT'S A TWO-WAY PROCESS

Unfortunately some advertisers are unaware of the Code, and breach the rules unwittingly. Others forget, bend or deliberately ignore the rules.

That is why we keep a continuous check on advertising. But because of the sheer volume, we cannot monitor every advertiser all the time.

So we encourage the public to help by telling us about any advertisements they think ought not to have appeared. Last year over 7,500 people wrote to us.

WHAT DO WE DO TO ADVERTISERS WHO DECEIVE THE PUBLIC?

Our first step is to ask advertisers who we or the public challenge to back up their claims with solid evidence.

If they cannot, or refuse to, we ask them either to amend the ads or withdraw them completely.

Nearly all agree without any further argument.

In any case we inform the publishers, who will not knowingly accept any ad which we have decided contravenes the Code.

If the advertiser refuses to withdraw the advertisement he will find it hard if not impossible to have it published.

WHOSE INTERESTS DO WE REALLY REFLECT?

The Advertising Standards Authority was not created by law and has no legal powers.

Not unnaturally some people are sceptical about its effectiveness.

In fact the Advertising Standards Authority was set up by the advertising business to make sure the system of self control worked in the public interest.

For this to be credible, the ASA has to be totally independent of the business.

Neither the chairman nor the majority of ASA council members is allowed to have any involvement in advertising.

Though administrative costs are met by a levy on the business, no advertiser has any influence over ASA decisions.

Advertisers are aware it is as much in their own interests as it is in the public's that honesty should be seen to prevail.

If you would like to know more about the ASA and the rules it seeks to enforce you can write to us at the address below for an abridged copy of the Code.

The Advertising ✓
Standards Authority.
If an advertisement is wrong, we're here to put it right.

ASA Ltd, Dept. T, Brook House, Torrington Place, London WC1E 7HN.

Give us ten minutes of your time and

When the Hardy Brothers set up in business over a century ago they didn't sit down and decide to make the finest fishing tackle in the world. They decided to make the kind of tackle with which they themselves enjoyed fishing.

They believed in perfect balance because a rod and reel should be a joy to use even when the fish aren't biting.

They looked for sensitivity because your tackle should be virtually an extension of your arm.

And they demanded strength because you can't blame your tackle if that big one gets away.

So they used the finest materials that were available to them.

They employed the best craftsmen they could find.

And, if something wasn't right, they experimented and redesigned until it was.

As a result, Hardy Brothers has been responsible for most of the important advances in tackle design this century.

We pioneered the split-cane rod.

We were one of the first manufacturers in Europe to set up our own plant for the making of glass fibre and carbon fibre blanks.

We've produced, over the years, the most impressive advances in reel design.

And today we manufacture the finest carbon and boron rods money can buy.

"It should never be forgotten that it is to Messrs Hardy of Alnwick we owe the supremacy we have obtained as rod makers. They have left all competitors hopelessly behind."
The Field 1902

Small wonder, then, that to own a Hardy rod has been the ambition of generations of fishermen not only in Britain but throughout the world.

TO SEE WHAT WE CAN DO, LOOK AT WHAT WE'VE DONE.

It was for Palakona split-cane rods that we first became famous.

Our reputation was earned because we used only those bamboos from above the snow line where the canes grow slower and thus acquires greater substance and hardness.

These were the only canes which gave us the steely temper we wanted.

We spent hours on simple processes like planing the angles so we could be

HARDY'S PATENT
Combined Spear and Butt Cap

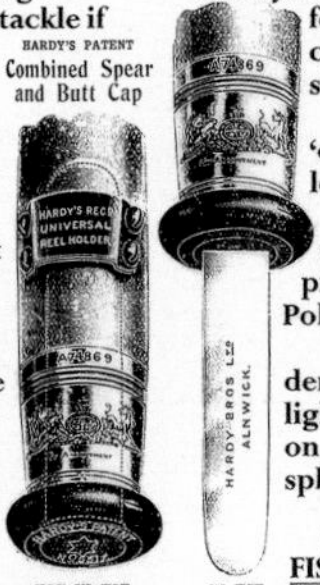

NOT IN USE.
Fig. 1.

IN USE.
Fig. 2.

absolutely certain that every section was true, every taper perfect and every hexagon exact.

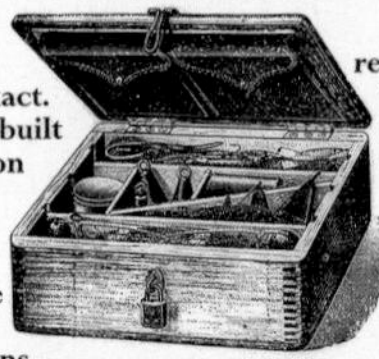

We constructed hollow-built cane fly rods with the precision of a Swiss watchmaker.

We innovated pine centred cane rods by removing the soft heart of the bamboo and laminating with strong, light pinewood sections.

THE BOAT ANGLER'S BOX.

We were large importers of Spanish gut and actual workers in drawing, twisting, plaiting and cast-making up until the advent of monofilament which rendered obsolete one of the most characteristic of anglers' rituals, the use of dampers and cast-box.

And in 1911 we introduced the 'Filip' silk fly line which we regard as the forerunner of today's distance casting with forward tapers and shooting heads.

Yet it is noticeable how often 'development' meant something less than radical change.

Nineteenth-century fly minnows, for example, were, in profile, identical to today's Polystickles.

And the modern demand for ultra-light rods followed on quickly from the split cane revolution.

Hardy's "STUD" Lockjoints
Pat. No. 14632/23.

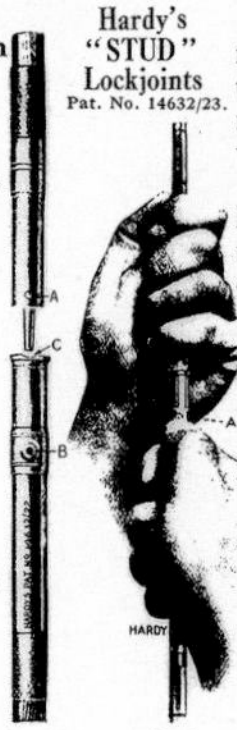

SOME OF OUR FISHING RODS ARE STILL GETTING BROKEN IN.

Hollow fibre glass was a natural for fishing rod construction.

This material combined with phenolic resin, was used for the successful Jet series of rods which we matched with Marquis reels to make exquisitely balanced outfits.

Where the old ways are best, however, we cherish them.

We still finish all our rods with scores of hand operations, sandings, bakings and inspections. Then several finishing coats are applied to achieve a unique ultra-smooth gloss finish.

Fig. 1.   Fig. 2.

Mosquito Veil and Gloves.

Anglers fishing in Newfoundland and other mosquito and insect infested countries will find these gloves and veils a great boon. The gloves have long sleeves and so perfectly protect the wrists. The veil covers the head and neck. It is provided with a fine hair window which does not affect the sight. In this window is fitted an automatic closing hole in a convenient position for the pipe.

So that, just as you would recognise a Rolls-Royce by the finish alone, so a Hardy rod is recognised by a finish that reflects its quality.

THE LAST WORD IN FISHING RODS. FROM THE PEOPLE WHO INVENTED THE FIRST.

In an age when mass production and corner cutting are the rule we still believe in traditional methods. Not because we're too old-fashioned to move with the times but because we know they give the best end result.

THE "BETHUNE" LINE WINDER.
(HARDY'S PATENT).

That's why Hardy rods are still made largely by hand. Where modern technology has some real improvements to offer, however, we accept them with gratitude.

Carbon fibre, for example, is so light and strong we're able to make our new Supertip Match rods of a very small diameter.

The result is a unique action which has to be experienced to be believed.

"Please let me offer my congratulations to you for making the 13' Matchmaker … the very best rod I have had the pleasure of using." P. Herron, Lincoln, 1976.

Take our Series 1 Match rod, for example. It's fitted with an incredibly fine spliced-in solid carbon tip which measures only 0.0076 cm at its extremity.

This allows you to play out a fish when using bottoms of only ½ lb.

Our Series 2, on the other hand, has more power and strength to give you extraordinary long range casting properties, even into the wind.

Add to that a superb sensitivity that enables you to tell the slightest touch of the bait, and you'll begin to appreciate why this new range of rods is thoroughly worthy of the Hardy name.

WE PUT ALL WE KNOW INTO ALL WE MAKE.

If there's one thing hour upon hour of fishing has taught us, it's the virtue of patience. Just as no fish was ever hurried onto a hook, so the craft of building a rod cannot be hurried.

That's why every new rod we make is a little bit better than the one we made before.

we'll give you a hundred years of ours.

Take our most recent introduction, Boron. Although it has tremendous strength, it's lighter in weight than aluminium so the angler can cast much further with the same amount of effort. It also has a tremendously smooth recovery from bending and this gives such velocity to the rod tip you can control it almost as easily as the tips of your fingers.

The Dry Fly Angler's Knife

"Until I used your 'Silex' I was a perfect duffer, always getting overruns and tangled up, a ruffled temper that made me say things that I should not."
Letter quoted in Hardy Catalogue, 1925.

One thing we do ask however: If you decide to invest in one of our boron rods, be sure to match it with a Hardy reel for ultimate performance.

OTHER TACKLE MANUFACTURERS OFFER YOU THE PROMISE OF A GREAT FLY REEL. WE OFFER YOU THE PROOF.

Our enthusiasm for doing our own design and development work has been evidenced by a flood of models over the years.

During the late 1930s the fly fishermen could choose from a mind-boggling twenty-four models.

There were Perfects and Silent Perfects in sizes from under 3 in., to over 4 in. in diameter.

You could buy a Uniqua in five sizes or a Uniqua Salmon in five more. And if you wanted something a little different from the rest of the crowd you could try a Bouglé or a Sunbeam, a Davy, a Cascapedia or a Barton. In all we produced twenty-eight models of named fly reels between 1886 and 1982.

If we add in the Centrepin style reels we might expand the list to as many as thirty-three.

1912 Hardy's New Patent Compensating Check.

Hardy's "BETWEEN" Waders

The line DD denotes approximately the position of the fire where it commences to consume the nicotine.

a section of Hardy's "Angler's and Sportsman's" Pipe.
THE COOLEST AND SWEETEST SMOKING PIPE MADE

Remember, too, that we produced fourteen spinning reels including the Altex, the first fixed spool reel with a helical gear and full-bale pick-up; the Elarex, one of the first salmon multiplier reels; bottom fishing reels like the Conquest and Eureka; and sea-fishing reels like the Zane Grey and the Alma Baker.

Cap to screw on E, when handle is not in use

Hardy's Improved 'Y-Shaped Collapsing Landing Net.
Fitted as made by us for Mr. Cholmondeley-Pennell, with Telescope Handle and Sling.

Today, at Alnwick, we still produce all our own reels.

The process involves the melting and casting of aluminium ingots for drums and frames, the machining of all parts, the moulding of reel handles, final assembly, inspection and packaging.

This is the only way we can subject every stage of every process to the most rigorous quality controls.

And make sure even the smallest details are exactly as we want them.

HOW CAN YOU TELL A GREAT ROD FROM A POOR ONE?

The short answer is that you can't, especially when it is new.

The rod may *The solid carbon fibre tip, reproduced here at actual size has a sensual sensitivity.*
1980 HARDY CARBON FIBRE MATCH RODS

look all right; it may be well finished; the action may seem to be fairly good, the fittings, the handle; everything may have the appearance of a first-class rod.

Yet you find that, after a little hard use, the action and the balance of the rod don't live up to their promise.

Perhaps the ferrules or reel fittings work loose or collapse.

Quality in such things can only be tested in use and it's too late to regret having bought an inferior rod after you've lost a fine fish which, had the tackle been sound, would certainly have come to grass.

Hardy's "Lash On" Gaff

So, in choosing your fishing gear, we cannot emphasize strongly enough that quality and soundness should be your first and most important considerations.

This applies to all the tackle you use because, just as a chain is only as strong as its weakest link, so your hold on

WITH IMPROVED CARRIER.

a fish is no stronger than the weakest point in your tackle between the reel and the hook.

Which is why, now you know all there is to know about Hardy fishing gear, you shouldn't need any incentive to buy it.

But we're giving you one anyway.

Because, if you fill in the coupon at the bottom of this page, we'll make you a member of the famous Hardy Pall Mall Club. This not only entitles you to receive an annual copy of our Pall Mall brochure, it allows you to take advantage of the very generous special offers which

we make club members from time to time.

Join now and you'll qualify immediately for a free Hardy line of your choice when you buy either a Graphite or Boron rod and fly reel through Hardy Pall Mall. You'll also receive a Hardy new products brochure and a copy of the Hardy 1982 catalogue.

He examined my rod, asked me to let him have a few casts with it, then came back, took his own rod, chucked it on the ground. "I am off home, I'll sell my rod to someone and get a 'Hardy' rod like yours."
Letter quoted in Hardy Catalogue, 1912.

We're making you this offer because we believe that in no other sport can the cost of unsuitable equipment be so high in loss of money, opportunity, confidence and time.

That's the reason we go out, time and time again, to fish with the tackle we make. Not because it's a duty, but because we enjoy it. And we want to share our enjoyment with you.

⬛ HOUSE OF HARDY
61 Pall Mall London SW1.

Tim
Delaney

Tim Delaney started his career in advertising in the mail room. He worked as a copywriter at Y&R and BMP before joining BBDO London, where he became creative director at 27 and managing director at 31. He founded Leagas Delaney, aged 34.

Though he is chairman of an agency with offices in London, Hamburg, Milan, Shanghai and the US, he is a working copywriter and over the years has won awards for his work in all the major awards schemes, notably D&AD, One Show and Cannes.

The D&AD President's Award, the President's Award Creative Circle and the British Television Awards Lifetime Achievement Award have all been bestowed on Tim in recognition of his contribution to the advertising industry. In 2007, he was inducted into the One Show Advertising Hall of Fame in the US, and Campaign's British Advertising Hall of Fame in 2008.

How I write copy:

— On my laptop.
— With every available fact about product and category to hand.
— In a quiet meeting room. Or on Sunday morning.
— At least a day after the Project Manager says it's needed.

Opposite
Client: Tripp
Agency: Leagas Delaney
Year: 2007

Next spread
Client: Linguaphone
Agency: Leagas Delaney
Year: 1988

At Tripp, we understand the temptations placed in front of the intrepid traveller. So we make luggage that ingeniously expands to give 25% more packing space. It also provides external pockets for things like tickets, passports and free airline magazines. To protect your ill-gotten gains, we employ a strong honeycomb frame and fit tough EVA front panels. And to appeal to your obvious acumen, we reduce the price: £100 to £60. It's exclusive to Debenhams.

TRIPP

The expandable suitcase. Now you can steal the bathrobe as well as the toiletries.

Tripp Summer range.
45cm, 60cm, 68cm (shown here),
76cm upright cases,
duffle bag, wheeled duffle bag,
wheeled tote, vanity case.
Red or black.
www.tripp.co.uk

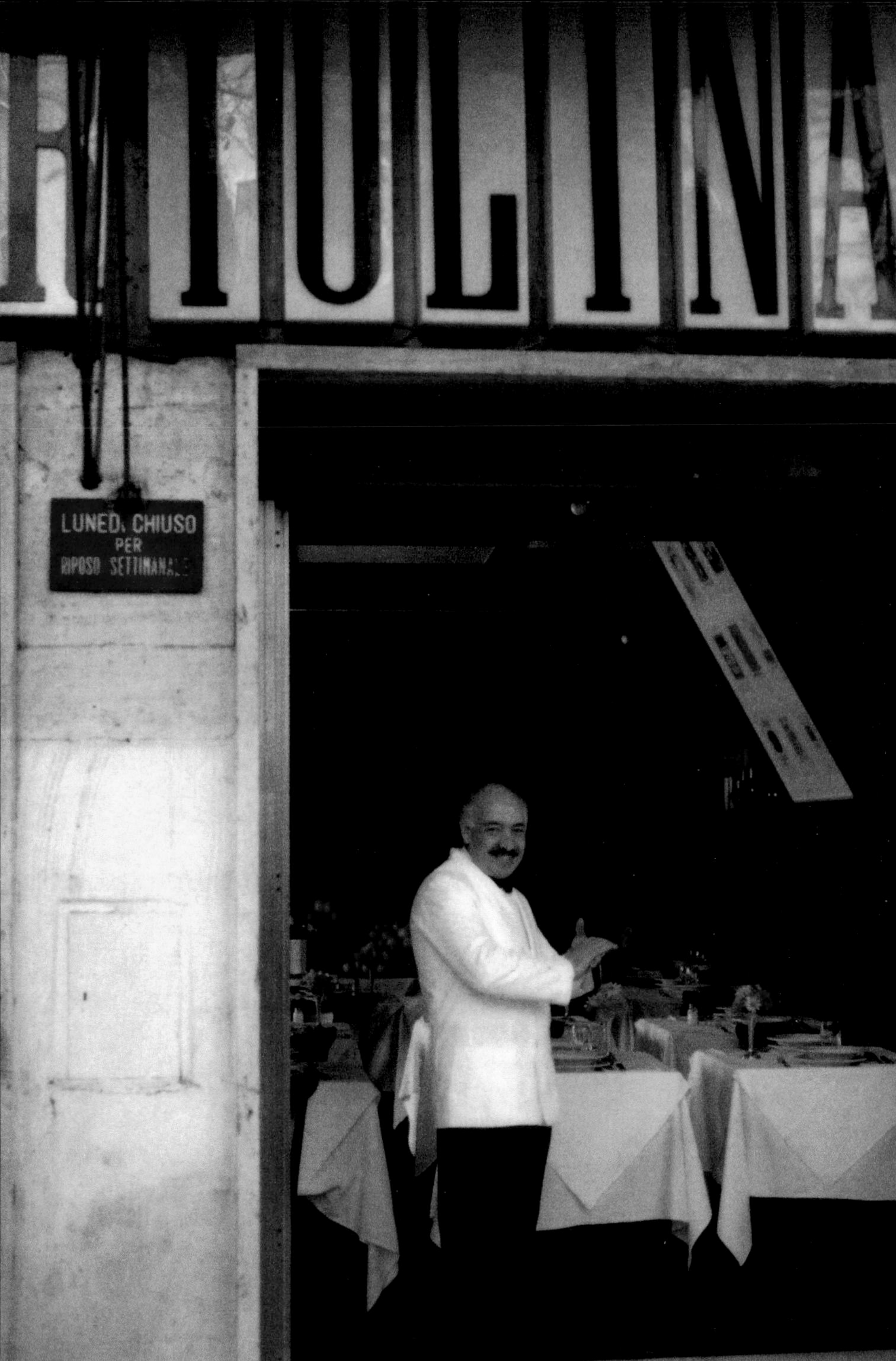

LUNEDì CHIUSO
PER
RIPOSO SETTIMANALE

'A table for two? Certainly you old trout?'

Have you ever doubted the sincerity of an Italian waiter's smile? Wondered what it was you said that made those Spanish shop assistants giggle? Or questioned why that French doctor gave you headache pills for food poisoning?

Haven't we all?

But imagine, for a moment, how different these situations might be if you could understand and talk to people when you're abroad.

At Linguaphone, we've spent the last 60 years helping people talk to each other. In fact since we began, Linguaphone has enabled over 5 million people to learn another language. And along the way, we have also learned some very important lessons.

Number one is that people learn faster if they're enjoying themselves. Number two is that people learn more easily when they listen to languages *before* they start reading about them.

Which sounds simple enough. And indeed it is. It's the very same way babies learn to talk.

Using a method developed by some of the most eminent linguists of our time, Linguaphone have taken this most elementary form of learning and speeded things up a little.

We use native speakers in life-like situations. The text book (you didn't think you'd get away without one did you?) is illustrated throughout with familiar objects with new names. Very quickly, you start imitating. Then conversing.

We use the same method to teach 30 different languages in 101 different countries.

Japanese use it to learn English. (Why don't more English businessmen learn Japanese?

Maybe we would still have a motorcycle industry.) Welsh people use it to learn Welsh. Someone somewhere uses it to learn Icelandic.

In this country, Linguaphone has helped men, women and children to further their educations and advance their careers.

No fewer than 27 British universities use it. As do many of the biggest companies in the world. Ford, Unilever, BP, American Express and British Airways among them.

If you want to know more about our language courses, just fill in the coupon.

And then the next time a waiter says something disagreeable, you won't have to smile graciously and agree with him.

LINGUAPHONE

Opposite
Client: Nationwide
Agency: Leagas Delaney
Year: 1989

Next spread
Client: Timberland
Agency: Leagas Delaney
Year: 1991

Page 110
Client: Pictet
Agency: Leagas Delaney
Year: 2008

Page 111
Client: Pictet
Agency: Leagas Delaney
Year: 2010

If you want to find out how banks became the richest, most powerful institutions in the world, go into the red one day.

Banks have not always been as big and profitable as they are today.

Believe it or not, all the big boys on the High Street were small businesses once.

(In 1955, Barclays only made just over £2½ million profit.)

How then, did the High Street banks achieve the status they enjoy today?

and, most important of all, easily understood.

Of course, the reverse is true with most bank current accounts.

Which is no doubt why they have Hollywood-style adverts telling customers how much they care for them.

At Nationwide Anglia, we believe in deeds not words.

You simply ring one phone number and punch in your personal code. Then, by pressing a few more buttons, you can pay your bills.

Or, just as easily, get instant confirmation of your balance or order a full statement.

From any telephone in the world, at any time day or night. And all in return for a £10 deposit, which is refundable.

COMMISSION
OVERDRAFT ADMIN
**** £26.00

Innovative ideas? Hardly. The first cheque was issued in 1659.

Dynamic management? You have called your bank manager a lot of things in your time, we bet 'dynamic' isn't one of them.

Customer satisfaction, then? No comment. No.

Quite simply, it is you, dear reader, who have made the banks so rich and powerful.

You, and millions of people like you, who over the years have put your hard earned money into their coffers and received little in return.

Indeed, when you have had the temerity to go into the red, you have paid dearly for it.

Thankfully, there is now an alternative to a bank current account.

Nationwide Anglia's FlexAccount.

An account based on a very simple idea: that it is your money and we should not forget the fact.

So if you go into the red with a FlexAccount you don't start attracting mysterious 'service charges'.

You won't suddenly find yourself having to pay for standing orders and direct debits for a whole three month period when you have only slipped into the red for one day. And we won't slap in a bill, sorry, 'arrangement fee' just for discussing and sorting out an overdraft.

All we ask of you is interest on the money you borrow until you're in the black.

We think this is reasonable, straightforward

So we pay FlexAccount holders interest on the money in their current account.

Not just to people with lots of money in their account, mind.

Every FlexAccount holder gets 2% net per annum on anything up to £99. 3% interest on sums between £100 and £499. And 4% when you're £500 or more in credit.

(Both the higher rates are paid on the whole balance, not just the amount over £100 or £500.)

All calculated daily and paid into your account annually.

This is the interest the High Street banks have traditionally believed is theirs.

Somewhat strange logic as it is your money that earns it.

Isn't there anything good about a bank current account?

Of course there is.

Cheque books, cheque guarantee cards and cash cards. Not forgetting other services like standing orders and direct debits.

All excellent facilities.

Which is why they are all available to FlexAccount holders.

But that's not all.

Being rather keen on new ideas, we also offer our customers something called a Home Banking Unit.

Which works like an unusually helpful, round-the-clock counter clerk.

Not everyone will want one, we know. But that's not the point.

It's another expression of our philosophy.

Another way of helping people manage their money and, ultimately, get more from it.

Does all this sound too good to be true? It shouldn't. It is, after all, common sense.

Which is no doubt why Channel Four television's 'Money Spinner' programme singled it out as being a service "which High Street banks would do well to take notice of."

So far they haven't. Just check your last statement.

If you went into the red, you'll find a deduction has been duly made.

No information about how it's computed. No breakdown. No nothing.

Is it really the best way to treat a customer?

We don't think so. Maybe that's because we are not one of the richest, most powerful institutions in the world.

For further information, just call into your local Nationwide Anglia branch.

Or write now to Claire Adams, Nationwide Anglia Building Society, Chesterfield House, Bloomsbury Way, London WC1V 6PW.

FlexAccount

We always remember whose money it is.

Nationwide Anglia Building Society

WE STOLE THEIR LAND, THEIR BUFFALO AND THEIR WOMEN.

THEN WE WENT BACK FOR THEIR SHOES.

The Red Indians were an ungrateful lot.
Far from thanking the whiteman for

labours is a shoe which comes with a heap big

Naturally, during the course of their disputes, the whiteman found it necessary to relieve the Red Indians of certain items.

Thousands of square miles of land, for instance, which they didn't seem to be using.

The odd buffalo, which provided some interesting culinary experiences for the folks heading West.

And of course the squaws, who were often invited along to soothe the fevered brows of conscience-stricken gun-runners and bounty hunters.

But perhaps the most lasting testament to this cultural exchange programme is the humble moccasin.

A shoe of quite ingenious construction. And remarkably comfortable to boot.

Even now, nearly two centuries after the first whiteman tried a pair on, they have yet to be bettered.

Which is why at Timberland, all of our loafers, boat shoes and walking shoes are based on the original Red Indian design.

How is this possible? Surely a shoemaker of our standing is capable of showing a clean pair of heels to a few pesky injuns?

Not really.

Although over the years, we have managed to make some modest improvements.

Rather than use any old buffalo hide, we always insist on premium full-grain leathers. And when we find a tannery that can supply them, we buy its entire output.

We then dye the leathers all the way through so you can't scuff the colour off and impregnate them with silicone oils to prevent the leather going dry.

It is at this point that we employ the wraparound construction of the moccasin to create the classic Timberland shoe.

Using a single piece of softened leather, our craftsmen mould and stretch the upper

around a specially-developed geometric last.

This has the effect of breaking the shoes in before you've even set foot in them.

It also extends the life of the shoe for many, many moons.

Our hand sewn shoes also hark back to the days before the whiteman came. No mass production. No deadlines.

Just a pair of nimble hands making shoes in the time-honoured way.

With just a little help from the twentieth century.

Like the high-strength nylon thread, double-knotted and pearl stitched to prevent it coming undone even if it's cut or in the unlikely event that it breaks.

The two coats of latex sealant, added to stop even tiny droplets of water sneaking in through the needle holes.

And the patented process which permanently bonds the uppers to the soles.

(If the Indians had only known how to cobble soles onto their moccasins, we probably wouldn't be in business today.)

As you would expect, the result of all our

Of scorching tarmac laces. Or Gore-Tex linings?

Come to that, what other shoemaker shows such concern for your feet when big rains come?

For example, as well as utilising all our traditional methods, our new Ultra Light range uses new technology to keep your feet dry.

They're lined with Gore-Tex to make them completely waterproof while allowing your feet to breathe. (Gore-Tex has 9 billion holes per square inch. We didn't believe it either but it works, so now we believe it.)

The soles are made from an incredibly lightweight and highly resistant, dual-density polyurethane.

And, in an uncharacteristic concession to fashion, some models even sport tightly woven waxed cotton cloth.

LEFT: TIMBERLAND UPPER, RIGHT: THE ORIGINAL MOCCASIN.

A far cry from the Red Indian moccasin?

We certainly hope not.

Because if we ever forget our origins, or change our old-fashioned way of making boots and shoes, one thing's for sure.

A lot of people are going to be on the warpath.

Timberland Shoes and Boots, 23 Pembridge Square, London W2 4DR. Telephone 01:727 2519.

Timberland

If you knew
more about us
we wouldn't
be so famous for
our discretion.

Geneva Zurich London Tokyo
Luxembourg Nassau Singapore Lausanne
Paris Frankfurt Madrid Milan Turin
Florence Rome Montreal Hong Kong

PICTET
1805
Independent minds

Every day our partners do something our clients really appreciate. They work.

Wealth Management
Asset Management
Investment Funds
Custody & Investor Services

Geneva Lausanne Zurich Basel London
Luxembourg Frankfurt Paris Madrid Barcelona
Turin Milan Rome Florence Dubai Singapore
Hong Kong Tokyo Montreal Nassau
www.pictet.com

PICTET
1805

Independent minds

Simon Dicketts

Simon Dicketts worked as a copywriter at Saatchi & Saatchi, where he was made joint creative director.

He has consistently won industry awards for outstanding press, television and cinema work for clients such as British Airways, Carlsberg-Tetley, *The Independent*, Pilkington, ICI, the Conservative Party and the Samaritans.

He was a founding partner of the New Saatchi Agency.

I suppose we all experience turning points in our careers. I'm not just talking about the usual landmarks like your first offer of a job or the first ad you write that actually gets into print and your mother sees, but moments in the game when you learn something that changes the way you approach things for ever.

One such moment sticks in my mind and this seems to be a good place to tell you about it. It goes something like this.

In the run-up to the 1984 election I was working on the Conservative Party campaign. (Whoops… I've lost my audience already… rule of copywriting, don't begin by alienating your readers, never mind, here goes…)

The Conservatives were already in power and seeking re-election. They were worried that people would have forgotten what life was like under Labour — naturally this was something that they thought was beyond the pale.

The brief was to produce an advertisement that would warn people what they would be letting themselves in for under a Labour Government.

Fergus Fleming and myself had been slaving away to this end in a sweaty little outpost of a God-forsaken area of the creative department dubbed "Milton Keynes" and as far as we were concerned we had cracked it.

Our headline read: "Putting a cross in the Labour box is the same as signing this piece of paper." Then there followed a series of ghastly facts and to top it all at the bottom of the page was a dotted line challenging the reader to put his or her name to it as if it were some dreadful hire-purchase agreement.

We were thrilled.

I had spent some hours researching and writing the copy and to cap it all the client had bought it.

Time to put our feet up and bask in the undoubted glory that would follow as the nation went to the polls to vote Conservative.

No. Time to learn something.

The door opened and there stood Charles Saatchi.

"You did this ad?" he asked, brandishing the aforementioned article.

"Yes," we replied, rising to our feet as lesser mortals tend to when they unexpectedly find themselves in the society of a "Demi-God".

"It's great," he said.

"Oh… well… thanks," we said as we sat down.

"Fergus," he elaborated, "it looks fantastic."

Fergus went a pretty colour which I was only subsequently to witness when he announced the birth of his first son.

"Now," he continued, "I need to have a word with Simon."

That's when he let me have it.

"Every ad is an opportunity. This could be a great ad. Every word you write now will be with you forever. Find the right tone and stick with it. Don't just write it as a series of facts, but find an attitude. And remember, once it's printed you can't change a thing. You want to be able to read this ad in years to come and be proud of it."

I followed his advice and the bugger was right. I read it today and I'm glad I did.

—

This lesson is no less relevant 23 years later.

I remind myself of it every time I sit down with a pen in my hand.

(I don't type. That's one lesson I've never learnt.)

I would like to add one thing. Copywriting doesn't mean copying writing.

We are not machines.

Develop your own style.

Celebrate your own individuality.

It's a lot more interesting.

It's certainly a lot more fun.

Opposite
Client: Conservative Party
Agency: Saatchi & Saatchi
Year: 1983

Next spread
Client: Conservative Party
Agency: Saatchi & Saatchi
Year: 1983

AS A PENSIONER HE'D BE BETTER OFF VOTING CONSERVATIVE.

As a pensioner in 1979 Michael Foot would have received £31.20 a week.

Now, under the Conservatives, he would receive £52.55 a week.

An increase of 68 per cent, way above any rise in prices over that period.

Under the Conservatives he would have received a Christmas bonus every year. A pleasant change after the cold Labour winters of '75 and '76.

As a pensioner he's better off voting Conservative.

Let's hope this time he puts his cross in the Conservative box.

It won't make him Prime Minister. But that's just as well for everybody.

PUTTING A CROSS IN THE LABOUR BOX IS THE SAME AS SIGNING THIS PIECE OF PAPER.

1. I hereby give up the right to choose which school my children go to and agree to abide by any decision made by the State on my behalf.

2. I empower the Labour Party to take Britain out of Europe, even though my job may be one of the $2\frac{1}{2}$ million which depend on Britain's trade with Europe.

3. I am prepared to see the Police Force placed under political control even though it could undermine their capability to keep law and order.

4. I agree that Britain should now abandon the nuclear deterrent which has preserved peace in Europe for nearly forty years. I fully understand that the Russians are not likely to follow suit.

5. I agree to have the value of my savings reduced immediately in accordance with Labour's wishes to devalue the pound.

6. I empower the government to borrow as much money as they wish from other countries and I agree to let my children pay the debt.

7. I fully agree to a massive expansion of nationalisation, whatever the cost to me in higher taxation.

8. I do not mind if I am forced to join a union. I do not expect to vote for the leaders of that union and do not mind if I am not consulted by secret ballot before being told to strike.

9. I sign away the right to buy my own council house.

10. I do not mind paying higher rates.

11. I am prepared to allow my pension fund to be used by the government to invest in any scheme that they see fit whether or not this shows a good enough return on my investment.

12. I understand that Labour's plans could mean that prices will double once more, as they did under the last Labour government.

13. I realise that the tax cuts from which I will have benefited under a Conservative government may be withdrawn at once.

14. I waive my right to choose any form of private medicine for my family.

15. I understand that if I sign this now I will not be able to change my mind for at least five years.

SIGNED.

CONSERVATIVE X

PUBLISHED BY CONSERVATIVE CENTRAL OFFICE

Opposite
Client: Index on
Censorship
Agency: Saatchi & Saatchi
Year: 1986

Next spread
Client: Pilkington
Agency: Saatchi & Saatchi
Year: 1985

If Samuel Beckett had been born in Czechoslovakia we'd still be waiting for Godot.

Samuel Beckett's Waiting for Godot is banned in Czechoslovakia. In fact any writing that doesn't reflect the opinions of the Czech government is banned.

Luckily Beckett is not Czech. But what of those writers who are Czechs? Index on Censorship is a magazine that is committed to exposing censorship

around the world and publishing the work of censored writers, film makers and photographers.
Work which you would otherwise not

be able to enjoy. To subscribe please write to us at 39c Highbury Place, London N5 1QP or you can telephone us on 01-359 0161.

Support Index on Censorship for crying out loud.

WE SENT A LARGE CONSIGNMENT OF LENS GLASS TO JAPAN LAST YEAR. MOST OF IT CAME STRAIGHT BACK.

If the Japanese didn't continually strive to produce the best cameras in the world it would be a different story.

But they do. That's why a good deal of the glass for their lenses doesn't come from Tokyo or Osaka. It comes from St Asaph in North Wales.

Last year Pilkington exported over 700 tons of high quality optical glass to Japan. Enough glass to make at least 20 million lenses.

Not just for cameras. For video cameras, photocopiers, binoculars and spectacles (three out of four Japanese photochromic sunglass wearers observe the rising sun through Pilkington Reactolite Rapide lenses).

Fortunately the Japanese aren't the only ones who know quality when they see it.

Pilkington produces almost one fifth of all the ophthalmic lenses in the western world and though ophthalmics represents only a fraction of the Group's output (about one twentieth) it's a market which is rapidly growing.

That's exactly why Pilkington is continually developing new areas.

Ultra sophisticated range finders. Holographic optics. Security equipment. Thermal imaging equipment.

Beyond the area of ophthalmics, scope for innovation in glass seems almost limitless.

Already Pilkington has developed a range of products as diverse as nuclear shielding windows and a glass pellet for livestock which actually dissolves in the stomach gradually releasing its vital minerals.

With 70% of our income now earned from abroad and with a worldwide turnover of more than £1,200,000,000 it seems our innovations are paying off handsomely.

It's certainly nice to hear of a British company succeeding so well in Japan when so often we hear the story the other way round.

It's also nice to know that thanks to Pilkington many of our foreign visitors get to see our more famous monuments in the best possible light.

PILKINGTON

Get off at the fashionable end of Oxford Street, drift into the achingly cool technology hall of London's most happening department store and view this year's must-have plasma courtesy of the sound and vision technologist in the Marc Jacobs sandals then go to dixons.co.uk and buy it.

Dixons.co.uk
The last place you want to go

Client: Dixons Store
Group
Agency: M&C Saatchi
Year: 2009

Opposite
Client: The Samaritans
Agency: Saatchi & Saatchi
Year: 1986

Why you should think more seriously about killing yourself.

We wouldn't want to alarm or shock unnecessarily.

But it is alarming that every year over 200,000 people in this country try to kill themselves.

And it is shocking because only a very few of them really want to die.

Over 95% of these people who try to kill themselves and survive are glad that they survived.

Out of those who didn't survive there will sadly be many who didn't really want to die because in most cases, an attempt at suicide is first and foremost a cry for help.

So is a call to the Samaritans.

The difference is that it's a cry that will always be answered.

That's exactly why a call to the Samaritans is a serious alternative.

This isn't to say that you have to be about to kill yourself to call the Samaritans.

We hope that people will call long before they reach that point.

The Samaritans are there to listen to anyone who needs someone to talk to, no reason for calling is ever too trivial.

A Samaritan will never censure, criticise or pass judgement.

All conversations, whether face to face or over the telephone are conducted in absolute confidence.

Samaritans are on call for 24 hours a day and 365 days a year. Anywhere in the country.

And there are daytime centres you can visit in nearly 200 cities and towns so there is bound to be one near you.

Anyone who does try to commit suicide and succeeds will never have the chance to change his or her mind.

That's why everyone should think more seriously about taking the easy way out and call the Samaritans.

Please.

The Samaritans.

Sean Doyle

In 1986, after failed attempts at becoming a journalist and a fireman, Sean Doyle joined the production department of Royds Advertising in Manchester. After failing at this too, he realised that writing ads was the only way forward for a man with a limited attention span and few qualifications.

Sean subsequently worked at BBDO, Simons Palmer Denton, WCRS, Leagas Delaney, DDB and AMV winning D&AD Pencils and Golds and Silvers at One Show, Campaign Posters and Campaign Press along the way.

In 2002 he launched Campbell Doyle Dye with Walter Campbell and Dave Dye. In 2007, he started Panic, a quick-turnaround creative operation (and in so doing, got to live his firefighting dream). In this capacity, he has solved problems for agencies including M&C Saatchi, DDB, The Assembly, R/GA, RKCR/Y&R, adam&eve, Ogilvy, Iris, Anomaly and Big Al's.

"Nah."
Tim Delaney

Best lesson in advertising I ever had, that. You'd go into Tim with around 30 ads (20 was the minimum, 40 was just creeping), and sometimes you'd be lucky and he'd pick two or three from the pile. Other times, he'd grimace, pick none, and just go "Nah". He didn't have to elaborate, or steer you anywhere, or even pick out some close-but-no-cigars. He just wanted you to carry on working. He knew that the more work you put in, the better the results would be.

It's obvious really. The more ideas you come up with, the less obvious the later ones are going to be, if only because you have to avoid repeating those first thoughts. So you're bound to get to a more original idea.

Such scant feedback would infuriate some people. And it *was* infuriating at the time because you didn't know where to go next. But when you're not told where to go next, you have to find out for yourself. So you just keep thinking, stewing, writing, until suddenly you find yourself — through the sheer act of doing, of working hard, of generating — in a place where you're on to something. (I believe cool people call it "the zone", I can't say for sure.) Tim didn't really teach. He wanted you to just get on with the job and teach yourself. And that's much quicker and more effective than any long drawn-out critique. Don't think, just do, and thoughts will definitely happen along the way.

Always be collecting

There are gazillions of ideas floating around out there, just awaiting collection. Just keep your radar on for anything remotely interesting, and snatch it. Be bothered to write it down or photograph it. Then file it away. It's amazing how a seemingly irrelevant object you see in the street can suddenly become the perfect answer to a problem. You can come up with some great ideas when you're not trying to come up with some great ideas.

Wake up early

Get into work before anyone else. Psychologically, physically, literally, you've got a head start on others. There's no noise. Plus your brain is less cluttered the closer you are to sleep so your thinking has more clarity. Your agency seems like a whole other world with no other people in it, and there's nothing like a change of environment to stimulate your creative juices.

Beware of the committee

We live in politically correct times. So everyone's allowed an opinion: the creative team, the creative director, the planner, the account director, the account exec, the junior planner. They could each have a different, valid opinion. But if you try and accommodate them all in your ad — valid as they may be — you end up with an idea that may tick a lot of boxes, but won't be brutally single-minded. And if your idea isn't brutally single-minded, it's bad. Be petty and defend even the tiniest detail.

Less isn't always more

Look at the two sentences below, both saying exactly the same thing.

"Women don't get the recognition they deserve."

"Ginger Rogers did everything Fred Astaire did. Only she did it backwards and in high heels."

Yes, the first one's shorter. Yes, it's more to the point. But which one might stick in your mind? Clue: you've forgotten the first one already.

Pick a side

Ask most creative teams these days "Who's the art director and who's the writer?" and you always get "Ah, we both do both." Which means they're both pretty good at doing ideas but maybe not quite as good as they could be at crafting them.

The idea is the most important thing, obviously, but the craft is only just behind it. When people are judging ads at awards-time, they're looking for those details that elevate a piece of work above the rest. The ones that get rewarded are the ones that have care lavished on every little element of them. Nothing wrong in being a specialist in one area.

Avoid brainstorms if you want

I say *if you want* because some people like them. I hate them. And I've always managed to fall mysteriously ill when one loomed on the horizon. If you hate the idea of sitting in a room with lots of other people, throwing ideas out, trying to make yourself heard, try and get out of it. Maybe you're shy. Maybe you can only work without noise. Maybe you're a better thinker when you're holed up in your own space. If people accuse you of being non-collaborative and stand-offish, well, you know, fuck 'em. You are what you are.

Opposite
Client: National
Newspapers of Ireland
Agency: BMP DDB
Year: 1998

To get people to advertise in newspapers, what better strategy than to demonstrate how different an ad could look? But rather than having all that blank space and a headline that spells the whole message out (like *Different, isn't it?*), it's much more rewarding for the reader when they have to do a little bit of the work themselves.

e.g.

$2.15

The Macallan 25-year-old Single Malt

IT'S NOT THE WINNING

IT'S THE TAKING APART

NIKE

Brian Moore. Harlequins & England.

Client: Nike
Agency: Simons Palmer
Denton Clemmow &
Johnson
Year: 1991

Opposite
Client: The Macallan
Agency: Campbell
Doyle Dye
Year: 2006

Next spread
Client: English Heritage
Agency: Leagas Delaney
Year: 1996

Great brand. Best agency of the early '90s. Account men who daren't return from the client with a non-sale. All the ingredients were there. It's sometimes good to take a clichéd expression and add one little thing. In this case that one little addition was the letter "a". Ballsy, powerful art direction by Mark Denton.

Good old Stella Artois. Paved the way for clients to show off about their products being expensive. Unlike Stella, though, with The Macallan there's no creative licence and exaggeration necessary. It's the truth. We did dozens of ideas but I like this one because it makes the "expensive" point intelligently, rather than cleverly.

A gorgeous-looking campaign, crafted by Dave Dye and Dave Wakefield. With those two, it was always going to look beautiful, so the headline didn't need to say "beautiful". Which meant there was room for a bit of wit here, to show that English Heritage wasn't some stuffy organisation.

IN 1092, William Rufus, angered that Carlisle was *proclaimed* part of Scotland, went north, drove the Scots out and ordered the building of a stronghold in the borderlands. Thus *Carlisle Castle* was constructed just half a mile outside the city. And ever since it has been the scene of numerous battles with different factions fighting for ownership. It was besieged by parliamentarians in the Civil War, then by Bonnie Prince Charlie during the Jacobite Rising. In order to repel such attacks, the castle defences have been extensively remodelled over the centuries. Perhaps the most notable 'guest' at Carlisle Castle was *Mary Queen of Scots*, a prisoner there back in 1568. You can see Queen Mary's Tower and take the very route she took during her daily walks around the grounds.

THIS year marks the 250th anniversary of the imprisonment of *Jacobites* inside Carlisle Castle following the *1745 Rising*. Led by Bonnie Prince Charlie, they succeeded in taking Carlisle Castle before marching southwards to claim the throne for Charlie's father, James Stuart. An *exhibition* within the castle tells the dramatic story of the Jacobites' movements. *How* they returned north in defeat with the Duke of Cumberland's men hot on their heels. *How* they were captured and imprisoned, many of them later to be hanged, drawn and quartered on the nearby *Gallows Hill*. In a dungeon, you will see the famous *Licking Stones*. A permanently moist wall which provided a little water for the Jacobites in this overcrowded prison.

WHEN

YOU BUILD A CASTLE

FOR A KING WHO'S RENOWNED

FOR CHOPPING

PEOPLE'S HEADS OFF, YOU BUILD

A REALLY NICE CASTLE.

Located in the small village of Belsay, 14 miles north-west of Newcastle, *Belsay Hall* consists of a well-preserved fourteenth-century castle, the ruins of a seventeenth-century mansion and one of the most important *neo-classical* houses in Britain. But the real jewels in the crown are the 30 acres of magnificent formal gardens, exotic quarry gardens and woodland that surround the buildings. A stroll through the grounds at Belsay

reveals sycamore, oak and ash trees, the Magnolia Terrace, the Rhododendron Garden, the lovely Meadow Garden. Much of what you see there reflects the eccentric character of Sir Charles Monck. He returned from his 19-month European honeymoon, 1804–1806, full of ideas to build a *new home* at Belsay in beautiful neo-Greek

WHEN Osborne House was completed in 1851 to provide a country residence for Queen Victoria, it was considered by Her Majesty to be 'small and snug'. However, to humble subjects such as you and I, it is anything but. *Osborne*, on the Isle of Wight, served as a peaceful seaside retreat where Queen Victoria and Prince Albert could escape the strict confines of ceremony. And a *magnificent* retreat it is too. Albert's passion for the Italian *Renaissance* is clearly evident, what with the Italianate terrace, the Andromeda fountain and the cement copies of the fine Medici Lions from the *Loggia de' Lanzi*, Florence. Inside you will see a classical Roman statue, the *Marine Venus*, a lovely fresco painting by William Dyce and lots of extravagant grotesque decoration. In the Durbar Room there's a change of country, this state banqueting hall having been designed in the Indian style. Other rooms worth visiting are the Royal Apartments, the Billiards Room and the Nursery Suite. And the perfect way to *finish your day* at Osborne House is to take a Victorian horse and carriage ride from the main building to the delightful Swiss Cottage, a present from the Queen to her children in 1854.

HENRY VIII aside, many other royals have spent time at WALMER CASTLE. Amongst

TO celebrate the 1996 Year of Visual Arts, Belsay Hall will come alive again from 4th May until 26th October. The '*Living at Belsay*' exhibition will feature the work of selected craftsmakers and artists who'll be refurbishing the entrance and the three main reception rooms. It's a novel idea which will see the *normally* bare rooms equipped with magnificent furniture, fine ceramics, glassware and wall hangings. A rare chance to see contemporary artistry in an historical setting.

Walmer Castle, Kent.

...distinguished visitors. Like Walmer Pitt the Younger, who was Lord Warden until his death in 1806. He would try and visit whenever his official duties would allow. A later Lord Warden, the *Duke of Wellington*, was equally taken with his 'charming marine residence'. His room is arranged just as it was during his stay, its plain, modest furnishings bearing testimony to the Iron Duke's preference for unsophisticated surroundings. You can see the very armchair where he died in 1852, his campaign-bed which still retains its original horsehair mattress and, in the WELLINGTON MUSEUM just along the corridor, the boots worn by the celebrated British war hero.

DURABILITY, not beauty, was the main requirement in the construction of *Walmer Castle*. However, the architects, not wishing to take any chances with the notoriously hard to please Henry VIII, wisely decided to address both issues. One of a chain of coastal artillery forts, Walmer was built to thwart any invasions by Spain or France. This was a real possibility as Henry's split with the Roman Catholic Church and destruction of many monasteries had infuriated the papacy. The castle differed from earlier mediaeval defences in that it had no high walls or lofty towers. In fact, so *attractive* was Walmer that only minor modifications were needed to make it the comfortable residence it is today. For more information on English Heritage and our role in preserving the nation's significant buildings please *call* 0171 973 3434 or *visit* any one of our 400 sites.

It's yours. Why not visit it.

ENGLISH HERITAGE

Client: Pepe Jeans
Agency: Leagas Delaney
Year: 1997

Opposite
Client: Christian Aid
Agency: SHOP
Year: 2008

Next spread
Client: Adidas
Agency: Leagas Delaney
Year: 1995

The idea was to give Pepe a bit of attitude, make it stand out from the cool-looking modelly ads of other jeans manufacturers. The brief was "Fuck off", as I recall. A tad more interesting than "Look great in Pepe Jeans".

This picture is a cliché: it's an ad for a charity and it shows the poor victim. So far, so bad. But with him speaking to you casually about a little thing like turning your thermostat down, it has a newness about it. That picture seems sort of wrong with that headline. But that clash is why it works.

Trail-running is all about getting out there and running without paths, without other people around, without straight lines. It's running at its rawest. It's going from A to B without knowing where B actually is. All very logical really.

Sorry to bother you.
Any chance of turning
that thermostat
down a degree?

 Climate change isn't some threat to the future. It's today's reality. Environmental disasters, such as droughts in Niger, are wrecking people's lives with more and more frequency. And it's going to get worse. Want to do something about it? Good, we need people like you. Visit our website to see how the actions of you and your workplace can change the world for the better. Or text CLIMATE1 to 84880 for an 'Actions' poster.* Climate changed. Let's get to work. www.climatechanged.org

MAKE YOUR OWN B.

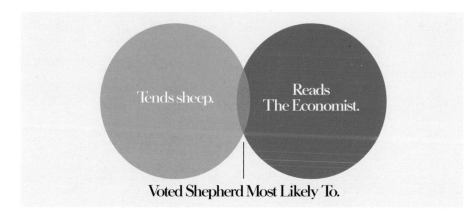

Tends sheep.

Reads
The Economist.

Voted Shepherd Most Likely To.

Client: The Economist
Agency: AMV BBDO
Year: 2000

Dave Dye had a great idea
to inject a bit of newness
into the *Economist* work:
Venn diagrams. (Although
he did see the technique
in my copy of *The Sun*.)
We did hundreds and whit-
tled them down to our 20
favourites. Others were:
"Reads *The Economist*.
Maverick. Has his name
below the door." And
"Reads *The Economist*.
Catholic. Earns lots, feels
guilty about it."

Next spread
Client: Mercedes-Benz
Agency: Campbell
Doyle Dye
Year: 2007

To highlight the safety
features of the Mercedes
E Class, we thought,
"What's the end benefit?"
Obvious answer: they'll
stop you being in an accident. So we simply pointed
these non-accidents out
in the form of official
announcements.

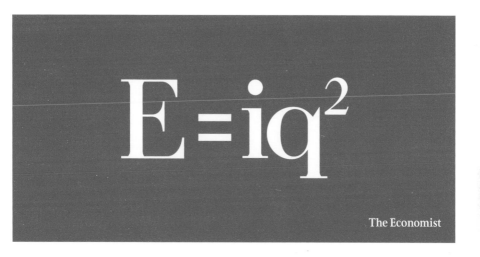

Client: The Economist
Agency: AMV BBDO
Year: 2001

The *Economist* brief was
"Intelligent". *Economist*
begins with E. Intelligence
is IQ. A bit of doodling
around on a layout pad and
it was just a short leap to
that headline. Not rocket
science, this job.

Active Body Control automatically adjusts the chassis settings to the driving situat

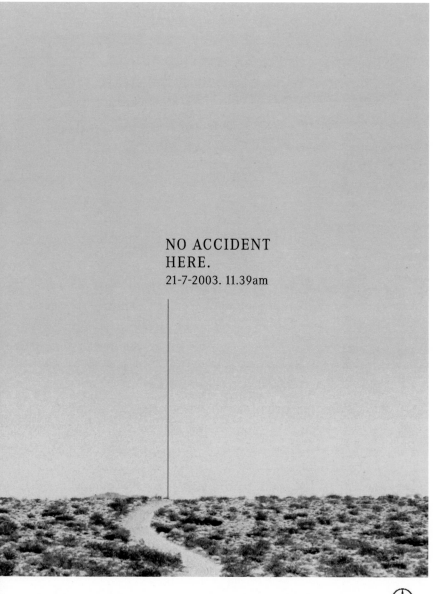

NO ACCIDENT
HERE.
21-7-2003. 11.39am

ves greater directional stability at all times and makes for a smooth, if uneventful, journey. Mercedes-Benz

Malcolm Duffy

Malcolm Duffy has worked through an alphabet of agencies, DMB&B, Colman RSCG, CDP and AMV BBDO to name but a few. In 1999 he set up Miles Calcraft Briginshaw Duffy with Jeremy Miles, Helen Calcraft and Paul Briginshaw.

The agency produced the cinema ad of the year (Aristoc), radio ad of the year (Travelocity), press ad of the year (Millets), the DM ad of the year (Met Police) and the TV ad of the decade (Hovis). Malcolm has now left the building.

When writing you must do whatever works for you. This is what worked for me. Pulling the product to pieces. Before putting finger to keypad, I liked to interrogate the product as though it was a spy. I'd pester the account people for facts and figures. And when they came up with them, I'd pester them for some more. You simply can't have too much information when you're writing an ad.

The Thesaurus. The English language is amazing. We seem to have a hundred words for everything. Why not make the most of it. David Abbott once caught me thumbing through a Thesaurus on the hunt for an *Economist* ad. "You'll not find the answer in there," he said. But for once he was wrong. There on page 588 was the word "magnate", and a few moments later was the *Economist* poster "Attracts Magnates". Four weeks later the ad ran. If you're working on something with an adult theme, may I recommend Roger's Profanisaurus, one of the greatest books ever written.

Don't write. Re-write. I liked to go through my work over and over and over. Then go through it again five more times for good measure. It always got better, not worse. I sometimes used to go through copy so many times I knew it off by heart. Ask yourself, is your copy worth memorising?

Read. You can't be a writer if you're not a reader. I've always got a book on the go. Devour as much good writing as you can get your hands on. Ads. Books. Articles. Packaging. Whatever. It doesn't matter. If good things are going into your head, good things will come out.

Make lists. If I ever found myself stuck in a writing rut I'd dig myself out by writing lists of appropriate words. Let's suppose I was writing an ad for soap and all I could come up with was "Joe's Soap. The Clean Machine." I'd open my Thesaurus and write down as many words as I could find to do with soap and cleaning. There were always lots. Then I'd write at least one headline for each word. There was soon a huge list to choose from. Many of them better than the first effort. And the ones I didn't use for a headline were often good enough to use in the copy. The beauty of simplicity. The best copy is always concise. If you want to write flowery stuff, become a poet.

The element of surprise. If your words can't surprise you, they won't surprise anyone else. Very few products are so amazing that all you have to do is tell people that they exist. That's why every word you write is so important. Use word-play, alliteration, quotes, observations. Whatever it takes to keep the consumer gripped. No one ever bored someone into buying a product.

Keep smiling. Copywriting is not an easy job. But it is a great job. You get to make things up. You get to work on lots of different brands. You get to learn lots of new stuff. You get to see your work in print. And you get paid for it. Not a bad way to spend a working week. And if none of these work for you, don't panic. You're a copywriter. I'm sure you'll think of something.

Client: The Economist   *Opposite*
Agency: AMV BBDO   Client: Apple
Year: 1994   Agency: AMV BBDO
                         Year: 1993

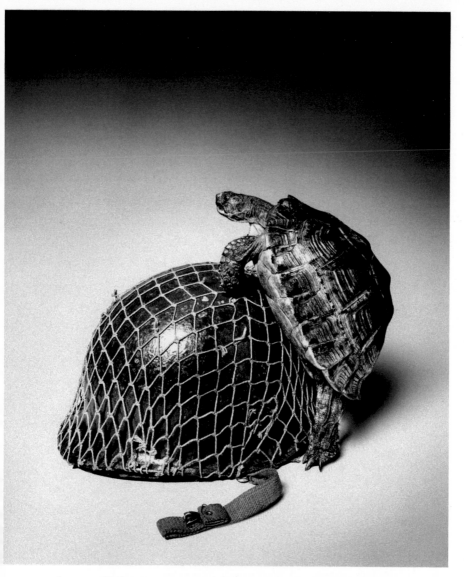

Compatibility is never a problem with Apple Macintosh.

Finding the right partner can be one of life's more painful experiences.

But not if your name's Apple™ Macintosh™ We're compatible with absolutely everything.

We work with other personal computers, host systems and their networks.

We can import and use MS-DOS® files, run industry-standard programs such as WordPerfect® and Lotus® 1-2-3™ and even run programs written in MS-DOS.

On top of all that, Apple Macintosh is renowned as the easiest personal computer in the world to use. Millions of people are more productive as a result and they find everyday tasks more enjoyable.

In fact, whatever type of work you do, and whether you're a dab hand or a novice in the field of personal computers, there's one thing you can be absolutely sure of.

Apple Macintosh is the perfect match.

 Apple™ Macintosh.™ The power to succeed.

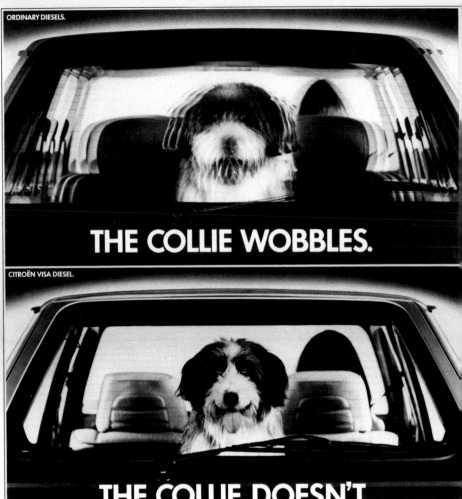

ORDINARY DIESELS.

THE COLLIE WOBBLES.

CITROËN VISA DIESEL.

THE COLLIE DOESN'T.

THE CITROËN VISA DIESEL. FROM £4,799.

WHAT'S YOURS CALLED?

YUGO
(So do we. 71.5 mph with the Mistral behind us.)

SEAT
(Yes, we've got four of those as well.)

COLT
(You get the power of two grown-up horses in our little thoroughbred.)

PANDA
(With bumpers front and rear we've been a protected species for years.)

POLO
(We've got a hole in the middle too. It's called a sunroof.)

NISSAN
(Nice huts, but will they last as long as a 2CV?)

CITROËN 2CV DOLLY
(What a sensible little name.)

The Citroën 2CV Dolly (now in blue and yellow) at £3,245. For your nearest
dealer dial 100 and ask for Freefone Citroën UK or write to Citroën Freepost at the address below.
Ask your dealer about 0%ᴀᴘᴿ finance available throughout November.

Client: Citroën
Agency: Colman RSCG
Year: 1987

Opposite
Client: Citroën
Agency: Colman RSCG
Year: 1986

The average smoker needs over five thousand cigarettes a year.

Get unhooked. Call 0800 169 0 169 or visit getunhooked.co.uk

SMOKEFREE

Client: Department
of Health
Agency: MCBD
Year: 2007

Opposite top
Client: Gossard
Agency: AMV BBDO
Year: 1996

Opposite bottom
Client: WebBaby
Agency: MCBD
Year: 2000

Next spread
Client: Olympus
Agency: CDP
Year: 1990

The Don McCullin exhibition. Featuring the work of Idi Amin, Pol Pot and Ho Chi Minh.

For over twenty years Don McCullin travelled to the battlefields of the world armed only with a camera.

In Cambodia his pictures bore witness to the work of the Khmer Rouge and their fanatical leader Pol Pot.

In Vietnam he was party to both the horrors of war and the dangers of war coverage. Forty-five journalists and photographers were killed and another eighteen are still missing.

In the Congo he found himself embroiled in a conflict made all the dirtier by the involvement of gun-toting mercenaries. And he visited places whose names have become synonymous

But if war and oppression gave us his most powerful pictures then surely peacetime has given us his most appealing ones.

From his travels in the East are photographs of New Guinea tribes, a religious festival on the banks of the Ganges, and scenes from the Sumatra Islands.

From our shores there are dramatic landscapes.

And from his own home there is a series of still lifes.

For this major retrospective includes McCullin photographs that have never been shown before.

McCullin used Olympus cameras for many of these pictures, and Olympus in return are proud to be sponsoring this exhibition.

His work can be viewed at The Royal Photographic Society, Milsom Street, Bath from June 29th to September 1st.

Don McCullin has seen it all. Now so can you. **OLYMPUS**

Jim Durfee

Jim Durfee, Carl Ally and Amil Gargano opened Carl Ally on July 2, 1962 and things began to happen — heroic wins, spectacular losses and headline controversies.

Never before had a single agency been endowed with such a magnificent array of talent: David Altschiller, Ron Berger, Ed McCabe, Tom Messner, Steve Penchina, Martin Puris, Dick Raboy, to name but a few.

As copy chief Jim hired, mentored and learned from this crew. Then came ten years of running Durfee & Solow with fellow writer Martin Solow. Which led to three years as vice chairman, corporate creative director of Della Femina McNamee. Which led to a merger forming Messner Vetere Berger McNamee Schmetterer Euro/RSCG. He was again a partner, in an agency with one office and only one measure of success. The quality of the work.

"Kill all your darlings."

If a single commandment could be burned into the mind of each beginning writer, it should be this one. If a single mantra were to be chanted by every experienced writer, it should be this one.

Mark Twain wrote these words, and lived by them. Here's why I try to. By shunning that darling of all darlings — the pun headline — I'm left with no-nonsense straight talk. Prospects can never get enough of that. By avoiding cutesy-clever copy phrases I eliminate the danger of show-off writing. And when I'm writing long, flowing, beautiful, heart-pounding sentences (like this one) I know I'm in danger of spewing ego-garbage. Which endangers clear thinking. So I start over. Well, usually.

Copywriting, of course, is not a matter of rules and regulations. Hell, then anybody could do it. Yet guidelines and checkpoints can be helpful. Here, in no particular order, are a few that work for me. Believe, really believe, that every word you write will be read and you'll write better. And be read more. Never lecture. Remember how boring lectures were in college? A headline that needs a subhead usually needs more work. Don't fall into the trap of writing to a prospect profile. In fact, don't "write" at all. Visualise the one person you want to influence, then sit that one person down across from you. Now talk to him or her through your pen, pencil, typewriter, word processor or whatever.

Every product has its own truth, its own believability zone. Stray and your readers will know. Oh yes, they'll know. Don't rely on your art director to save you. A strong idea, simply presented, is far more effective than a weak idea strongly presented. There is no such thing as long copy. There is only too-long copy. And that can be two words if they are not the right two words. If you find yourself developing a creative philosophy, your growth is over. Stagnation has set in.

Write short sentences with small words and few adjectives. They are easier to read. And more interesting and believable. Never write an ad a competitor can sign.

When you get your copy to the point where you're really, really happy with it, cut it by a third. Take the embarrassment test. Imagine yourself standing before your family, reading your copy aloud. Still proud of it?

Listen hard as you write. Are you hearing the prospect say, "Yes! Yes! That's what I want to hear. More! More!" Write for yourself. Never write for your creative director. Neither of you will be happy with the result.

Every writer needs an editor. If you find a good one, treasure the relationship. I have not only been blessed with a great editor, she consented to marry me 22 years ago. And now about these ads.

Opposite
Client: Lotus
Agency: Durfee & Solow
Year: 1983

Next spread
Client: Hertz
Agency: Carl Ally
Year: 1969

Sometimes an ad is stronger without copy. When you write a headline that induces the reader to become emotionally involved, he'll write his own copy. And it'll be better than yours.

If you're being attacked, don't defend. Attack back. In the great rent-a-car war, it took only 90 days, with ads like this, to demolish a powerhouse Avis underdog campaign that had been hurting Hertz for years. And "We're No. 1" became the cry of the land.

At least some part of your life should be on your own terms.

No. 2 says he Than who?

We wouldn't, for a minute, argue with No. 2. If he says he tries harder, we'll take him at his word.

The only thing is, a lot of people assume it's us he's trying harder than.

That's hardly the case. And we're sure that No. 2 would be the first to agree.

Especially in light of the following.

A car where you need

The first step in renting a car is getting to the car. Hertz makes that easier for you to do than anybody else.

We're at every major airport in the United States. And at some airports that are not so major. Ever fly to Whitefish, Montana? Some people do. And have a Hertz car waiting.

No matter how small the airport you fly to, if it's served by a commercial airline, 97 chances out of 100 it's also served by Hertz or by a Hertz office within 20 minutes of it.

We also have locations throughout the downtown and suburban areas of every major city.

In all, Hertz has over 2,900 places throughout the world where you can pick up or leave a car. Nearly twice as many as No. 2.

Can't come to us? We'll come to you.

We have a direct line telephone in most major hotels and motels in the U.S. It's marked HERTZ and it's in the lobby. Pick it up, ask for a car, and we'll deliver one to the door. You often can't get a cab as easily.

What kind of car would you like?

When you rent from Hertz, you're less likely to get stuck with a beige sedan when you want a red convertible. We have over twice as many cars as No. 2.

Not only is our fleet big, it's varied. We do our best to give you what you want. From Fords, to Mustangs, to Thunderbirds, to Lincolns and everything in between. Including the rather fantastic Shelby GT 350-H.

What kind of service will you get?

When you rent a new car from us or anybody else, you expect it to be sitting there waiting, ready to go, looking like new.

On that score we claim no superiority over our competition. They goof once in awhile. We goof once in awhile.

Except when we goof it bothers us more because people don't expect the big one to goof. And to make up for it, if our service is not up to Hertz standards we give you $50 in free rentals. * Plus an apology.

No. 2 gives a quarter plus an apology. And

*There's one thing you have to do for us: fill out our Certified Service form and mail it to our main office in it's self-addressed envelope. Upon verification we'll send you $50 in rental certificates by return mail.

tries harder.

advertises that he "can't afford" to do more.

We feel the other way about it. We can't afford to do less.

Besides, the $50 comes out of the station manager's local operating funds. This tends to keep him very alert... and our service very good.

Hot line.

When you're in one city and you're flying to another city and you want to have a car waiting when you arrive and you want it confirmed before you leave, we can do it for you. Instantly. In any one of 1,038 U.S. cities. No other rent a car company can make that statement.

The major reason we can do it is because we recently installed one of the world's most advanced reservations systems.

After all, with the supersonic jets in sight and one hour coast to coast flights in prospect, you'll need some quick answers.

We can give them to you today.

About credit.

If you've got a national credit card with most any major company, you've got credit with us.

A businesslike way of doing business.

If you own your own firm or are instrumental in running a firm, you know what a nightmare billing can be.

Have your company rent from us and we'll help ease that nightmare. We can even tailor our billing cycle to fit your paying cycle.

We'll bill by the rental, by the month, by division, by department, by individual, and by blood type if it'll help you.

Speak up No. 3.
Is it you that No. 2 tries harder than?

Hertz

Paul
Fishlock

When the realisation he'd never be a rock star set in and the novelty of being a removal man wore off, Paul Fishlock was very fortunate to stumble into advertising. More fortunate still to be allowed to stay and, over the years, learn from some of the legends in this book in both London and Australia.

He was a founding partner of Sydney agency Brown Melhuish Fishlock (BMF), which he and his partners built into Australia's largest independent agency.

After BMF, Paul spent a few years as executive creative director/chairman of The Campaign Palace. Currently, he is principal of Behaviour Change Partners and chief marketing officer of 878TEN.

Maybe it's just me, but I've never written a piece of copy I didn't want to change. Actually, I know it's not just me. Looking back through the original *Copy Book*, I was reassured to see restless editing as a recurring theme. Draft. Write. Re-write. Throw away. Write again. Edit. Re-write. Write from memory. Time's up. Damn! It was just starting to come together. So it was with two eager hands that I grasped the opportunity to revisit something I wrote half a career ago.

Reading it again, an "I-am-not-worthy" paralysis at writing about writing in a book of writers echoes down the columns. There's a lesson in that beyond any merit you may or may not find in the content. Readers like authenticity. In ads it's all too easy to be slick and shallow and they can spot it a mile off. Don't be afraid to let how you feel about your subject come through. It should be a deafening conviction in the benefits of what you're selling. If it isn't, close your laptop and don't open it again until it is.

So what can I add to my 1995 contribution that won't be said better by one of my copywriting neighbours? As a card-carrying dinosaur, how about this unfashionable suggestion: despite all the brouhaha that everything's changed forever, the fundamentals of copywriting haven't. Why? Because, at their best, they tap into hard-wired drivers of human behaviour, which evolve over thousands of years not ten minutes.

Readers approach our copy with the same question they always have: "Is what you're selling better than what I'll otherwise do or buy?" If you can't convince them it is, nothing happens and you've wasted your client's money. It's as true of a Tweet as it is of a DPS broadsheet (pause for sentimental sigh).

To the greater wisdom between these covers I also offer five modest observations: all things I've long suspected but with age, experience and advancing curmudgeonliness, I am now more convinced of than ever.

We are not in the entertainment business we're in the influence business. It's my version of something Dave Trott said to me (and every other wannabe) some 30 years ago: "Our job is not to make people think what a great ad, it's to make them think what a great product". Mr Trott, you're a genius. In this elegant line is not just why advertising exists but why it usually goes wrong. With Dave's permission, I'll put it above the door if ever I do another start-up. Look, I love entertaining ads as much as you do. I love it when people say one of mine is one of their favourites. I love how cleverness and humour can make your message more engaging and memorable. But entertainment alone is not why we get paid. Don't forget to sell. Our history is littered with lauded, awarded campaigns that have catapulted their authors to fame but failed to do the one thing they were supposed to do. You know who you are.

Copywriting is more science than you may think. If you accept a copywriter's job is to change behaviour, how can you *not* have a world-class curiosity about how to change behaviour? Read up about psychology and brain science — it's fascinating and useful. Not to replace your genius but to make you an even greater genius. Creativity underpinned by proven principles of persuasion works better than creativity flying blind.

Creative prizes are a false God. Some brilliant advertising wins awards; ideas we should all stand up and applaud. But flaky advertising wins the same awards; it's inevitable given beauty pageant judging that puts gags and visible cleverness on the home straight before everyone else even starts. And shameful cheats stand with both of them on the podium clutching identical prizes. Profound cheats who should be disembowelled for fabricating everything from client to media and regular cheats who should simply hang for thinking "award" versions of ads are OK because everybody does it.

The end result is that creative awards are a totally unreliable currency of good and bad advertising. Anyone who measures copywriters, agencies, networks or countries on their prizes alone is a fool. Never set out to win an award. Set out to create a brilliant piece of persuasive advertising. If it doesn't smell like something that won a prize last year, don't change it.

We influence some of the least important decisions in people's lives. Real people aren't as interested in their choice of toothpaste as you are. It may be life and death for agency and client — careers, school fees and mortgages depend on it — but often the best thing you can do for Mrs Smith is help her drop something in her trolley without thinking. Life's too short to do a cost benefit analysis every time you want to buy something. This is not an excuse for lazy copy, it's a case for harder-working copy. Stand in the supermarket, bar or showroom and watch people at the exact moment they decide whether to buy your product or your competitor's. Your ad may have charmed her in her living room but if it doesn't work here, it doesn't work.

Beware management. Nothing to do with MDs changing headlines just a career warning flag. Become a great copywriter and becoming group head, creative director or ECD will one day beckon. It will feel like a logical next step, with more money and make your mum proud but it's likely to be a totally different job from the one you're good at and love doing. While some copywriters thrive on management others die painfully from resource utilisation spreadsheets, firing friends to meet budget and having to be your worst client's best buddy. So check the crown fits you before you put it on — it's hard to go back. (On the other side of the coin, remember even brilliant non-management 40+ copywriters are chips to seagulls when the network cost-cutters come to town.)

I know I should re-write this. I could lose 200 words, sharpen the syntax, rhythm and make it a better read for you. But the deadline has beaten me. It always does. D&AD are screaming for me to press "Send". Sorry.

Maybe I'll write something I'm happy with for the 2025 *Copy Book*.

HERE'S WHERE'

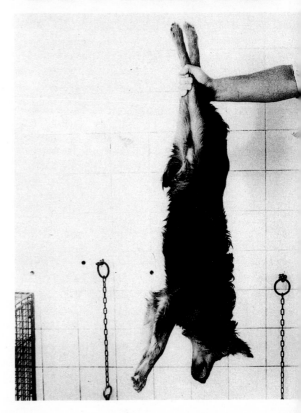

Client: Australian Writers
& Art Directors Association
Agency: Saatchi & Saatchi
Year: 1991

DEAD DOG. MY AWARD?

THIS YEAR AWARD WILL BE GIVING LESS TO CHARITY.

Community service and charity advertising has always been a special case when it comes to awards.

It has its own categories in every major advertising festival around the world. AWARD is no exception. However, we've spotted a problem.

Not only have community service and charity ads been able to enter their own categories, they've also been able to enter the general ones. A small space charity ad, for example, gets three bites at the guernsey; the Community Service and Charity section, the Small Space section and the Newspaper section.

Hardly fair on a packet soup ad that only gets one go. And often resulting in a book that looks more like a Charity Awards Annual.

So we've made a few changes for AWARD'91. Community Service and Charity ads will now <u>only</u> be judged in their own categories. Likewise, Small Space ads.

A minimum size for posters has been introduced to stop press ads being entered on the grounds they were pinned to the wall.

And Christmas cards, wedding invites, birth announcements, etc get their own category and are no longer a direct threat to direct mail for proper clients.

Details of changes are in the 13th AWARD Call for Entries booklet. If you still don't have a copy, call Mary or Sandra on (02) 267 6907 or (02) 267 6916.

But get a move on, the deadline for entries is June 7th. And if you've been pinning all your hopes on getting several gongs for one charity ad, all is not lost.

Just think of the money you'll save only having to enter it once.

1991 CALL FOR ENTRIES.

AWARD appreciates the assistance of Saatchi and Saatchi, John Currow and the NSW RSPCA for production of this advertisement —

Look at the person sitting opposite you. Just a quick glance. Try not to stare. What do you think they do for a living? How much do you think they earn? More than you? Could you do their job? Think of five possible christian names for them. And one nickname. Are they married? To what kind of person? Imagine their home. Their furniture. What do they keep on their mantelpiece? What colour bathroom do they have? Consider the ANY DISTINGUISHING MARKS section of their passport.

We're not allowed to tell you about Winston cigarettes, so here's something to pass the time.

What does it say? What should it say? Where are they heading now? And why? To meet somebody? Who? For what reason? Do they look as if they're late? And if they suddenly leant forward and offered to buy you dinner, what would you do? But before you pass too harsh a judgement on this poor, unsuspecting fellow-traveller, here's something else to think about. There's another Winston ad, just like this one, directly above your head.

LOW TO MIDDLE TAR As defined by H.M. Government
DANGER: Government Health WARNING: **CIGARETTES CAN SERIOUSLY DAMAGE YOUR HEALTH**

Client: Gallaher
Agency: JWT
Year: 1983

Opposite
Client: Olympus
Agency: Collett
Dickenson Pearce
Year: 1988

A rare sight indeed.
Abominable prints from an Olympus.

On April 14th 1987, a group of climbers in the Himalayas stumbled across mysterious footprints in the snow.

Could they be the tracks of an Abominable Snowman?

Fortunately, Chris Bonington's team were armed with a couple of our Olympus compact cameras at the time. So they clicked away, confident that the world would soon see clear evidence.

The tracks had been made by a two-legged creature moving fast across the snow in running bounds. Closer inspection proved that they were not those of man or any creature known to man.

The Tibetan porter had no doubt in his mind.

These were the marks of the 'Chuti' – the smaller of the two

Yeti – said to live in the high mountain forests of the region.

"It was an extraordinary moment" said Jim Fotheringham, leader of the climbers at the time "four experienced mountaineers snapping away like wedding photographers."

Most of us are unlikely ever to be called upon to record the tracks of a Yeti half way up Mount Menlungtse.

But when it comes to your holiday snaps, it's reassuring to know that a small Olympus can take a great set of prints.

OLYMPUS CAMERAS

Richard
Foster

Richard Foster's early career was spent at BBDO and Collett Dickenson Pearce, working on Sony, Birds Eye, Heinz, Barclaycard, Parker Pen and Heineken, among others.

In 1980 he joined the board of the fledgling Abbott Mead Vickers, where he spent the next 25 years helping to build AMV into Britain's biggest and most creatively-awarded agency.

He has worked on many award-winning campaigns, most notably for Volvo, Sainsbury's, NHS anti-smoking, the RSPCA and *The Economist*.

His work has won awards at all the major creative competitions, including a Black and five Yellow Pencils at D&AD.

Today I'm writing the copy for a Sainsbury's olives ad.

The rough is pinned on the wall in front of me. (I always have the rough in front of me when I'm writing a piece of copy. It helps get me started.) The visual is of a Sainsbury's Queen olive in a glass of martini. The Queen olive is a very big olive, so it's hogging the glass. The headline says: "Would you like a martini with your olive?"

The first thing I have to do is tell people that this is a big olive and not a small martini. I have a jar of Queen olives on my desk, together with a jar of ordinary olives. I take out an olive from each jar and put them side by side on a plate. As I'd hoped, the Queen olive looks about twice the size of the ordinary olive. So I write (in longhand, as always) "The Queen olive is twice as big as ordinary olives."

Before I finish the sentence I've already got the next line. "And twice as delicious." I immediately realise that "twice as delicious" is a matter of opinion, so I make it a matter of fact. "And, some would say, twice as delicious."

I need to expand on "delicious". I take the Queen olive from the plate and eat it. I write what I taste: "Its flesh is plump, but firm, with a luscious fruitiness that makes it the perfect appetiser..." It occurs to me that a martini is a kind of appetiser, so I add (in brackets, of course) "... with or without the martini."

As I said, this is an ad for Sainsbury's olives, which means Sainsbury's entire range of olives. There are nine olives in the range. All but one of these olives come from Spain. More than that, they come from Seville, the best olive-growing district in Spain. The odd one out, damn it, comes from Greece.

Of the eight Spanish olives, seven are green and one is black. The Greek olive is also black. Of the seven green olives, one is the Queen olive and the other six are Manzanilla olives. Of the six Manzanilla olives, one is whole, one is pitted, two are stuffed and two are marinated. Of the two black olives, the Spanish one has a strong flavour and the Greek one is just Greek.

How should I arrange all these different olives in the copy? I lead with the Seville story. I re-read my opening lines and continue: "Like all Sainsbury's Spanish olives, our Queen olives come from Seville, the most renowned olive-growing district in Spain."

Now I have to introduce all the other olives in the range. I decide to get the Manzanilla olives over with in one fell swoop. I write: "We also sell the more familiar Manzanilla olives, either whole, pitted, stuffed or marinated."

I then continue to explain that one of the stuffed olives is stuffed with pimiento and the other with almonds, and that one of the marinated olives is marinated in olive oil with garlic and chilli and the other in olive oil with herbs.

It's too long. I'm going to have to boil it down. So I rewrite the end of the paragraph as follows: "… stuffed (with pimiento or almonds) or marinated (in olive oil with garlic and chilli or with herbs)."

Now I'm on the home straight. All I have to do is talk about the two black olives, mention the fact that Sainsbury's have the widest range of olives, and then clinch the sale with a call to action.

I start to re-read the entire piece. I only get as far as the opening line. "The Queen olive is twice as big as ordinary olives." I don't like the word "ordinary", it's too ordinary. Common-or-garden olives? No, I've seen common-or-garden too many times. The common olive? No, too derogatory. Wait a minute, Queen olive… royalty… commoner.

"The Queen olive is twice as big as commoner olives."

Time for lunch.

——

Since I wrote my original piece for the *Copy Book*, an extraordinary number of people — not all of them junior colleagues trying to ingratiate themselves with me — have told me how much they enjoyed reading it.

Even now, hardly a year goes by without someone remarking flatteringly upon it.

So when they asked me if I'd like to update my piece for a new edition of the book, my initial reaction was to leave well alone.

But a lot has happened in the past 23 years.

I've given up drinking, for one thing. And smoking.

And I've given up going to work. (I knew the game was up when they offered me a four-day week and a 20% salary cut — as if I'd work longer hours for less pay!)

But I still haven't given up writing ads — or perhaps I should say, it hasn't given me up.

I've gone freelance. (I know, the last refuge of the dinosaur creative.)

It seems there are still a few people out there who value the power of the written word in their advertising.

Enough, anyway, to keep me gently employed for a couple of days a week (roughly my career average work rate, as it happens).

Quite a lot of what I write these days appears on the Internet rather than in magazines or newspapers. But this has no bearing on how I approach the job.

If someone asks me to do an online banner I pretend it's a 96-sheet poster. (If they ask me to do a skyscraper, I politely decline — unless the proposition can be successfully conveyed in words of less than six letters.)

And I love virals — not least because they are immune from the imbecilic machinations of the BACC (more grandiosely known as the Broadcast Advertising Clearance Centre).

By and large what I do these days is the same as what I used to do 30 years ago. With the one notable exception that I seldom get to write anything longer than a few sentences.

One of my clients (I have only two) recently referred to an ad I'd done for him as "the long copy one" — it contained 37 words. Including the headline.

Not that I'm complaining, mind. I charge by the day, not by the word.

And it still takes me quite a lot of days to come up with a really splendid line like "Why kiss ass when you can kick it?"

As Mark Twain (or was it Blaise Pascal?) famously wrote, "I'm sorry this letter's so long, I didn't have time to write a short one."

This piece, for example, is the longest thing I've written for some years. And yet it has only taken me, ooh, let me see...

Good heavens, it's nearly 4 o'clock.

Time for my nap.

Opposite
Client: Health Education Council
Agency: AMV
Year: 1987

The copy exhorts the reader to put this ad under smokers' noses. I sincerely hope some of them did.

If only.

Nobody has ever smoked an entire cigarette.

In fact, about two-thirds of the smoke produced a cigarette goes straight into the atmosphere.

Which in a room, pub, restaurant or cinema can create an extremely unpleasant atmosphere.

Breathing other people's cigarette smoke doesn't get up non-smokers' noses.

It gets down their throats and into their lungs.

According to the British Medical Journal (and we quote) "substances released into the air from tobacco smoke can be assumed to cause at least some cases of lung cancer."

The article goes on to say that the children of parents who smoke have more chest infections than the children of non-smokers.

If you smoke, we hope you'll spare a thought for the majority who don't. And if you don't smoke, but live or work with people who do, we hope you'll put this advertisement where they can't miss it.

Right under their noses.

Don't force smoking down other people's throats.

HEALTH EDUCATION COUNCIL

FOR A FREE LEAFLET "BREATHING OTHER PEOPLE'S TOBACCO SMOKE" WRITE TO THE HEALTH EDUCATION COUNCIL DEPT 682 22 24 CLARKE ROAD MOUNT FARM, MILTON KEYNES MK1 1JQ

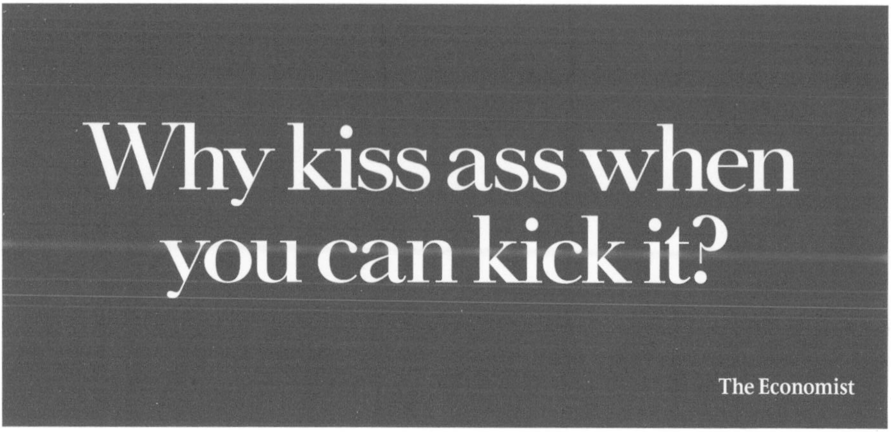

Why kiss ass when you can kick it?

The Economist

Client: The Economist
Agency: AMV BBDO
Year: 1999

A poster that ran only
once at a rugby interna-
tional at Twickenham.
So I thought I'd give it
another airing here.

Opposite
Client: JKR
Agency: Grey
Year: 2006

One of the few ads I've
done recently with what
could be called body copy.

Next spread
Client: Sainsbury's
Agency: AMV BBDO
Year: 1995

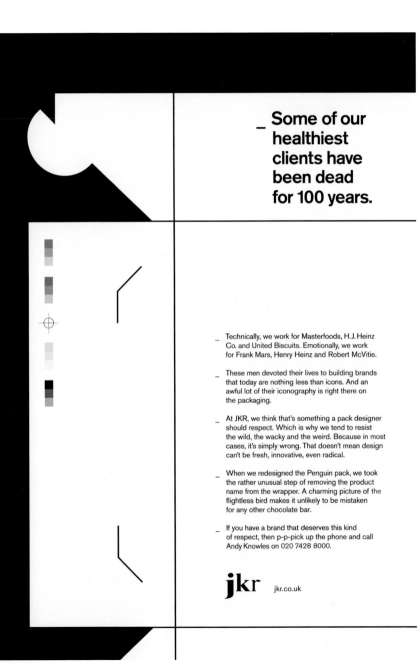

_ Some of our healthiest clients have been dead for 100 years.

_ Technically, we work for Masterfoods, H. J. Heinz Co. and United Biscuits. Emotionally, we work for Frank Mars, Henry Heinz and Robert McVitie.

_ These men devoted their lives to building brands that today are nothing less than icons. And an awful lot of their iconography is right there on the packaging.

_ At JKR, we think that's something a pack designer should respect. Which is why we tend to resist the wild, the wacky and the weird. Because in most cases, it's simply wrong. That doesn't mean design can't be fresh, innovative, even radical.

_ When we redesigned the Penguin pack, we took the rather unusual step of removing the product name from the wrapper. A charming picture of the flightless bird makes it unlikely to be mistaken for any other chocolate bar.

_ If you have a brand that deserves this kind of respect, then p-p-pick up the phone and call Andy Knowles on 020 7428 8000.

jkr   jkr.co.uk

Would you like a martini with your olive?

The Queen olive is twice as big as commoner olives.

And, some would say, twice as delicious.

Its flesh is plump, but firm, with a luscious fruitiness that makes it the perfect appetizer (with or without the martini).

Like all Sainsbury's Spanish olives, our Queen olives come from Seville, the most renowned olive-growing district in Spain.

We also sell the more familiar Manzanilla olives, either whole, pitted, stuffed (with pimiento or almonds) or marinated (in olive oil with garlic and chilli or with herbs).

All these olives are green olives, but our range would be incomplete without the black variety.

Hence Sainsbury's Calamata and Hojiblanca olives.

The Calamatas come from Greece, where they are usually to be found adorning the classic feta salad.

Hojiblancas are stronger in flavour than their green cousins which makes them the perfect partner to paella or pizza.

As you may have guessed by now, Sainsbury's offer a wider range of olives than any other supermarket.

So if you want the choice of the choicest olives, choose Sainsbury's.

SAINSBURY'S Where good food costs less

suicide  homicide

passivesmokingkills.org

Client: The Roy Castle
Lung Cancer Foundation
Agency: CHI
Year: 2007

A recent freelance poster.
Actually, I did it ten years
ago at AMV for the NHS
client, but it never ran.
(Never throw a good
idea away.)

Opposite
Client: Amoco
Agency: Vernons
Year: 1972

My first whole-page
broad-sheet colour ad and
less than a square inch of
colour. Astonishingly, the
client changed his logo a
fortnight after the ad ran.

Give us time, give us time.

Of the 38,000 petrol stations in Britain, something like 360 are ours.

Don't laugh.

It was only in December 1963 we opened our first.

Like nearly all the ones that followed, it was run by a tenant, not a manager.

The difference being that a tenant makes his money according to how much petrol he sells.

While a manager gets paid the same wage however well, or badly, he does.

We don't have to tell you who gives you the warmer welcome.

The trouble is, with so few Amoco stations around, there may not be one near you.

Take heart.

360 stations in seven years works out at about one new one a week.

Next week could be your week.

Lifelike, isn't it?

We really must hand it to our advertising boys.

They've achieved something we've always thought was impossible:

Demonstrate the lifelike qualities of Sony's unique Trinitron picture on the page of a newspaper.

(Excellent though colour printing is nowadays, it could never quite do justice to our colour picture.)

And if the demonstration is ingeniously simple, so is the Trinitron system.

Instead of the customary three small electron lenses, Trinitron uses just one large one.

By focusing the colour beams through the centre part of the lens, we can produce a picture of exceptional sharpness and clarity.

Another department in which Sony set a shining example, is brightness.

Which is where our Aperture Grille comes into its own.

It's made up of stripes, not holes, thereby allowing more of the colour beams to reach the screen.

But perhaps the real beauty of our television lies in its solid state circuitry and low running temperature.

For it is these things that make the Trinitron so reliable.

And there's only one thing better than a lifelike picture.

A lifelike picture that lasts.

SONY.

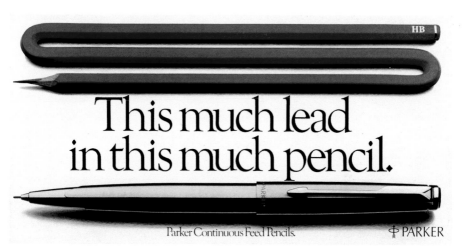

Client: Parker Pen Co.
Agency: Collett
Dickenson Pearce
Year: 1981

I reckoned this ad had
pencil written all over it.
Fortunately, so did the
1981 D&AD Poster jury —
a black one, no less (the
Pencil, not the jury).

Opposite
Client: Sony
Agency: BBDO
Year: 1976

I was so pleased with this
ad I congratulated myself
on it in the opening line of
the copy.

Neil French

Born 1944. Expelled from minor public school at 16. Rent-collector, account executive, bouncer, waiter, singer, matador, rock band manager, promoter, account executive again and copywriter. Joined Holmes Knight Ritchie in London 1980. Joined and left Batey Ads in Singapore 1986. Joined Ball Partnership also in 1986 as vice chairman & regional creative pooh-bah; got fired 1991.

Pottered about directing and consulting for a bit, then re-joined Ogilvy as Asian regional creative director, which morphed into worldwide creative director of Ogilvy, and then the dizzy heights of WPP worldwide creative director; a basically undoable job, but one that allowed him to work with some nice people at Y&R and Grey as well. It all came to an end in 2005 and he's now merely a single dad. Best job he ever had.

'Straordinary, really.

Asking fifty-three people who spend their lives writing advertisements to tell others exactly how they do it. So, since you've actually shelled out good money for this scam of scams, I guess I'll have to make it sound difficult, or scientific, or something. If you're looking for folks who take all this seriously, there are conceivably one or two in here.

My advice is, if you come across 'em, think how much money they make, and ask yourself, did they get that stinking rich by handing out the real secret of success to every bozo capable of navigating his way to the "How To" section of an airport bookstore? Right? Quite so. Anyway. Here it is. "My Way". By Neil French. Aged 74.

First and foremost, avoid like genital warts the temptation to start writing. Once I've read the brief, I tend to waddle off and play pool, or hang about with unsuitable women for a while. On the one hand it allows the important bits of the brief to sink in, and the reams of dross to fade into richly-deserved obscurity, and on the other, it's a far more sensible way of spending the time than sitting in an office counting the number of times a junior account executive uses the word "creative".

When I can only remember one thing about the brief, and just before I forget there was a brief in the first place, and assuming I'm not on the black, I write that one thing down and get the account people to write a strategy round it. This is not, of course, the "correct" way to go about things, but in my experience it's the only way to get the strategy to match the ads. In any case it keeps the account people out of the pool-halls and knocking shops. They do so lower the tone of a place.

Next, I look at every other ad in the category, so I know what my ads mustn't look like. This is quite possibly the most important part of the entire wossname, come to think of it.

I have this heartfelt theory that people hate ads. Ads interrupt TV programmes and bulk out newspapers and mags and are generally a waste of perfectly good trees. So I try to avoid writings "ads". Or at least I try to make my stuff look different, so that it doesn't scream off the page "Hi! I'm an ad! Ignore me!"

And at the very least I make sure that my stuff doesn't look like any competitors'. If you gather a wad of ads in a category, you'll often find they form a sort of genre. It becomes established over time that "car ads look like this" and "bank ads look like that". Stands to reason that if you can make a car ad that looks like a bank ad, you'll stand out in the category. Got it? OK.

Maybe I should say, right now, that I don't work with an art director. I do my own.

And I do my own because I was tired of being disappointed when my concepts came back looking, somehow, "wrong". I realised then that, at the instant a writer has an idea, he usually has a glimpse of the finished "look" of the piece, and that glimpse is part of the idea itself. So now, even if my ads are horrible, at least they're exactly how I saw them in the first place. I'm never disappointed. Everyone else may be, but I'm not.

At this point I decide what sort of an ad it's going to be. There are only two sorts: a copy ad or a picture ad. Anything half and half is wimpy, in my view.

If it's a copy ad, it's either going to be masses of words, with a nod in the general direction of the product, so we still get paid, or a single sentence of pithy prose writ large or little with a pack shot. In the latter case, you use the phrase because you can't think of a sufficiently jolly picture, and in the former the wodge of copy is, in itself, a design element. It says "My, but these people have a lot to say for themselves", so even if the consumer shows the good sense not to read the whole sermon, he's left with an impression, at least. And we still get paid.

If it's a picture ad, it's a hugely-amusing snap with, if really necessary, some explanatory jotting beneath or within, for the benefit of the terminally bewildered. If it's this sort of ad, I do a little picture, write the line, and toddle off to the beach. No point in knocking yourself out for no good reason, what?

But if it's a long-copy job, it all gets jolly technical. Please concentrate, from here on.

Firstly, I get a good bottle of red; ideally, Rioja; possibly a Vega Sicilia or a Castillo Ygay, from the cellar, and remove the cork. Then I find a large expensive wine glass, of the type that goes "ting" for a long time after you've tinged it, and I place that in close proximity to the bottle and myself. This takes years of practice to perfect, but persist; I think you'll find it worthwhile.

Then I pour some of the wine into the glass and I think about the ad. Snatches of sentence, natty little phrases, excellent words, all come to mind. But I never write them down. All this while I am simultaneously drinking the red, slowly, from the tingy glass (I warned you this was the tricky part), but I'm withstanding the temptation to pick up a pen. When I've finished the wine there frequently doesn't seem a lot of point in thinking about bloody ads any more, so I have a little lie-down.

When I wake up, I let rip. Anything that survives the little lie-down is obviously memorable, and goes in the ad. Anything I've forgotten obviously isn't and doesn't.

Now, I'm no good with slide-rules, and I can't type, so I do everything by hand. I take a sheet of tracing paper and in pencil draw the shape and design of the ad, very accurately. I then take an Extra-Fine Pilot Hi-Techpoint, stick my tongue out about half a centimetre between my lips and commence. I decide on a point-size for the type, and whether it's going to be serif or sans, and start in the top left-hand corner.

When I see the bottom right-hand corner looming up in my periphery vision, I start to wrap up the argument, and waffle along till the space is full. Then I stop.

I rarely re-write, except to amend awkward typography; firstly because it's tedious and secondly because I can never seem to keep the flow, once I start to tinker.

I only have one rule and I recommend it to you. In any ad, most people will tell you, there is a minimum of four elements: headline, picture, copy, logo.

Forget captions, tag-lines, diagrams — they're all optional add-ons. The minimum of elements in ninety percent of press ads is four.

If you can do an ad that really works, using only *one* of those elements, you've got a winner.

Two elements only, and it'll be pretty good. Three and it'll still look better than anything else in the paper. If you can't get below four, it's possible that the basic idea isn't strong enough, or you haven't expressed it well enough.

Reductio ad absurdum. Try it. It works.

Finally, I can't advise you how to write. There's a school of thought that tells you to submerge your own personality, and be the voice of the client. I can't do that. I'm always me, chatting away on *behalf* of the client. If I always sound like me, that's OK, because I am, and the public is nowhere near as gullible as they're made out to be. They can tell if it's bullshit.

I wish I could show more ads, and more variety. But since this is a book about copy, most of what follows are copy-ads. Sorry about that.

Client: Panadol
Agency: Young & Rubicam
Year: 2004

Next spread
Client: The News
Proprietors of America
Agency: Ogilvy Worldwide
Year: 2001

Nobody reads long copy any more.
Here's why.

More importantly, absolutely nobody reads *newspapers* any more. That is a well-known fact, right?

And yet, tragically ignorant of this, many thousands of journalists spend their lives pointlessly gathering information, news and opinions, and writing about it. Day in, day out, day after wasted day.

Sadder still, many more thousands of lost souls are glumly occupied in setting the result in type, designing the newspapers and printing the damn things.

And strangely enough, millions and millions of otherwise seemingly-sane people one assumes, go out and buy (yes, buy) a newspaper, every day. This is because they need a cheap substitute for an umbrella, an inexhaustible supply of drawer-liners, or kitty-litter for a herd of terminally-incontinent cats.

But nobody actually reads the newspaper, surely?

Dearie me, no. Whatever next?

Next is the news that Elvis, having been abducted by aliens, has returned as a small rodent, and is living with his auntie, in Papua New Guinea.

Go away.

You're not still reading this drivel, are you?

Why, for heaven's sake? Believe me, it's not going to get any better. Go and do something useful. Count your socks.

Go along now. Shoo!

(Have they gone?)

Right, then. Sorry about that, but you've got to

An American bloke goes on holiday to England. On his return, he's telling his pat all about it.

"I was coming out of a shop one day, and it was raining hard outside, so I took shelter in a doorway.

Another feller was sheltering too, and he turned to me and he said, 'Nice weather'. Well, of course it wasn't nice weather at all. In fact it was terrible weather…and then, I got it! This was an example of the famous British irony. I loved it!

And I've been using irony ever since. Like the other day, I was having this barbecue for the family and a bunch of neighbours, and I burned the burgers.

And Joe, from next door, was standing there, and I turned to him, and I looked at the burgers, and I said, 'Nice weather'."

(Pause for what…bewilderment, I suppose…and back to business.)

Can we acknowledge, then, that all the hundreds of words printed in this newspaper aren't put there *just* to make your fingers dirty?

Irony aside, people buy newspapers so that they can read them.

And since this is obvious to anyone with the intellect of a soap-dish, why is the paper not chock-full of ads for big, sexy brands?

The short answer is stupidity. And the combined stupidity of ad agencies, researchers, and (perish the thought) clients can be a terrible thing to behold.

Basically, remember, you can prove just about anything. If you want to prove that people don't read long copy, you start by proving that newspaper readers only read a small proportion of the editorial articles in any given issue.

We once produced a campaign that proved, beyond all reasonable doubt, that you could launch a beer in the press, even more successfully than you could on T.V. and at a fraction of the cost.

The big-brand beer manufacturers were not persuaded. Having been panicked for weeks by a campaign that widdled all over their T.V. commercials, they ignored the evidence once the panic was over.

One somehow doubts that the opinions of the copywriters engaged in this campaign are going to sway the beloved prejudices of most clients.

The present economic oops-a-daisy is really only a symptom of the fact that most businesses are run by buffoons. And that the world's occasional booms take place in spite of their poltroonery, not because of their brilliance.

When a new company begins its first meteoric rise (actually, meteors fall, don't they? Maybe this is a sadly prophetic metaphor), it's because the guy who started the company is not a clown. But as his company grows, he has to hire more people, and it seems but a nanosecond before the executive floor is echoing to the flap of big shoes, and the beeping of red noses.

The only time it's controlled is when the top man takes back his advertising into his own hands, as a way of avoiding the depredations of his minions, who are so diligently throwing buckets of confetti at one another, one floor down.

"You talkin' to me?"

So, Rule One of advertising is 'decide who you're talking to.'

There is no Rule Two or Three.

them not our sort of person at all.

Now, where were we?

Erm...nobody reads newspapers; that was it. Well, I suppose we might admit that the people who write the newspapers read their own stuff. So do their mums, unless there's wrestling on the T.V.

This particular exercise in the art of futility was intended to be one of a series of ads headed "How to write a newspaper ad" — surely a headline so mind numbingly dull as to rival the marvellous "Small earthquake in Peru. Nobody hurt", as the most boring ever written.

And the fact is that the vast majority of the folks who bought this rag are never, ever, going to write an ad, and still less give a rat's bottom about those who insist on doing so.

Most of them will have flicked the page at a glance at the headline. This does not prove that they don't read long copy. It merely proves that long copy (or indeed any copy) has to be relevant to the audience.

But withdrawing copy from the mix, in an attempt to make it more palatable to a wider audience, is plain nuts. It merely reduces any degree of effectiveness it might have had.

Thus this epic is on the one hand insanely incestuous, and on the other, appears to contradict the very point it hopes to make.

Sod this. Light relief, please.

Anyone still with us will recognise the first bit of this saga as a plodding attempt at heavy irony. A useful tool for debunking myths, is the old irony-ploy.

But did you know that there's an unfortunate myth that Americans don't understand irony? Since they apparently don't read either, it's probably academic, but for what it's worth, and to give us all a break, here's my favourite irony-story.

...ture, irony will be in italics, but not all franctised words are ironic. Everybody clear on this?)

But the seeds of doubt have been sown. The fuzzy logic goes like this:

People don't read all the words in the newspaper.

Therefore, people don't like to read.

Therefore, we must avoid ads that depend on words.

Newspapers are full of words, so we must not advertise in them.

So newspapers become a 'secondary' medium, which is never used for its unique strength.

So the ads aren't very good.

So nobody reads them.

Bingo. A self-fulfilling prophecy.

Send in the clowns.

But people will read something that interests them. And my bet is that, by now, the only people reading this are advertising folk. Mostly creatives.

So, now that we're all alone, and just between ourselves...it's the clients, isn't it?

How many times have you been in a client meeting and he's announced, "People don't read copy any more." This, coming from a man with a newspaper poking out of his briefcase. And if you point this out, he says, "Well, I do, of course. But the public doesn't."

You've noticed that this isn't in italics.

The bloke seriously believes that he and and the public are different species. This is also the genius who says, when you present an ad, "Well of course, you know, I understand it, but the public won't."

(A good exercise with this variety of idiot is to substitute the word 'women' for the word 'public' and play it back to him.)

But you can't fight really determined stupidity, in the end.

picture, small picture, no picture, no copy, long copy... the consumer and the product will sort out all those problems for you.

But newspapers are so often your secret weapon. And here is the real point of this ad.

People *buy* a newspaper. Do you think they buy it but don't read it? That they don't value it? Think again.

T.V. is on the face of it, free. Radio is free. Posters are free. Internet advertising, damn it to hell, is free. And advertising in each and every one of them is hated and despised as an imposition, an interruption, and an annoyance.

Not so with newspapers. When did an ad last spoil your enjoyment of the paper?

Sure, newspaper ads these days tend to be so boring that you ignore them. But that's not the same as being an irritation.

And it's your business to change that. Now's the time to own the medium.

Newspapers are portable. You can read them anytime. Not just when the programmers decide you can.

They are private. You don't have to share your newspaper, or argue with your entire family about which page to read.

You need both hands to read your newspaper. You can't double-task. On the other hand, the paper makes an excellent barrier against the rest of the world.

Your entire vision-field is filled. Even your periphery-vision. For a few minutes, the newspaper is your world.

Nobody opens a newspaper to provide 'background' or as part of life's wallpaper. Reading is a considered decision.

Newspapers are not an entertainment medium. That's why they are called *news* papers. Readers are in the mood to be informed. Nobody reads the newspaper to escape from reality. They read to get involved.

In other words, if you can't get people to read your ad in a newspaper, it's nobody's fault but your own.

the end.

As our contribution to road safety, may we point out that drinkers of our beer will never drink and drive, because after three nobody ever remembers where they parked the car.

12% alcohol, and available soon in selected bars with nice comfortable floors.   X.O. Beer. Take it lying down.

Client: Singapore Press
Holdings
Agency: Freelance
Year: 1993

Here's the first ad in a campaign ostensibly for "XO Beer". It didn't actually exist as a product when we ran the campaign; the intention was to convince advertisers that you could sell beer in newspapers. But there was such a demand that a local brewer started making the stuff. We tested two approaches: one with a picture and a pack shot; one with a headline and a pack shot; six of each. Recall was about the same, except that people could actually parrot the entire headlines back to us. So in my book, they win. The strategy, by the way, was basically, "Gets you drunker quicker".

Opposite
Client: Chivas Regal
Agency: The Ball
Partnership
Year: 1988

An ad for Chivas Regal that broke every booze-ad rule, aimed at the Chinese drinker.

Next spread
Client: Dove
Agency: Ogilvy Worldwide
Year: 2002

THIS IS AN ADVERTISEMENT FOR CHIVAS REGAL.

IF YOU NEED TO SEE THE BOTTLE,
YOU OBVIOUSLY DON'T MOVE IN THE RIGHT SOCIAL CIRCLES.

IF YOU NEED TO TASTE IT,
YOU JUST DON'T HAVE THE EXPERIENCE TO APPRECIATE IT.

IF YOU NEED TO KNOW WHAT IT COSTS,
TURN THE PAGE, YOUNG MAN.

Twenty fascinating but utterly useless facts you really don't need to know about skin.

1. The smoke from burning giraffe skin is used to treat nosebleeds among some tribes in Africa. These tribes always travel with a spare giraffe and a box of matches, in case they bump into a tree.

(Not really: I made that last bit up.)

2. Surprisingly, elephant skin is extremely sensitive to sunburn. Now, why nature should have decided this was a good plan for a large animal living exclusively in very sunny climates is a mystery. But there it is. Take it or leave it.

3. Sharks have skin that is smooth when rubbed in one direction and abrasive when rubbed in the other. In fact, it was used as sandpaper, before they invented sandpaper. Not a lot of people know that. So if you leave a trail of sawdust every time you scratch your back, you're probably a shark.

4. Lots of animals, snakes and tarantulas, for instance, shed their skins every so often. They just clamber out of it, like overdue-for-laundry long woolen underwear, and walk away... Well, not all of them. Frogs and salamanders eat their old skin. Words, frankly, fail us.

5. Polar bears are black. No kidding, they've got black skin but wear white fur coats, like Puff Daddy. Polar bears do not wear shades, or indulge in rapping, to our knowledge.

6. How do mommy-hedgeghogs have baby-hedgehogs? Going "ouch!" quite a lot, one would think. But no; baby-hedgehogs are born in a little bag. So that they don't hurt mommy.

Isn't that just unbelievably cute?

7. The Burmese python has heat sensors in its lips. This apparently helps them locate prey. Which, presumably, they then kiss to death. Anyway, a popular python nickname is 'Hotlips'. Try it out next time you meet one.

8. The skin of the crested newt tastes horrible. This is said to be a defence against predators.

On the other hand, since this wouldn't work until you were actually being eaten, it seems a somewhat questionable means of defence.

Revenge maybe.

9. The African plated lizard is usually sort of brownish. But in the breeding season its head turns purply-pink. A similar phenomenon in humans can be observed in New York singles bars.

10. The New Guinean Pitohul has a toxic secretion on its skin and feathers, making it the world's only known poisonous bird. So if you see a 'Pitohul-in-a-basket' on a menu, probably avoid it.

11. How do hedgehogs make love?

"Carefully" is the accepted answer. So it's kinda strange that some African tribes use hedgehog skin as a fertility-charm. But then, these are people who inhale giraffe-smoke to cure nosebleeds, so what do we know?

12. Frogs don't drink. That's a fact.

Alcoholics Anonymous have very few members who are of the frog persuasion.

They do, however, absorb moisture through their skin, and consequently have terrible trouble keeping their swimming pools full.

13. The Hagfish exudes a slimy, gluey stuff, which apparently ensnares predators. How in the world it ever seemed like a good idea to stick yourself to the animal that intends eating you, is beyond us. It would seem to make you a sort of takeaway lunch. But still...

14. Amazingly the salamander does the same trick... only his secretion has the strength and bonding-speed of rubber cement. This explains why you see so many animals wandering about with their faces festooned in salamanders.

Not.

15. The Golden Poison Arrow Frog, from Colombia, has a skin-secretion so deadly that it cannot even be touched by bare hands. Guess what local hunters use this secretion for... attaching little bells to party-hats?

Nope, try again.

16. The Sumatran Rhinoceros is the only rhino with any noticeable hair on its body. Very butch, the Sumatran rhino, but this also explains why none of them have ever turned out to be Olympic swimmers.

17. The bullfrog breathes through its skin while underwater. As soon as it gets out of the water, it starts breathing through its nostrils. Nobody knows why it doesn't just go on breathing through its skin, but possibly it doesn't want to become a slave to habit.

18. Hognose snakes play dead when threatened. They not only lie very still but also exude a really disgusting, foul, rotting-flesh smell.

It probably works, but frankly, you wouldn't want your daughter to marry one.

19. Some toads have rather knobbly skin that exudes hallucinogenic slime.

Devotees avail themselves of this 'high' by scraping the slime from the back of the animal, or, in more urgent cases, licking the toad. Our question has always been what sort of person would think it a great idea to lick a toad in the first place, before the dubious properties of its sweat were discovered.

20. The average female human has about four pounds of skin, which, if spread out, would cover about fifteen square feet. And if filled with feathers, would make an attractive duvet.

Mind you, if you use your skin as a bedspread, all your bits would fall out, and you'd have to carry them about in a large plastic bag. Which is easily obtainable from a local supermarket.

21. <u>And one you do.</u>

(Dove is all *you* need to know about skin care.)

Opposite
Client: Beck's Bier
Agency: The Ball
Partnership
Year: 1991

For Beck's, the strategy
was "expensive lager",
and since we couldn't
bring ourselves to rip off
the lovely UK work for
Stella Artois, we went for
an interminable read.
There are three in the
series, and they're my
all-time favourite ads.
I did them with Ben Hunt.
I like the headline treatment on this one.

A FEW ENCOURAGING WORDS FOR THE TOTALLY INCOMPETENT.

It's perfectly alright to be incompetent for hours on end.

I am. And so is everyone I know.

Of course, being of this persuasion, I shall never be able to afford a bottle of Beck's Beer. Which is why the people who sell Beck's Beer got me to write this ad.

They see it as a sort of public service announcement; as a way of consoling those who moan at the unfairness of it all. A way of making the 'have-nots' feel glad that they 'haven't'.

So here, for the first time, are the great names: The people who were so bad in their chosen sphere of endeavour that they achieved greatness.

People who believed that success is overrated.

And who believed, as G. K. Chesterton once said, that 'If a thing's worth doing, it's worth doing badly."

THE WORST BOXING DEBUT

Ralph Walton was knocked out in 10½ seconds of his first bout, on 29th September, 1946, in Lewison, Maine, USA.

It happened when Al Couture struck him as he was adjusting his gum-shield in his corner. The 10½ seconds includes 10 seconds while he was counted out.

He never fought again.

THE LEAST-SUCCESSFUL WEATHER REPORT

After severe flooding in Jeddah, in January 1979, the Arab News gave the following bulletin: "We regret that we are unable to give you the weather. We rely on weather reports from the airport, which is closed, on account of the weather. Whether or not we are able to bring you the weather tomorrow depends on the weather."

THE WORST SPEECH-WRITER

William Gamaliel Harding wrote his own speeches while President of the USA, in the 1920's.

When Harding died, e. e. cummings said, "the only man, woman or child who wrote a simple, declarative sentence with seven grammatical errors, is dead".

Here is a rewarding sample of the man's style. "I would like the government to do all it can to mitigate, then, in understanding, in mutuality of interest, in concern for the common good, our tasks will be solved."

THE MOST UNSUCCESSFUL ATTEMPT AT DYING FOR LOVE

When his fiancee broke off their engagement, Senor Abel Ruiz, of Madrid, decided to kill himself for love.

Reviewing the possibilities available on such occasions, he decided to park himself in front of the Gerona to Madrid express. However, jumping in its path, he landed between the rails and watched, gloomily, as the train passed over him.

He suffered only minor injuries, and promptly received First Aid at Gerona Hospital.

Later that day, he tried again. This time he jumped in front of a passing lorry, again only acquiring some more bruises. His rapid return to the hospital led doctors to call a priest, who made Sr. Ruiz see the folly of his ways. Eventually, he decided to carry on living, and to seek a new girlfriend.

Glad to be alive, he left the hospital and was immediately knocked down by a runaway horse; he was taken back to Gerona Hospital, this time quite seriously injured, for the third time that day.

THE WORST JUROR

There was a rape case at a Crown Court in Northern England in the late 1970's at which a juror fell fast asleep, during which time the victim was asked to repeat what her attacker had said prior to the incident.

To save her embarrassment, the girl was allowed to write it on paper, instead. This was then folded, and passed along the jury. Each member read the words which, in effect, said "Nothing, in the history of sexual congress, equals the comprehensive going-over which I am about to visit upon your good self."

Sitting next to the dozing juror was an attractive blonde. After reading the note, she refolded it, and nudged her neighbour, who awoke with a start.

He read the note, and looked at the blonde in astonishment. To the delight of the entire court, he then read the note again, slowly. Then he winked at the blonde, and put the note in his pocket.

When the judge asked him for the piece of paper, the recently dormant juror refused, saying that 'it was a personal matter'.

This is what the label on a bottle of Beck's Beer looks like. Since its the closest you'll probably ever get to one, we've given you a dotted line, so you can cut it out, and put it on your wall as a kind of ikon. When you've finished cutting it out, plasters can be bought from any pharmacy.

THE LEAST-SUCCESSFUL WEAPON

The prize for the most useless weapon of all time goes to the Russians, who invented the dog-mine. The rather ingenious plan was to train the dogs to associate food with the underside of tanks, in the hope that they would run hungrily beneath the advancing Panzer divisions. Bombs would be strapped to their backs, which endangered the dogs to a point where no insurance company would look at them.

Unfortunately, they associated food solely with *Russian* tanks, and totally destroyed half a Soviet division on their first outing.

The plan was quickly abandoned.

THE WORST BUS SERVICE

Can any bus-service rival the fine Hanley to Bagnall route, in Staffordshire, England? In 1976 it was reported that the buses no longer stopped to pick up passengers.

This came to light when one of them, Mr Bill Hancock, complained that buses on the outward journey regularly sailed past queues of elderly people; up to thirty of them sometimes waiting in line.

Councillor Arthur Cholerton then made transport history by stating that if the buses stopped to pick up passengers, it would disrupt the timetable.

THE LAST WORD

"They couldn't hit an elephant at this dist..." The last words of General John Sedgwick, spoken while looking over the parapet at enemy lines during the Battle of Spotsylvania, in 1864.

OH, ALRIGHT, THEN; HERE ARE SOME MORE

Typography has never been our strong point, so here are a few more determined losers, to fill out the column: The Welsh choir who were the sole entrants in a competition, and came second; the Swiss pornographer who was heavily fined because his wares were insufficiently pornographic; the writer of this ad, who, unable to master the art of précis, copied the entire thing, word for word, from Stephen Pile's 'Book of Heroic Failures', thereby incurring almost certain legal action.

There, feel better now, don't you? After all, the price of a bottle of Beck's Beer may well be so high as to be audible only to highly-trained bats, but at least you're not the only one who'll never be able to afford it.

(Oh, no. Three more lines. How about a jingle? Beck's diddly-dee-de-dah, Beck's, tiddly-pom. The end).

Dan Germain

Dan is brand director at innocent, the healthy drinks company. He's worked there since the company started in 1999, and in 2014 was named Designer of the Year in the United Kingdom, beating Apple's Sir Jonathan Ive and Sir Paul Smith among others.

These days his duties include overseeing the creative and brand direction of innocent; everything from ads to products to company culture, across Europe. He also works in the areas of sustainability, purpose and ethics, maintaining the brand's most important values, and figuring out where that might take innocent in the next 10, 20, 50 years.

Creating the tone of voice and the brand culture from scratch are Dan's proudest achievements, and he is still searching for ways to keep the business both useful and interesting.

I read the first edition of this book when I was learning how to be a writer.

It was really useful, as I had never worked in an advertising agency or a design agency or met many people who claimed to be copywriters.

So this book was a window into a world I knew very little about.

To now be in this book is quite strange. I'm very proud. And I think the best thing to do is to explain why I think I'm in this book.

I helped three of my friends start a business in 1999. The business is called innocent and we made healthy drinks. We're still called innocent and we still make healthy drinks.

Right there at the beginning, we didn't know what we were doing. We didn't know how to make the drinks, we didn't know how to design the packaging and we didn't know how to do marketing. But we had a go anyway.

One responsibility that fell to me was that of writing things. There was a space to fill on the back of the label and we thought it would be good to write whatever we fancied there. Little stories about the drinks or us or the Mafia or dinosaur eggs or being scared at night. We thought it would be good to write about whatever we fancied because it might be more interesting than just writing about fruit.

And people seemed to like those little stories. They would email us and tell us their favourites, or write their own versions, and of course they would tell us when our stories were crap. But it was all a good thing, because it was the start of a conversation that we've been having ever since.

People in advertising and marketing talk a lot about conversations. It's an overused term to describe the relief you have when you find out that someone has actually read the stuff you've written. The gratification comes a little more quickly these days — you can write a tweet and someone will tell you you're an idiot in less than a minute. But back then we'd write the label, argue about it, make it better, set it, print it, stick it on a bottle, get it to the shops, and just when you'd forgotten what you'd written, someone would buy a drink, read the label and email us via the address on the label to tell us we were idiots. Delayed gratification.

Anyway, once we started writing stories on bottle labels, we realised that there were lots of other places where we could write things. Websites, posters, point of sale materials, festivals, social media, email newsletters, books and adverts. We spoke the same way wherever we wrote stuff because it was us writing the stuff. I think that is known as having a consistent tone of voice. We didn't really have rules for doing it — it was just the sound of me and my friends trying things out.

There were lots of people who I worked with or spoke to who helped me write better. My friend Rich (one of the innocent founders) was my best writing partner. We wrote books together, made adverts and messed about until we came up with good work. And plenty of people have worked and still work in our in-house creative and social teams, and have continued the tradition of writing excellent copy for innocent. Some of the stuff in the accompanying pictures was their work, with me interfering from the sidelines.

I still work at innocent and I write less than I used to. My job now is to make sure we don't stray from the right path (as a company and as a creative organisation), and to help the people who write the words for innocent do a great job. By the time you read this book we'll be writing our own copy in eleven languages, so we have a Writers' Club — a clandestine group of copywriters from around the world who meet every few months to share work, moan, laugh, cry and drink beer together. It's a good way to keep the voice alive.

Finally, if I had to share a few short tips on how I think the best writing is done, I'd probably give you these three:

1. Take a train. Or even a plane. There is something about movement and not being anywhere that helps me write better.

2. Stare out into the cosmos. Remembering how small and accidental you are reminds you that what you're doing isn't that serious or difficult.

3. Start. The hardest bit is starting. Once you're writing, it's fine. It's the bit before you start that kills you.

Thanks for reading.

Opposite
Client: Innocent
Year: 2009

The cover of *A book about innocent,* published by Penguin Books.

Hello. This is a book about innocent.

It tells the story of setting up the business and the things we've learned. We started making smoothies in 1999 – on the first day we sold 24 bottles; now we sell over 2 million a week, so things have moved on a bit since then. This book is about the things we've discovered along the way; about running a business and getting started, about having ideas and thinking different, about building a brand from nothing and recruiting great people, and about everything we could think of that might be remotely helpful. We hope it will prove useful to anyone thinking of starting their own business, or those who already have, or anyone who wants to think about different ways of working. We think our ideas are pretty universal – they could apply to any business, or pretty much any organized endeavour. And rather than be weird and secretive and keep all of our ideas to ourselves

innocent
our story & some things we've learned

we thought we should share. Plus, maybe our mums will read this book and finally believe us when we say we haven't rung home for a while because we've been a bit busy at work.

Client: Innocent
Year: 2010

Opposite
Client: Innocent
Year: 2012

Next spread
Client: Innocent
Year: 2002

Ponchos produced for the
2012 London Olympics.

The innocent wee-ometer:
a guide to hydration.

the innocent wee-ometer™

A night out with Keith Richards.

Office party.

No one can see the smell of asparagus.

Half a shandy.

Smoothies and juices are great, but we all know you're supposed to drink a bit of water too. An easy way to check that you're getting enough water is to use our patented innocent wee-ometer™. Just compare your wee to what's on the chart - the darker your wee, the more water you need to drink. A nice pale yellow (Wee Nirvana®) is what you should be aiming for.

"Blow into the bag
please Sir."

Beetroot surprise.

Wee Nirvana®.

I can pee
clearly now.

Malcolm Gluck

From being a pioneer student at Watford College (1962/3), Malcolm Gluck went on to become copy chief of DDB London, copy chief of AMV, and then CDP, Ogilvy & Mather, Lintas, and, finally, Priestley Marin-Guzman & Gluck. During this period he also ran Intellect Games and published the advertising magazine *Adze*.

He became wine correspondent of *The Guardian*, writing a weekly column called Superplonk for 16 years. His annual Superplonk wine guide was a best-seller until 2004. He also wrote and presented his own BBC2 TV series, *Gluck Gluck Gluck*. He continues to appear regularly on TV and radio discussing wine.

His first fiction, *Chateau Lafite 1953 & Other Stories*, was published in 2010 along with the poetry collection *Five Tons of Jam* (written under the heteronym John Orland). He has written over 40 books.

How copy was once written. Is it any wonder no one writes like it today?

Well, try.

If you are a tyro advertising copywriter in the third millennium what you are about to read will strike you as the droppings of a dinosaur. But it is said the study of dinosaur dung is useful (it even has a name, coprolite paleontology) and may provide important clues as to how life has developed. In that spirit, then, I shall continue, mindful that no one writes long copy ads any more, or even writes ads (as opposed to causing them to be created via teamwork). It is also probable that newsprint is doomed. Modern advertising is, then, as like the business I worked in from 1963 to 1992 as the iBook I write on now is to the yellow writing pad and the Faber HB pencils issued to all Doyle Dane Bernbach copywriters when I joined that agency's London office in 1966 (supplemented by an office-issue Remington portable typewriter, Roget's *Thesaurus*, the pocket Oxford dictionary, and, at my own expense, Fowler's *The King's English*). Overlooking the gender in the last book, and even as the England football team were winning the World Cup, I was studying Fowler on "mixed metaphors", "enumeration", the "spot-plague", and "unequal yoke-fellows".

Doyle Dane Bernbach was a terrifying place for an unlettered lout such as myself who, though raised from an early age on a diet of words, had received his most meaningful educational excitements in public libraries. Under the tutelage of copy chief John Withers, and shaking in my Chelsea boots (for in offices along the copy department corridor scribbled three further wise men, John Salmon, Dawson Yeoman, and David Abbott), I spent three months working on a single piece of copy for Mothercare. I was paid £26 a week, to go up to £30 a year later when Mr Withers decreed that I was fit to remain. He taught me about split infinitives and dangling modifiers, the double-entendre and the negative pun. He also introduced me to *grand cru classe* bordeaux.

I approached copywriting, prior to DDB, as Robert Graves had advised Alan Sillitoe on the writing of poetry: compose a strong, irresistible opening line which is unrelated to the title (for which we may substitute, for our purposes here, "headline"), and write a powerful narrative middle which makes a seductive case for what it is you wish to get across, and to finish always have a memorably witty ending. DDB forced me to refine these vague admonitions. DDB taught me how to think, not just how to write.

Working at an agency where Socratic reasoning was the norm I soon learned not only to apply Occam's razor to every sentence (every thought) but to make a piece of copy a compulsive delight to read. I learned that if a line (let alone a word) could be taken out and the copy still stood up, if it did not suffer in any way, then it could be quashed. I had fallen, with Mr Withers' help, under the spell of Sir Arthur Quiller-Couch, the late Victorian writer and critic. On the pinboard in my office, in 72-point upper-case type, there was stuck Quiller-Couch's great injunction "MURDER YOUR DARLINGS." In zealous sanguinary style, I became a serial murderer of my own and anyone else's copy (when I became that Tyrannosaurus, the Copy Chief).

What relevance, dear old fart, I hear you asking me, can this possibly have to the age we now live in? In the age of texting, Twittering, Facebook, MySpace, e-tailing, and ads where the propositions are not based on a rational appeal to a reader via a genuine advertising idea but an emotional bludgeoning built around computer-generated imagery aimed at a viewer which even from the back seat of the Odeon starkly betrays the horrible grubby fingerprints of planners all over it, the craft of copywriting is, surely, more or less dead. I have not seen a print ad or a TV or cinema commercial in the last 20 years which would have been signed off at DDB (let alone the early AMV or CDP).

Indeed, I am told that copywriters no longer have offices where they can write undisturbed and relish their solitude but sit at something called a work station in an open-plan office in front of a computer terminal. How it is possible to write in such a bustling hell is beyond me. But then I've never had to try.

My approach (in my own office) was to scribble down several dozen opening lines, before committing one to the typewriter wherein lay rolled a virgin sheet of saffron yellow copy paper. The sentence sat there, stark and accusatory, under the headline which I typed in first. This was then followed by a frenzy of writing on the pad as I more or less listed everything I had to say. I then paused. I stretched my legs. I did clues in the *Times* crossword. I cleared my mind of the task in hand for several minutes. I then attacked the main body of the copy again until a second and longer pause came when I would, with the help of a telephone, organise an evening with a distant young lady, at the theatre or dinner at a restaurant. I then typed up what I had written on the pad, made a few amendments and corrected typos, and tried out a few end lines.

Which brings us to lunchtime. This was a prolonged mental exercise lasting three hours and several bottles of lovely wine were consumed (with possibly calvados to follow) in the company of one or other of my colleagues. On my return around 3.30 or 4PM from this daily habit, which was essential to create as much distance as possible between me and the copy (thus removing my ego from it and creating a more objective stance), I would see that what I had written in the morning was tosh. I would throw it away (amongst the myriad of things DDB provided for its copywriters was a green metal waste-bin). This ritual was repeated for three or four days; slowly a curious process had taken place in my mind: I discovered what it was I wanted to say and roughly how I wanted to say it. Occasionally, to add to the essential breaks in the daily writing routine (the *Times* crossword proving so feeble as to last less than 15 minutes, say), and distant young ladies being intransigent or unbiddable via the telephone, I would go and chat to an art director or perhaps one of the prettier media buyers. The former were the more culturally challenging (art directors really were art directors in the days of which I speak). They would ask how I found the latest Philip K Dick, or what I thought of Bill Evans' left hand on "Round Midnight" on his latest EP, and if I had anything original to say about Adrian Mitchell's new play or Stanley Spencer's monstrous hangings at the Tate. We rarely, if ever, discussed advertising.

Anxious to have an opinion on everything, one was forced to become extremely diverse. DDB therefore became my university. Writing copy there was an intellectual experience. It was like being on a drug. I was daily so stimulated I would have paid to work there. (By the time I reached CDP, alas, I was so totally blasé as to write copy in my sleep.)

Usually it took two weeks for a long piece of DDB copy to settle itself down and become a promising shape. For a short piece, and if I had the luxury of the time, it took three weeks. Of course, some pieces of copy were more urgent, and took only two days, but this was the exception. Never did I discuss with anyone else what I was writing. Only when I was satisfied with it, to the extent that over a week of playing with it I had been unable to change a significant word, would I show it to the art director. Only if it passed that test, and now daring to think I had achieved something succinct and profound, did I dare offer it to Mr Withers or ask Mr Abbott or Mr Salmon or Mr Yeoman for an opinion.

It seems to me now that the biggest problem to overcome with writing advertising copy is keeping it natural, fresh, and seemingly effortlessly arrived-at; as if the words had just been baked and were still warm to the touch. If taking three weeks to write a piece of copy results in a mannered and remorselessly self-conscious read, the writer has failed. What is the secret of writing copy which does not make you feel a failure?

Reading it out aloud to yourself. Again and again.

I read out loud a lot of what I write today, even when I am turning out 25,000 words in a month. A lot of the time I am pacing my study, arguing with myself.

A man in the street who talks to himself is listening to a fool. A copywriter who talks to himself is having a conversation with a genius.

Opposite
Client: Christian Aid
Agency: DDB
Year: 1968

An ad turned out over a weekend during the Biafran war. It raised a great deal of money.

Next spread
Client: The Guardian
Agency: Priestley Marin-Guzman & Gluck
Year: 1989

A simple trade ad to reveal that a younger hip audience reads the newspaper. In those days John Barnes, the England forward, was young and hip.

Fresh food is now flying in to Biafra.

Good nourishing stuff it is, too.

Sausage-flies are full of protein.

So Biafran mothers feed them to their children. It's the only way to keep them alive.

And if they can't stomach sausage-flies, there are always rats and lizards.

But sausage-flies are the easiest meat. At night they flock to any bright light they see.

Which is more than can be said of relief planes.

They can't get through with food and medical supplies, because an air route can't be established.

And Nigeria and Biafra can't agree on the best way to set up routes overland.

So thousands of people die of hunger and disease.

Both in Biafra and Nigeria.

3,000 deaths a day is one estimate.

What can be done?

Why do we, Christian Aid, ask you to give us money when we can't immediately use it to help Biafrans?

At the moment, we're stockpiling non-perishable food and medicines on the island of Fernando Po off the Nigerian coast.

The minute we can get it into Biafra we will.

(We've already flown 1,400 tons of stockfish into starvation areas now held by Federal troops.)

But our main concern is for Biafra and Nigeria when the fighting ends.

Because that's when the biggest fight begins.

We need money to rebuild schools and hospitals.

To buy farmers seeds and equipment.

To fly in irrigation experts, agriculturalists, doctors, engineers, and teachers.

We need the money now.

We need the money now because we have to plan for the future now.

Christian Aid people will be working in Nigeria and Biafra years after the war is over.

The same as they are still at work in the Congo, the Arab countries, South America, India, and all over the world.

Of course helping the hungry will be our first thought.

But you can't plant next year's harvest with dried fish. **Christian Aid.**

We cannot deny it. Left wingers enjoy The Guardian.

It comes as no surprise. A readership so youthful is bound to be a sporting crowd.

Indeed, according to the National Readership Survey we have more well educated ABC1 readers under 45 than any other quality daily: 342,000.

True to form they dress fashionably and drink stylishly. Better, in fact, than the readers of any comparable newspaper.

Perhaps they wear well because they lead such active lives. Among our 1.31 million readers we can, for instance, count on 125,000 golfers and 221,000 tennis players.

And at least one professional footballer.

The **Guardian**

Opposite
Client: Tern Shirts
Agency: DDB
Year: 1967

Next spread
Client: Jamaican
Tourist Board
Agency: AMV
Year: 1978

Wives bought their hus-
bands' shirts in those days
and so the client introduced
a range with varying sleeve
sizes. I blush to read it
now, talking to women as
if they were just adjuncts
to a male lifestyle.

I never read so many
books before or since on
behalf of any client. I
became an unofficial
historian of the island
between 1970 and 1979.

Is your husband in another man's arms?

When you buy your old man a white shirt, things don't always work out right.

The collar's his size, but the sleeves are someone else's.

To make matters easier for both of you, we offer the Tern Spin-King shirt.

We make its sleeves in five lengths. From 32 to 36 inches.

He should fit in quite comfortably.

You, however, should like Spin-King for other reasons.

The non-iron cotton the shirt is made from has been specially treated.

It comes out of the tub needing less ironing than any other non-iron cotton shirt.

For all this, of course, we expect something in return.

45 bob.

Write to George Stevens, Tern Shirts, Tottenham, and he'll tell you which shops will take your money.

Our Newcastle has a view of the Caribbean,
our Bath has cannonball trees, our Hampstead has coconut groves,
and our Manchester has orchids growing wild.

If you thought by visiting our island you would get away from it all, we have some surprises.

Our three counties of Middlesex, Cornwall and Surrey contain some very familiar names.

You'll find our Newcastle in the mountains above Kingston and the ocean.

While our Bath is grounded between Soho and Hampton Court.

Bath's a spa of course. And if its mineral springs don't soothe your ills try the Botanical Gardens.

You'll see right away why the cannonball tree is so called from its seed pods. But nothing prepares you for the complex beauty and perfume of its flowers.

Rich like spiced jasmine the scent is the most thrillingly tropical in the island.

Our orchids can't compete. Even on Hampstead heath where a flower farm nestles among the coconut groves.

Or in Manchester where the orchids climb the orange trees. And humming birds hover like bees.

Glasgow's hereabouts. So is Marlborough and Penzance.

Our Aberdonians, however, live the other side of Maidstone just up the road from Windsor.

(Near the rum distillery. Not to be confused with Windsor Castle which specialises in delicious pimento.)

In our world, Northampton and Leeds are near the Santa Cruz mountains.

(Since it was Columbus's ships which first stumbled upon our island in 1494 it's only fair the Spanish get a word in.)

We also have a Belfast, and castles at Edinburgh and Dublin.

In our Oxford we grow coffee. In our Cambridge bananas.

While our Londoners live a bus ride from a 7 mile stretch of beach the colour of crushed gold.

Our Kensington, you'll find, is free of parking problems. And any jams in Highgate or Islington will be guava or paw-paw.

However, while we may be able to offer you a home from home somewhere, nowhere can we provide matching weather.

We don't know what cold is. And in our island you'll find a diversity of landscape and people unequalled on the planet. People especially.

Jamaicans make Jamaica the warmest place in the Caribbean.

Even in chilly London we're *warm*. Contact us, the Jamaican Tourist Board, at Jamaica House, 50 St James's Street, London SW1 (tel: 493 3647) and we'll tell you how you can spend 14 days in our country for only £418, including the airfare and hotel.

Or drop by your travel agent.

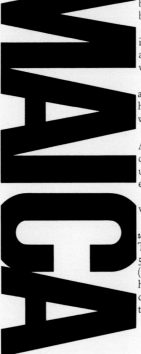

Steve Harrison

Steve Harrison started as a 30-year-old trainee writer at Ogilvy & Mather Direct (now OgilvyOne Worldwide). Within a few years he had become creative director and European creative director. After that he helped set up HPT Brand Response, which became Harrison Troughton Wunderman.

He ended up as HTW's chairman, creative director and (briefly) Wunderman's global creative director. By then he'd won more Cannes Lions in his discipline than any creative director in the world and twice as many domestic gongs as his nearest local rival.

That discipline was always direct and, true to his roots, he would like anyone with a comment or query on what follows to drop him a line at *harrisosteve@ googlemail.com*

It was probably my grounding in direct mail that taught me my obligations to the reader. I was usually entering their homes uninvited and because of that I always felt that my first responsibility was to them — and not the client.

I wasn't there to foist a product or service on the prospect. It was my job to show how the thing I was writing about could solve the reader's problems.

For example, the M&G work was written when the FTSE 100 was at its lowest for 15 years. We therefore had to reassure our anxious prospects (the affluent over-50s) and position M&G as the one brand that a) understood their fears, b) knew what it was doing, and c) could be trusted with their money.

To do this we set out to write headlines that elicited the response "bloody hell, that's interesting, tell me more." (Whatever the brief, I suggest you try this, too.)

In fact, the headline "In our opinion…" got so many "bloody hells…" that on the morning it appeared, the BBC invited M&G's Marketing Manager to appear on *Newsnight* to explain his contrarian approach.

Writing an arresting headline that addresses the prospect's problem should always be your starting point. But usually that's all it is: a "starting point". For, having done the extremely hard work of gaining the prospect's interest, you'd be crazy not to use this rare opportunity to then persuade them that they'd be better off with the thing you're selling.

The first paragraph is the hardest, for this must segue from the headline into your sales argument. Once again the reader's point of view is paramount and you should try to reflect their opinion, experience or attitude at that moment. After that, use an imaginative mix of empathy and facts to move them deftly to where you want them to be.

It helps if your copy has a natural, conversational style. To achieve this, as Jim Durfee has suggested, imagine you're sitting opposite your prospect and then, in the guise of the brand you're representing, write as you'd speak.

This means using language they'll understand instantly. Which words are they? Well, of the 80 most-used words in the English language, 78 have an Anglo-Saxon root. These are the short, simple words we use every day.

There's one short, simple word you should use a lot. Read your copy and check that "you" appears three times more than "I" or "we". This helps you write about the subject from the reader's perspective.

Once you've finished the first draft, leave it a few hours. Then imagine the reader — busy, distracted, sceptical. Ask yourself: is my big idea abruptive and relevant enough to get their attention? Have I really shown I understand their problem? Have I clearly described my solution? Have I anticipated their doubts and told them exactly what they need to do to enjoy the advantage I've described?

Then delete the unnecessary and rewrite the ambiguous. And rewrite... and rewrite...

Others have told you the next stage: get someone to read your copy. All I'd add is this: don't rush up and say, "This goes in 15 minutes, whaddyathink?" Explain the prospect, the proposition and the idea, and then give them time to mull it over. Make sure you've chosen someone who is confident enough to tell you "it's crap", and knowledgeable enough to tell you why. Of course, the most confident and knowledgeable person should be your creative director. Once you have their approval, the copy can go. And you can relax. Momentarily.

Many clients will feel compelled to tweak, amend or completely rewrite your work. Never dash off their changes but listen carefully to what's been "suggested". Then rework that which is valid (or truly mandatory) and resist the things that damage the argument. In both cases, be ready to explain why you are doing what you're doing.

It's hard, often infuriating work. And most writers can't be bothered. But it's your job to protect your idea and copy. Yes, the suits (this book's unsung heroes) play a big part and your creative director should be on the phone to the client in your Love-Forty moments. But the responsibility for getting the work out as intended is yours. And days or weeks later, when your ad, letter, email or whatever appears, you'll be glad you assumed that responsibility. And so might the most important person of all, the reader.

Next spread
Client: M&G Investments
Agency: HTW
Year: 2002

Pages 218–219
Client: M&G Investments
Agency: HTW
Year: 2002

Pages 220–221
Client: Bloomberg TV
Agency: HPT Brand
Response
Year: 1999

Try to say something
arresting, relevant and
useful to your prospect in
your headline and copy.
This ad was aimed at
frightened, confused
investors and appeared
when the FTSE 100 was
at its lowest for 15 years.

Plan your copy before you
start to write. Understand
your prospect and the
problem they're experienc-
ing. Be sure of the solution
you're providing and all the
facts that back it up. Work
out how you're going to
get from where they are
to where you want them
to be. Only then should
you turn on your PC.

Written properly, a letter
should get response
and shift perceptions.
This one accompanied
a label-less bottle of
Champagne that went
to 23 top media buyers
who were responsible
for big spending airline
accounts; 22 called
straight back and one
immediately moved

£500,000 of Virgin
Atlantic's spend. What's
more, after I'd made the
association with Dom
Perignon, all were left
with the desired image
of Bloomberg TV as a
brand synonymous with
great wealth.

In our opinion, there's never ever been a better time to invest in the stockmarket.*

At the moment, we believe the stockmarket is having the equivalent of a January sale.

Shares have fallen 13.3% in the last 12 months.

And, to us, it seems there are plenty of bargains to be had.

Others, however, might say you'd be throwing good money after bad.

Wouldn't you be better off selling your existing shares – before it's too late – and putting the money somewhere nice and safe, like a building society?

To answer these questions, we'll have to travel back to the dim. (largely

But what of the people who took their money and put it in a building society?

Well, they'd have known it was perfectly safe and secure.

However, that very same £1,000 would have only grown to £1,077 in the same period.

In case you're wondering who we are.

We introduced the UK's first unit trust on St George's Day, 23 April, 1931.

We successfully lobbied for regulation of the industry back in 1939 – which is why you can trust unit trusts.

In 1954, we introduced the UK's first regular

Bargain hunters beware.

If you look at the chart opposite, you'll see you can snap up shares in a lot of famous names for a fraction of the price you'd have paid just a few months ago.

However, it pays to shop around and, when you consider there are over 800 companies listed on the stockmarket, it takes a lot of expertise and effort to emerge with the very best deals.

While it can be exhilarating fun trying to do this yourself there are

The secret of investing is the same as the secret of good comedy – timing.

Get this right, and you could be laughing all the way to the bank.

The secret lies in what the experts call 'buying at the bottom.' And there are some who think that moment has already past.

We ourselves believe the recovery will happen sooner rather than later.

Which is why, if you don't count

Some of this week's special offers.

	Was	Now
Cable & Wireless	1022p	912p
Royal Doulton	70½p	12¾p
Marconi	800p	31p
Redstone	165⅛p	1p

These were correct when we went

How do you protect yourself against a volatile market? Invest in it more often.

When the markets are jerking up and down like a bunjee jumper, what's the best thing to do with your money if you have some to invest?

Some would say wait for things to calm down and put it in the safest place of all, the building society.

We, however, would disagree.

In our view, avoiding the markets is the last thing you should do. Because, quite simply, you'd miss out on the huge bargains that are to be had.

The problem is, picking the right time to snap them up.

So, how do you

Unfortunately, many people haven't realised this. So they teeter on the brink of the markets throughout the year. Then, in February and March, they leap in with all their money to beat the ISA deadline.

To see how costly this can be, look at this comparison. Imagine you'd had £3,000. Now, see how it would have fared over the past five years if you'd drip-fed it at £50 a month.

Then, look at how your investment would have performed as a £1,200 lump sum put in toward the

As any experienced gardener will tell you, you get better growth if you water little and often rather than soak once in a while. It can be the same with investments.

Why you can trust unit trusts.

Since we launched the first unit trust in the UK in 1931 millions of people have found them to be a profitable, reliable and safer way of investing in stocks and shares.

There's a very simple reason why. Your money is pooled with that of other investors to create a much larger fund. So, even the smallest investor has the clout of George Soros.

A fund manager then invests this, on your behalf, across a wide number of shares, bonds or other investments such as cash or property depending

By investing each month, you can smooth out the ups and downs of the market. If the unit price falls, your monthly contribution will purchase a larger number of units at a lower price.

And if the price rises, BINGO, this larger holding of units will make your investment more valuable – although, of course, your £50 a month will buy you less.

Call us for a free copy of our Guide

rewarding time to invest is, actually, all the time.

Don't jump in feet first.

Investing a little on a regular basis takes the pressure off trying to pick the one perfect time to make your investment.

Quite simply there isn't "one perfect time."

In case you're wondering who we are.

We introduced the UK's first unit trust on St George's Day, 23 April, 1931.

We successfully lobbied for regulation of the industry back in 1939 — which is why you can trust unit trusts.

In 1954, we introduced the UK's first regular savings plan, in which you could invest just five shillings a week.

We were the first UK fund manager to invest in international markets with our Japan & General Fund in 1971.

We launched the UK's first pure corporate and high yield corporate bond funds.

We introduced the UK's first no initial charge PEP.

M&G Investment Management are one of the largest investors in corporate bonds in the UK.

We manage investments for 544,505 individuals in the UK.

M&G Investment Management currently looks after £111,975,000,000 worth of investments — make that £111,975,001,526.

half as much.

Would you like another example of how it pays to drip-feed your investment?

OK, let's pick a period when it was decidedly more difficult to make money. January 1973 to December 1977. It witnessed one of the worst, and prolonged, stock market collapses of the last century.

If you'd invested a lump sum of £3,000 with us at the beginning of this period you'd have emerged with £3,967.

However, if you'd invested your £3,000 in regular £50 a month lumps then you'd have come out with an impressive £4,980.

That's a profit of 66%.

Worth getting out of bed for, certainly.

Now we can't promise you future profits based on past performance like this. However, we can suggest a way of ensuring you have as few sleepless nights as possible.

We have a whole range of unit trusts for you to choose from. (Actually we should call some of them OEICs — see the box below.)

We have some that are right for people who are looking to get one big lump sum when they finally cash in

What is an OEIC?

a) A ludicrous, flightless bird found only in the Galapagos Islands?
b) A beer-swilling, pot-bellied, ex-public schoolboy?
c) An Open Ended Investment Company which works in similar ways to a unit trust except that an OEIC is legally constituted as a limited company?

their investment. We have others that payback frequently on a more regular basis. And there are some that offer you the best of both worlds.

However, let's stick to our theme and talk about a unit trust that allows you to drip-feed your investment.

In one fell swoop this would take away both the worry about picking the right time to invest and the worry about picking the right individual company to invest in.

The answer is The M&G Savings Plan which allows you to put away a regular monthly investment.

market. As we said, we invented the unit trust and it's very likely we will have one that will match your needs.

We also have other innovative ideas which might help you capitalise on the current economic uncertainty. If you'd like to take advantage of them, please do not hesitate to get in touch.

Call M&G free on: **0800 072 6142** quoting reference TDG (lines are open 8.00am to 8.00pm, seven days a week; for your protection calls may be recorded) or complete and return the coupon below. We'll gladly send you a copy of our booklet which contains our thinking.

Or visit www.mandg.co.uk

Alternatively, contact your IFA if you have one.

Please send me a copy of your Guide to Investing.

Name:

Address:

Postcode:

Email:

Tel. No.:

Are you an existing M&G customer? Yes ☐ ref: XXDG   No ☐ ref: QXDG

Please return to: The M&G Group, FREEPOST 9131 (There, you're 27p better off already), Chelmsford, CM1 1FB.

M&G
INVESTMENTS

Clive Reed
OPTIMEDIA
84-86 Baker Street
London
W1M 1DL

23rd March 1999

The Bloomberg Television Viewer
has a penchant for fine wines, fast cars
first class air travel and a lot of day-time telly

Dear Clive,

I have sent you and three of your colleagues at OPTIMEDIA a bottle of Dom Perignon. You've probably all received the 1992 vintage. As you may know, 1992 was the last truly great year for Champagne and if you were to ask for it in your favourite restaurant you would pay something in excess of £200.

I said, however, that it is "probably" the 1992. In fact, the bottle you have in front of you could be a Champagne so magnificent that you are unlikely to see it in any restaurant or wine shop in London – the Dom Perignon 1966.

If you'd like to discover the true identity of the bottle in front of you, please call me on 0171 330 7704.

Whichever year it turns out to be, I hope you enjoy your Dom Perignon. The idea of sending it to you was actually suggested by the man for whom I work, Mike Bloomberg.

As he said, "what better way to get you in the mood to think about the Bloomberg Television viewer than to settle down with a nice glass of champagne."

You see, the Bloomberg viewer is quite partial to more than the occasional glass of Dom Perignon. More pertinently, they are very familiar with sipping it at 35,000 feet whilst flying First Class.

In fact, for someone like yourself who is seeking the wealthiest of frequent flyers, on behalf of British Airways, no medium provides more accurate targeting than Bloomberg Television.

Bloomberg Television is the only UK business channel which provides continuous coverage of the world's markets, in-depth interviews with market makers and analysis by financial experts. Walk round the City of London and you'll find it is as ubiquitous there as MTV is in the advertising agencies of Soho and Fitzrovia.

Quite simply, Bloomberg Television is essential viewing for many of the UK's most affluent and influential individuals. Precisely the kind of people who you are targeting for British Airways. Let me give you some figures on Bloomberg viewers:

96.2% took an air trip last year.

78.4% took three to five air trips in the past year.

54.7% took six or more air trips in the past year.

On average these people took 8.8 air trips in the past year. Few of these were short hops across the Channel. Indeed, over one third of Bloomberg viewers were away from home for more than four weeks.

In short they are precisely the kind of individuals that British Airways needs to be talking to.

Now I would never suggest that British Airways cease advertising in the more mainstream media. I would, however, simply say that if you want to target the rich frequent flyer, then use the medium they use most frequently. Bloomberg Television.

I'd be delighted to give you more details. So, when you call about your Champagne, please ask me any questions you like about our service. I can also tell you about our advertising rates, which I think you'll find most attractive. I look forward to hearing from you.

Yours sincerely,

S. Clements

Sue Clements

Steve Hayden

Steve Hayden began his career as a copywriter at General Motors. After honing his craft at various agencies, he was recruited to Chiat\Day where he and Lee Clow made advertising history as co-creators of the "1984" Superbowl spot for Apple. In 1986, Steve moved to BBDO to become chairman/chief executive officer of West Coast operations. He led the team that made Apple an iconic brand, at the same time tripling the size of the agency.

In 1994, Ogilvy asked Steve to join as "brand steward" for their IBM global account. While leading IBM's renewal, Steve played a key role with other major brands, earning almost every major award and accruing an enormous amount of recognition for the agency. While on Ogilvy's worldwide board, Steve drove engagement with digital communications, pushing the firm to become a leader in interactive media and integrated communications.

If you want to be a well-paid copywriter, please your client. If you want to be an award-winning copywriter, please yourself. If you want to be a great copywriter, please your reader.

Copywriting is perhaps the only non-criminal human activity that allows you to make a comfortable living off your character defects. These will usually include, but are not limited to, pride, anger, gluttony, greed, lust, envy, sloth and fear.

All of them are useful, depending on the circumstances, so make sure you're familiar with each in all its facets. This may be why some of the more successful copywriters are so familiar with the original black book, the Bible.

It not only explains everything you need to know about human frailty, but also serves as a very useful style guide (where do you think all those "Ands" in copy come from?). It's also the most powerful selling document ever written. In a world full of parity scriptures, it's persuaded billions to buy the totally intangible, often at the ultimate price a human can pay, for nearly twenty centuries. Forty, if you just count the scary parts.

It also embodies the principle of Anonymous Power. No one knows who wrote it. We barely know who translated it. But they were very, very good. How many of us, even after winning a D&AD Pencil, have our work referred to as The Word of God?

Thus, it's not a bad idea to emulate them rather than the flashier types you come across in awards books. In other words, make your work The Word of Proctor, or The Word of IBM, or The Word of Callard & Bowser.

Which brings us to hearing voices, and developing your own. A few great copywriters like Hal Riney and Howard Gossage can get away their whole lives with one voice.

Most of us, though, have to adapt our style to our clients, our audiences, our countries, and our mortgage payments.

That's why it helps to meet the president or managing director of whatever it is you're writing about. If they were great speakers and brilliant thinkers, and if you were able to sweep aside the stupidity and cupidity that drive most business, what would they sound like? Your job is to create your clients' Best Self. So look for the angel in them, and bring it out.

Now then, there's the matter of getting people to read your copy. Large promise, as Johnson pointed out, is the soul of the advertisement.

Search for some way to relate the tiny, constricted world clients live in to the larger, sunnier world people actually care about. Deodorants aren't about keeping dry, they're about being loved. Computers aren't about getting more work done, they're about power. Cars aren't about transportation. Food isn't about hunger. Drink isn't about thirst. And so on.

It's always useful to get yourself genuinely excited about a product or a service that seems incredibly dull to everyone else. Package delivery, for example. Find how to relate it to the large world, and you'll make yourself famous, at least in the copywriter's anonymous fashion.

The opening line of your copy is probably more important than the headline. A creative director at FCB once told me that four percent of the readership will slog through seventy percent of body copy no matter how bad it is. Your job is to beat those odds.

The Bible, save for Genesis, is a great source of book titles, but only occasionally for opening lines. For these, study Country and Western lyrics, the very font and wellhead of common emotion, everyday irony and freighted pith.

My favourite Country and Western lyric: "If your phone don't ring, it's me."

A brilliant example of morphemic loading for everyone who toils in the dank trenches of commercial prose.

Most people's lives are brutish, dull and long. If you can bring a momentary diversion, a promise that there is something interesting going on out there that might make a difference, they will love you.

If you are lying, of course, they will tear you to pieces. So make the truth as interesting as it can be, and never look down on your audience. They're wiser than you, will live longer and have faster Internet connections.

Now, one last piece of advice.

Avoid drugs if you possibly can, alcohol as much as you can, and cigarettes at all hazard.

You will spend most of your life creating artificial pearls for genuine, well, clients. If you win awards, they will hate you for it. If you don't win awards, they'll dump you for someone who does.

Ultimately, this can drive you to addiction and death, unless you're able to achieve a healthy perspective on your existence as a copywriter. After all, it's the only career in the world that allows you the life of an artist and the income of a foreign-currency manipulator.

So make sure you give at least ten percent of your earnings to worthy causes. Give your own time in love and service to others. Learn compassion and beware of the ego sickness that devastates so many in our trade.

Of course, that does bring us back to the Bible, preferably the version scripted by the anonymous scribes of King James' court. It's better written.

Baked Apple.

Last Thanksgiving, a designer from Lynn/Ohio Corporation took one of the company's Apple Personal Computers home for the holidays.

While he was out eating turkey, it got baked.

His cat, perhaps miffed at being left alone, knocked over a lamp which started

a fire which, among other unpleasantries, melted his TV set all over his computer. He thought his goose was cooked.

But when he took the Apple to Cincinnati Computer Store, *mirabile dictu*, it still worked.

A new case and keyboard made it as good as new.

Nearly 1,000 Apple dealers have complete service centers that can quickly fix just about anything that might go wrong, no matter how bizarre.

So if you're looking for a personal computer that solves problems instead of creating them, look to your authorized Apple dealer.

You'll find everything well-done.

The personal computer. **apple**

For the authorized dealer nearest you, call (800) 538-9696. In California, call (800) 662-9238. Or write: Apple Computer Inc., 10260 Bandley Dr., Cupertino, CA 95014.

Client: Apple
Agency: Chiat\Day
Year: 1981

Opposite
Client: Apple
Agency: Chiat\Day
Year: 1980

I don't believe the cleverest ads always have clever headlines. We ran this ad in 1981, welcoming IBM to the personal computer market. Somewhat like Belgium welcoming Hitler to the border. Oh well. The clever bit was that, even though Apple was tiny at the time, this ad made a two-horse race out of a twenty-horse race, and Apple-IBM have forever after been hyphenated.

We began setting Apple's brand persona back in 1980 with ads like this — true stories of how Apple computers fit into people's lives — without the bits and bytes, speeds and feeds featured in most computer ads.

Welcome, IBM.

Seriously.

Welcome to the most exciting and important marketplace since the computer revolution began 35 years ago.

And congratulations on your first personal computer.

Putting real computer power in the hands of the individual is already improving the way people work, think, learn, communicate and spend their leisure hours.

Computer literacy is fast becoming as fundamental a skill as reading or writing.

When we invented the first personal computer system, we estimated that over 140,000,000 people worldwide could justify the purchase of one, if only they understood its benefits.

Next year alone, we project that well over 1,000,000 will come to that understanding. Over the next decade, the growth of the personal computer will continue in logarithmic leaps.

We look forward to responsible competition in the massive effort to distribute this American technology to the world. And we appreciate the magnitude of your commitment.

Because what we are doing is increasing social capital by enhancing individual productivity.

Welcome to the task apple

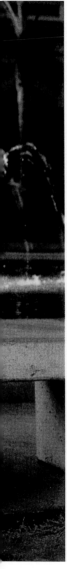

PowerBook.

"One of the best-designed products of the year."
–Time

"One of the best products of the year."
–Fortune

"Hardware product of the year."
–InfoWorld

Client: Apple
Agency: BBDO
Year: 1991

The PowerBook launch in the early '90s was some of the best print we ever did for Apple at BBDO. This is one of my favourites, featuring Steve Wozniak, Apple founder, and his son Jess. I wrote the copy with Chris Wall, and came up with "The next thing" theme for the campaign, which Apple never particularly liked, because it was inspired by Steve Jobs' NeXT. Years later, Hewlett-Packard complimented the campaign in the sincerest way imaginable with their "The computer is personal again" campaign, with celebrities demonstrating all the ways HP PCs served them.

"One of the best new products of the year."
–Business Week

It's the next thing.

Opposite
Client: KFAC
Agency: Boylhart,
Lovett & Dean
Year: 1978

Selling a classical music
radio in LA is only slightly
less challenging than
selling bikinis in Reykjavik,
but I thought this tried
and true advertising form
would at least get us
readership. It also got me
a job at Chiat\Day.

BEFORE
This is me before I started listening to KFAC. Overweight, poor, unhappy and alone.

AFTER
This is I after 16 short years as a KFAC listener. Rich, trim and sexy.

How classical music changed my life.

The other day at Ma Maison, as I was waiting for the attendant to retrieve my chocolate brown 450 SLC, the Saudi prince I'd been noshing with said, "Say, Bill, how did an unassuming guy like yourself come to be so rich, so trim, so...sexy?"

My eyes grew misty. "It wasn't always this way, Ahmed, old buddy..."

My mind raced back to the Bad Time, before the investment tips, the real estate empire, before Dino bought my screenplay and I bought my Columbia 50...

Once I was a lot like you.

Working at a nowhere job, hitting the singles bars, watching situation comedies in my free time. I tipped the scales at a hefty 232, but my bank balance couldn't have tipped the bus boy at the Midnight Mission.

Finally, I hit bottom...picked up by the Castaic police for barreling my old heap the wrong way over some parking lot spikes.

My last friend in this lonely world, Hardy Gustavsen, set me straight while he was driving me back to L.A.

"Bill, get hold of yourself! Start listening to KFAC!"

"Gosh, Hardy, don't they play classical music? I'm not sure I cotton to that high brow stuff!"

Aside from a couple of summers at Tanglewood and Aspen, and one semester in Casals' Master Class...

I knew absolutely nothing about classical music.

"Bill, who would be wrong if you got better?"

Looking into his steely blue eyes, I realized Hardy was right. I resolved to give KFAC a shot.

At first, it was quite painful. Listening to all those 100-piece groups was confusing—I was used to having the drums on the right and the bass on the left and the singer in the middle. All those semidemihemiquavers made my head spin.

But I started to feel the beneficial effects of classical music listening in just one short week.

In no time, I was using napkins with every meal, I switched from Bourbon to an unpretentious Montrachet and I became able to hear sirens even with my car windows rolled up.

Soon I was spending every night with KFAC and a good book, like Aquinas' *Summa Theologica.*

I realized that some of the wealthiest, most famous people in this world listened to classical music—Napoleon, Bismark, George Washington, Beethoven...and many others who are yet alive today.

Then I met Marlene. The first girl who knew there was more to *Also Sprach Zarathustra* than the theme from *2001.* And I fell in love.

Today, I'm on top of the world with a wonderful wife, close friends in high places and a promising career in foreign currency manipulation.

Can classical music do for you what it did for me?

A few years back, scientific studies showed that when dairy cows are played classical music the quantity and quality of their milk dramatically improves.

Now if it can do that for plain old moo cows, imagine what it can do for you!

You might use it to control disgusting personal habits and make fun new friends. The possibilities are endless!

Can you afford KFAC?

Is lox kosher?

Even though marketing surveys show that KFAC's audience is the most affluent assemblage of nice people in Southern California, yes, you *can* afford KFAC! Thanks to their Special Introductory Offer, you can listen FREE OF CHARGE for *as many hours as you like* without obligation!

Begin the KFAC habit today.

Remember, the longest journey begins by getting dressed. Don't let this opportunity slip through your fingers. Tune to KFAC right NOW, while you're thinking about it.

And get ready for a spectacular improvement in your life.

Warn your family and friends that you may start dressing for dinner.

You may lose your taste for beer nuts.

And the next time you're on the freeway thinking about playing with your nose, you'll find yourself asking:

"Really. Would a KFAC listener do this?"

Steve Henry

Steve Henry was founder and creative director of HHCL — the agency voted Campaign's Agency of the Year three times and Campaign's Agency of the Decade in January 2000. This unique award was given because of HHCL's "iconoclastic attitude both to the work and the way it does business".

Steve has won most of the major creative awards, including the D&AD President's Award and Black Pencil, the Grand Prix at Cannes, the Grand Prix at the British Television Awards, the President's Award at the Royal Television Society awards and the President's Award at Creative Circle (twice).

In 2008, Steve was included in Campaign's inaugural Hall of Fame, a collection of the 40 most influential people in British advertising over the last 50 years.

In 2011, Steve founded Decoded, a company that teaches anyone to code in a day. He also writes a blog on the Campaign website about creativity.

Life's too short to read body copy. Let's face it — life's too short to read this book.

Skim it. Look at the pictures. Nobody reads body copy.

Sometimes, I have this fantasy that a piece of copy goes out. And it hasn't been read by anybody — not even by the proof-reader. And, hidden down in paragraph 13, is a typo that reveals the secret of the universe. But nobody gets to see it. (Because nobody reads body copy.)

Actually, increasingly, people don't read ads at all. They read — content.

People don't look at ads, or judge ads, or consider ads. They consume — content.

Ads are things they avoid.

Working in the ad industry, you think people are interested in ads. But they're not.

Go home at Christmas, and talk to your relatives, and see how much they know about what you do.

Then divide that by 50, to give you a picture of how strangers feel about your latest campaign.

Ads are like wasps at the picnic. They get in the way of what people want.

Or they're like the loony on the bus. "Thinking of buying some dog food?"

Er, no. I don't have a dog.

People consume content, not ads. So you have to make content, not ads. You have to entertain. And words can still play an important part in that.

So my advice on writing body copy is — don't bother. My advice on writing content that is paid for by your clients is two-fold.

One, always be entertaining. Clients should be thinking, not "what ads do I want to make?" But "what ads would I like to see?"

Two, do it differently. The most important thing about any commercial communication is to do it differently. Write it upside down, in Jamaican patois, or with every fifth letter missing.

Having said all this, I went to dig out some examples of body copy from the plan chest and immediately realised that I hadn't been quite as revolutionary as I wanted to be.

My first, panicky thought was to send in ads with as few words on them as possible — like the old *Time Out* poster with a candle burning at both ends, or the First Direct poster with a deliberately bland shot of rather stubby grass stretching across 96 sheets of prime London poster-site.

Then I thought, grow up, mate. This book is about words, and you don't despise words that much, do you?

Because let me confess something right now. Although I fully understand the futility of writing body copy, I really like doing it.

So I dug out some ads with words on them. And I hit another problem. As a creative director, you don't always get to write the ads you most want to. So some of these ads aren't my body copy at all.

MTV. This was an MTV trade ad in which we introduced the idea of "optional body copy". The copy was put on a rubdown inserted into the magazine. You could add as much of it (or as little) as you wanted to by rubbing on the sheet like a transfer. This came from a team called Justin Hooper (copywriter) and Christian Cotterill (art director).

A BMW April Fool's ad from WCRS. I like this because I had to write to a style set by Robin Wight, but I was able to inject some of my own sense of humour into it.

Idris Soft Drinks. A chance to indulge — which I feel I only half-took. Undoubtedly this is the sort of ad which David Abbott would have written much better.

Thames TV. I love the way the copy is spread out around the page, so you avoid that normal block-wodge look of body copy. The ad was a lot of fun to write.

First Direct. In this campaign, small cut-out heads enjoyed short dialogues in small-space press ads. They had the feel of cartoons (i.e. they looked approachable), but I felt they were very fresh and different.

Next spread
Client: Idris
Agency: HHCL
Year: 1992

Idris Soft Drinks.

Most of the ads in the campaign were written by other people (Naresh Ramchandani, Dave Buonaguidi and Steve Girdlestone). I can't remember who wrote this one.

Call me perverse if you want to, but I like body copy that doesn't look like body copy. Which isn't that surprising when you consider that I first learnt about advertising from a man who took a very individual approach to copywriting.

Fresh from studying English Literature at Oxford University, I was told by Dave Trott that the best bit of body copy he'd ever seen was on a Land Rover ad from TBWA. I looked at it and there were actually no words on it at all. Just symbols.

He was right.

Now the question you've got to ask yourself is this. What's the next bit of genuinely revolutionary body copy going to look like? Not like anything in this book, that's for sure. Because these ideas have all been done before.

REMEMBER...

THAT TIME AFTER SCHOOL, in the summer, when you could go outside and play till ten o'clock at night? ¶ THAT LONG DRIVE to the seaside, when you

first saw the blue of the sea through a gap in the hills? ¶ PUTTING UP A TENT in the garden, and drinking Lemonade made cloudy by the real lemons in it, as the sun shone through the canvas? ¶ GETTING

OFF THE BUS a stop early, so you could spend the fare money you saved on sweets? ¶ PLAYING 'TAG' in the garden all afternoon, as the shadows lengthened across the lawn? ¶ GOING FOR A LONG WALK, just with

your best friend, and giving yourself a reward in the sweet shop a mile away from home? ¶ MAKING AN ICE CREAM float, with vanilla ice cream and Cream Soda, and taking it carefully outside

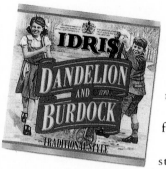

with your two favourite comics? ¶ PICKING WILD BLACKBERRIES, and thinking you could run away and survive for ever on the delicious, free fruit? ¶ ROLLING DOWN A long bank, and standing up and feeling all dizzy as you ran up the bank to do it again? ¶ THE TASTE OF Dandelion and Burdock (if you ever drank it, how could you ever forget it)? ¶ PLAYING CATCH AGAINST a wall, and giving yourself a target of 10 in a row, to help England win the match?

¶ COMING HOME ONE DAY, to find that your family was the proud owner of a dog, and you had to think of a name for it?

¶ TRYING GINGER BEER, made with real ginger, because your father said it was a great drink, and finding out he was right?

IDRIS
TRADITIONALS

How long does it take
to make a cup of tea?

 about the same time
as it does to open
a current account
that pays 9% interest.

put the kettle on then.

first direct

0800 22 2000

**first direct is a division
of midland bank plc.**

interest is paid monthly on any amount
in credit increasing to 9.25% for £500+.
rate quoted is net p.a. and may vary.

Client: First Direct
Agency: HHCL
Year: 1993

Opposite
Client: Thames Television
Agency: HHCL
Year: 1990

Thames TV trade ad.

Next spread
Client: BMW
Agency: WCRS
Year: 1986

BMW April Fool's ad.

THE WORST THINGS AN ADVERTISING AGENCY CAN SAY TO ITS CLIENTS.

1. "Great news. We've merged."

13. "Sorry. Looks like we can't afford London on the schedule."

2. "Meeting...what meeting?"

3. "You know what's causing the problem here. Your logo's too big."

12. "I know we've made a hash of your advertising for the last 10 years. But we'll really try hard from now on."

4. "Can I give you a lift to the station? My Ferrari's just outside."

11. "Blimey. Did we do that?"

5. "Here, this'll make you laugh. We've gone a bit over budget."

10. "You'll notice we've left your sales conference off the timing plan."

6. "Sorry about the punch-up in reception."

9. "Here's the finished film. I guarantee that people will be able to make sense of it in research."

7. "Hello. I recognise you from somewhere don't I?"

8. "Yea, yea. But clients don't know much about advertising, do they?"

YOU CAN'T AFFORD NOT TO ADVERTISE IN LONDON. YOU CAN AFFORD TO ADVERTISE ON THAMES.

THAMES TELEVISION

XXI

(CAMPAIGNS FROM £73,000. SPOTS FROM £500   EVEN LESS FOR LOCAL ADVERTISERS).

WHEN YOU CROSS THE CHANNEL, OUR STEERING WHEEL CROSSES OVER WITH YOU.

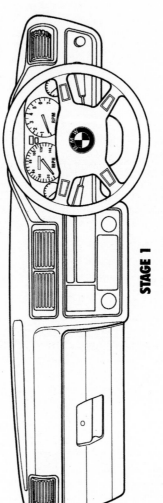

STAGE 1

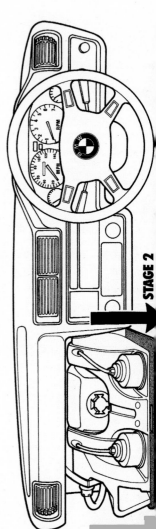

STAGE 2

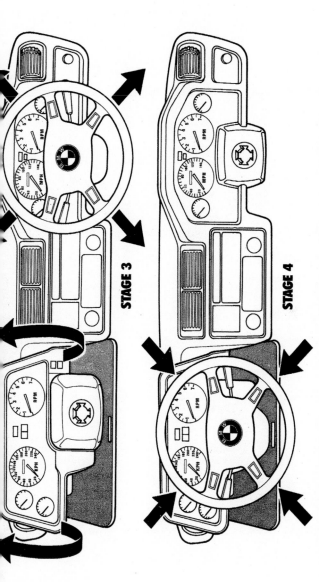

STAGE 3

STAGE 4

Since the 'Droit de Seigneur' act, passed in 1867, the French have always driven on the right-hand side of the road.

This is not merely a matter of inconvenience for British drivers; it is also a potential safety hazard. And yet car manufacturers have been ignoring the problem completely.

With one notable exception. Because BMW engineer Aap Riifühl discovered, just three years ago, that the problem could be tackled; and, with ingenious modifications, a test vehicle was designed that incorporated a unique BMW feature – the multi-dashboard facility.

By incorporating a second-unit steering wheel socket and instrument panel into a conventional glove compartment, Dr Riifühl was able to provide the basis for a secondary driving position.

The fascia, naturally enough, conforms to 'Continental' standards – with a kph speedometer, and the 'Lawson' fuel gauge reading in litres.

Then, by the insertion of a lynch-pin into the steering wheel column, fellow engineer Hans Grabbem was able to devise the first quick-release steering wheel. (Incorporated, too, into the column is a secondary 'Continental' horn – the 'Vorin-Drivers' 80 decibel air-horn.)

The final problem, of the foot-pedals, was easily resolved; Herr Grabbem made them transferable, too, with a dual position facility.

At present, this option is only available on the BMW 3 Series, but it is expected to be available on all models in time for the proposed opening of the Channel tunnel.

And then, for the first time, British drivers will be able to drive abroad without getting in on the wrong side of the natives.

Client: MTV
Agency: HHCL
Year: 1994

MTV trade ad.

This AD is BROUGHT to you with OptioNaL boDY copy. PLEASE ADD ACCORDING to TASTE.

Attitude — with. Style — Yes pleASE. 24 HOUR. AUDieNcE — ADULTs tHat ARE YOUNG. YOOT. AUDiEnCE STATUS — LOADED. READY TO SPend. ?oPTIONS — EURO or U.K. ONLY brANDS. CALL BRUCE SteinberGt DiRector of aDVertising SALES ON 071 239 7533. SERVING SuggEStioN — try Adding SPARE COPY TO ANOThER aD to mAke it moRE INTEREStiNG.

Susie Henry

After Wycombe Abbey and Goldsmiths College of Art, Susie Henry's first job was working for Ossie Clark at Quorum.

She wrote and illustrated a children's book that didn't sell, and later fell into advertising.

She had the great good fortune to be hired by David Abbott at FGA. There followed an award-winning run at DDB.

Susie went on to become the first woman creative with her name on the door of a London agency. Her final move was to Saatchi & Saatchi. In 2001 she returned to the agency for a further five years as creative consultant.

Susie has six D&AD Pencils, two of them for Commercial Union.

She now lives in Edinburgh, where she lectures in Creative Advertising at Edinburgh Napier University.

It's time to put my cards on the table.

My passport says copywriter. I've been a copywriter for 36 years and I've absolutely loved being in the business of creating ads and the industry has been kind to me. But the copywriting bit, and by that I mean the text, the real nuts and bolts of the ad, well, that's never come easy.

Looking back at other entries from the 1995 *Copy Book* I see I'm not the only writer to feel this way. Phew.

If it were just about sliding in those vital selling points and wrapping things up with a witty endline — I wouldn't have much of a problem. But good copy rarely happens like that. It's a complicated process, weaving all the threads into a persuasive argument, creating an empathy that gets the reader nodding. It's jolly hard, and the great trick is to make it look easy.

Now that everyone's on Macs and email, creative departments are spookily subdued places — so different from the buzzing dens of banter that I remember. It was impossible to write copy with all this larking around, so I would retreat home.

Which is where I am today — home now being Edinburgh rather than sw London. If I'm to have any chance, I have to sit in splendid isolation. No chat, no music, no distractions whatsoever. Which, being an irrepressibly sociable person, gives me the glums immediately.

Hey ho, on we go.

Revisiting my 1995 piece I see I refer to my art director "sharpening his chinagraph". How quaint! Do art directors in this digital age still use such things? So much has changed.

I may be 23 years older but at least I'm not stuck with that "big hair, big earrings" look. I have, however, stuck with the same ads that featured in the first edition of this book. That's because Commercial Union changed my advertising life. It also gives me a chance to reminisce.

I was at DDB and it was the account that no one wanted to work on. Why would we want an insurance brief when there were accounts like Volkswagen and Heinz in the building? I'm talking about a time when the only financial services advertiser on TV was the bank that took customer care to new heights with the ludicrous notion of "The bank manager in your cupboard" and the only memorable press campaign was "The man from the Pru."

After two months of thinking and lunching (for that was the way of it then) Bill Thompson and I had a campaign, based on true stories from CU's own claims files.

What struck us was that insurance is never front of mind until that moment when disaster strikes. You prang your car, your home gets flooded, a baboon nicks your camera. These things happen.

Commercial Union had an impressive track record of customer service in dealing with claims, only they'd never told anyone about it. Let this be your advertising campaign we said.

I wrote the line "We won't make a drama out of a crisis" and pinned it on the wall. Bill gave it the thumbs up. So did the account team. No planners in those days you understand.

Our creative director, Dawson Yeoman, liked what he saw.

So onward to the board of CU.

The press campaign ran as full pages in the national press. Unbelievably, there were no changes to the original concepts shown at the presentation. But then, focus groups had yet to be invented. A national TV campaign followed.

It was the start of a 20-year relationship that saw me and CU through four agencies together. OK, this is in serious danger of getting sentimental. Time to fast-forward to the here and now.

Yes, I'm still writing. But that final frontier, the body copy, doesn't get any easier. There are some great writers in this book, and I pay special tribute to David Abbott who taught me, encouraged me and laughed at my jokes. He and all those in the premier division are brilliantly capable of seizing on a crumb of information from the brief and making it something so deliciously edible you just keep coming back for more.

When I was young and starting out, I remember showing my book to one creative director, who commented "You write like a Butlins Redcoat." Gosh, I thought, is that good or bad? Looking back, it was probably very bad. But these days my Redcoat style is more likely to be called "accessible." How the advertising landscape has changed.

In 1995 there were very few female contributors to this book. So few in fact that poor old Neil French thought we were all blokes. I hope that this new edition will go some way to redress the balance.

Opposite
Client: Commercial Union
Agencies: DDB, Waldron
Allen Henry & Thompson,
KHBB, Saatchi & Saatchi
Years: 1970s to the
present day

The message finds its way
into the language.

The contributors to the subsequent editions of *The Copy Book* have a distinct advantage over the 32 original copywriters. They can look back on what the rest of us wrote, how we felt about the process, our quirky little rituals and tactics.

What strikes me is there's no magic formula. At least, I haven't found it yet.

Opposite
Client: Commercial Union
Agency: Doyle Dane
Bernbach
Year: 1978

Next spread
Client: Commercial Union
Agency: KHBB
Year: 1995

One of the original Commercial Union press ads written in 1978. The campaign won a D&AD Yellow Pencil the following year.

The drama continued for two decades. One of the later press ads in the campaign.

While others were assessing the damage, we were paying for it.

On the morning of January 11th 1978, you might have been forgiven for mistaking the streets of Sheerness for Amsterdam or Venice.

After a night of near hurricane force winds and waves as high as houses, the East Kent coastline was, quite simply, blown to bits.

In the light of this thirty mile trail of devastation, it became clear to us at Commercial Union that there was only one way we could be of real help.

Not with tea and sympathy. Or vague promises of compensation.

But rather, by agreeing to claims immediately. On the spot.

Now, it's not every day you'll find us popping in on policy holders, with a view to popping a cheque in the post.

After all, like any other insurance company, every claim we deal with involves certain formalities.

There are details to be noted down. Policies to be checked out. Assessments to be made. And so on.

A process that can take anything from five minutes to five months. Or even longer.

Speaking for ourselves, we prefer to simplify the paperwork, for the sake of a speedy settlement.

Which is precisely how we coped with the mopping up of East Kent.

On January 12th, with the storm damage barely a day old, we set up an emergency claims centre in Canterbury.

Within two working days we had our own team of claims inspectors out and about on the waterways, personally totting up the cost of repairs.

In all, we paid out £115,000 from just one branch, to more than 400 policy holders.

So they could start rebuilding their lives, while others were still getting estimates.

We won't make a drama out of a crisis.

C U ASSURANCE

he recipe said "Sauté lightly with a knob of butter."

Godfrey tossed the confetti-thin King Edwards into a pan and reached for his pepper grinder.

There could be no denying, the apron suited him.

Patting the pocket for the friendly rattle of Swan Vestas, he moved towards the hob.

His head momentarily lost in steam as he peered into the rumbling pot of stewed rhubarb on the back burner.

The aroma mingled menacingly with the pilchard mornay, gently toasting under the grill.

But here was a man who liked his flavours well-defined. In an atmosphere that would have sent others reeling, he sniffed the air with obvious pleasure.

He turned on the gas and struck a match.

What followed was nothing short of hair-raising.

For beneath Godfrey's luxuriant curls lurked a pate as smooth as a billiard ball.

Normally well-anchored by an ingenious combination of glue and clips, the mop had mischievously worked itself loose in the steam.

Without warning, and with deadly accuracy, it plopped into the flames.

His mercy dash to the soda syphon was, alas, too late to save the charred tufts.

It was a tragic case of toupee flambé.

The chef was understandably distraught. To replace the golden locks would cost hundreds. Money he didn't have.

At two minutes past nine the following morning, a man in a dark brown Homburg walked purposefully into his local branch of Commercial Union.

It was Godfrey.

The frizzled evidence of his culinary catastrophe in a carrier bag by his side.

One peep, and the girl at the claims desk understood the problem.

Cheered by the promise of a speedy settlement Godfrey went on his way.

Sure enough, a cheque in full compensation arrived within days.

Telephoning his thanks to our young lady, he summed up his appreciation quite simply.

He took his hat off to her.

'Without Commercial Union I'd have been stuck in a HAT for weeks.'

COMMERCIAL UNION

We won't make a drama out of a crisis.

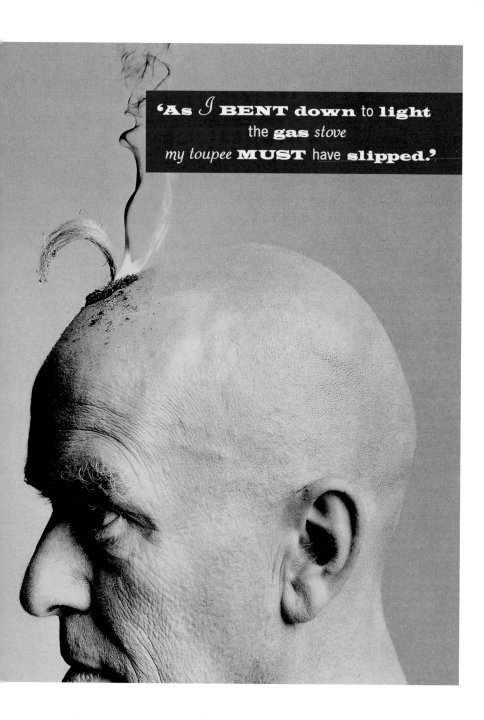

Adrian Holmes

Adrian Holmes got his first copywriting job in 1976, having studied Film and Photographic Arts in London.

He worked at a frankly alarming number of agencies, including Grey Advertising, Saatchi & Saatchi, CDP and WCRS, before finally settling down as joint creative director of Lowe Howard-Spink in 1989.

He rose to become worldwide chief creative officer in Lowe, before moving to Y&R in 2005 as its executive creative director, EMEA.

Adrian has won awards at Cannes, D&AD, The One Show, Campaign Press Awards and British Television Awards. In 1994 Adrian served as President of D&AD.

He is still a copywriter at heart, and manages to squeeze in the odd ad between meetings.

This is my favoured approach to writing a piece of copy.

After carefully studying the copy brief, I put one of Beethoven's late String Quartets on the gramophone and sit down at my desk overlooking Hyde Park.

I extract one sheet of handmade 150 gm/m² Swiss vellum from my drawer, and place this in front of me.

I unscrew the cap from my 1936 Waterman tortoiseshell pen and fill it from a bottle of Prussian blue engraver's ink which I have specially blended for me by a man in Cairo.

Approximately two hours later, I am ready to review the results. These typically constitute the following:

i. A series of increasingly frenzied zig-zag indentations in the paper where I've tried to get the goddamn 1936 Waterman pen to write anything at all.

ii. My preliminary design proposals for a sixteen-wheeled combined spaceship/all-terrain vehicle.

iii. A lot of half-hearted opening sentences and jottings, all of them crossed out, and then the crossings-out carefully inked in so as to achieve an eye-catching chequerboard design.

iv. Not a lot else.

The truth of the matter is I've never found writing copy a particularly easy business. A good 90 percent of what I commit to paper ends up being scrubbed out, abandoned halfway, completely rewritten or thrown into the bin in disgust.

There are of course writers — the Mozarts of our business — who seem to be able to *extrude* wonderfully crafted copy straight onto the page like so much toothpaste.

With me, it's more a case of hacking and hewing away at an unyielding rockface, with just the occasional nugget to show for my labours.

After nearly twenty years of writing, it would be nice to think that things have got a bit easier. But they haven't.

My hacking and hewing techniques might have improved a little. And each piece of copy seems to produce a slightly less mountainous slag heap than it used to.

But I still find the going tough. And the bits of writing I'm most pleased with always turn out to be the toughest to do.

However, for what they're worth, here are my Ten Tips for Copywriters — techniques I've either developed myself or picked up along the way.

They've certainly helped me down at the bottom of the mineshaft. I hope they do the same for you.

1. Make the most of your deadline.
Call me irresponsible, but I always wait until the traffic man appears at the door, purple-faced and screaming for my copy. *Then* I write it. I find there is a direct correlation between rising panic and burgeoning inspiration. Incidentally, I've fully exploited this technique for writing the piece you're reading now. My apologies to all at D&AD.

2. Before starting your copy, work out where it'll end.
To me, the process of writing a clear, logically-argued piece of copy is a bit like erecting a telephone line from A to B. The first thing you do is to establish the route your poles are going to take, and then put them up in a nice orderly line. Only then do you actually string the wire between them. In other words, get your basic structure right before you're tempted to start writing. If I don't observe this discipline, I usually end up in a hopeless tangle of wire.

3. Keep the reader rewarded.
Any copywriter has to strike a deal with the reader. And as far as the reader is concerned, the deal is this. *I'll keep reading for as long as you keep me interested.* So always ask yourself: have I expressed this in as original a way as possible? Have I been ruthlessly concise? Have I kept my side of the bargain?

4. Don't over-egg the mix.
Beware loading your prose with too many jokes and verbal conceits. As a rule, the plainer you keep things, the greater effect of the occasional flourish.

5. Read poetry.
And why not? Indeed, I think the best copwriting is a form of poetry. We fuss and fret about the way things sound just as much as poets do. So study their techniques, see how they use language, rhythm and imagery to achieve their effects. Anyway, it's good for you. What do they know of copywriting that only copywriting know?

6. Read your copy out loud to yourself.

This may well earn you some funny looks. If it helps, pick up a phone and pretend you're presenting the copy to someone on the other end. There again, this may earn you funny looks from switchboard. Either way, make sure you do it. I know of no better way of revealing awkwardnesses of expression. For instance, try reading that last sentence out loud. See? Straight in the bin.

7. Don't get too precious about your words.

Normally I'm no fan of research — except when it comes to my own copy. I get my art director to read it, I get other writers down the corridor to read it, in fact I pester anyone who'll spare me the time. I ask them: are there any bits which you had to go back and read again? Any jokes that didn't quite work? If there are, I re-write them. No questions asked.

8. Treat your copy as a visual object.

For some reason, copy that looks good on the page has a knack of reading well, too. One trick I have is to stand back from the finished typescript until I can't actually decipher the words. Does it have balance? Do any of the paragraphs seem excessively long or heavy-looking? Does it, in short, look inviting to the eye? I work closely with my art director and the typographer to achieve this. If they want extra words here, or to lose a paragraph there, I usually try and oblige.

9. Observe the sonata structure.

There is a convention in classical music whereby a piece is said to be divided into three distinct phases: the Exposition, the Development and the Recapitulation. In writing terms, this is just a posh way of saying that the end of your copy should somehow refer back to the headline thought. It's nice if you can pull it off — but if you can't, you can at least tell everyone down the pub that you have decided to break free of the tyranny of the sonata structure in your writing.

10. The good is the enemy of the great.

You've completed your 15th draft. You finally sit back and say to yourself: yup, that's good.

Congratulations. Now tear it up and do it again.

Only better.

I told you this writing business was tough.

Opposite
Client: Canon
Agency: Lowe
Howard-Spink
Art Director: Rod Waskett
Year: 1991

Getting copy started can be one of the trickiest parts of writing an ad. In this case I remember feeling mightily relieved when I had the notion of a hi-fi magazine reviewing a pair of ears. The ending strikes a distinctly jazz note.

Next spread
Client: British Tinnitus
Association
Agency: Saatchi & Saatchi
Art Director: Paul Arden
Year: 1986

My mother happens to be a sufferer of what she calls "bells in the head" and it was the surreal image conjured up by that simple turn of phrase that led us to the idea you see here. (The verse is hers, by the way.) Re-reading the copy now, I flinch at one or two bits of clumsy phrasing. This feels like draft number 15 and not 16.

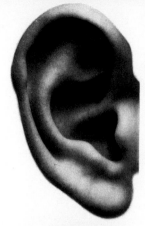
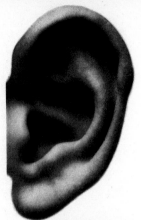

They're odd shaped, quirky looking things.

But they do give you great stereo sound.

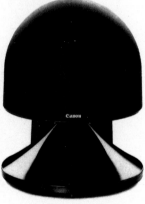

They're odd shaped, quirky looking things.

But they do give you great stereo sound.

Supposing a pair of ears came up for review in a hi-fi magazine. Just what would the reviewer say?

No doubt there'd be references to their 'startlingly accurate frequency response'.

Praise would be heaped on the 'uncannily natural sound reproduction'.

And there'd certainly be a mention of 'the superb stereo effect wherever the listener is sitting'.

Well, there's a coincidence.

Because that's exactly the kind of thing that hi-fi reviewers have been saying about Canon's new S-50 loudspeakers.

The reason they've been saying it is a breakthrough called Wide Imaging Stereo technology.

No, that's not a marketing man's feeble attempt to deafen you with science.

It's a radically different method of creating stereo sound images.

And, as you'll observe, it's resulted in a radically different looking stereo speaker.

For a start, the enclosure is not the familiar box-shape, but domed.

And instead of pointing outwards, it's directed downwards onto a precisely angled 'acoustic mirror.'

This reflects sound out into the room, and in doing so achieves something quite remarkable.

A stereo 'hot spot' at least six times the size produced by conventional speakers.

Most impressive. But what does that mean in plain English?

It means simply that you can enjoy balanced stereo sound over a much larger area of your living room.

In other words, whether you're sitting on the left end of the sofa, or the right end, it'll still sound as though you're sitting exactly in the middle.

If you'd like to witness this remarkable phenomenon with your own ears, may we suggest you call in at your local Canon Audio outlet listed opposite.

On the other hand, to understand more about the technical story behind the S-50, we'd recommend a pair of scissors.

They're odd-shaped, quirky looking things. But they're great for cutting out coupons.

Some of the things we've removed from people's heads.

We know a lady who's had a slice of bacon frying inside her head for the last thirty years.

We know a man whose only idea of silence is the incessant roaring of a jet aircraft.

And we know a little girl who wishes somebody would answer the telephone she hears ringing all night.

These people we know aren't mad (although a few may end up in psychiatric wards).

They aren't in the grips of some fatal disease (although every year an average of five or six commit suicide).

They are sufferers of a little known condition called *tinnitus*: from the Latin meaning 'the ringing of bells.'

Put simply, tinnitus is a malfunction of the inner ear that causes the brain to 'hear' sounds that aren't really there.

A lady from Hythe in Kent recently described her sounds in a poem she sent us:

Bells are malign that ring for me.
No pause or blessed lull.
Only this wild cacophony,
This howling in the skull.

Today the British Tinnitus Association needs funds more urgently than at any time in its history.

Particularly as the search for a cure is proving to be a long and expensive one.

If you'd like to help us, please send anything you can to the BTA, 105 Gower Street, London WC1E 6AH.

Or, if you have a credit card, dial 01-387 8033 (extension 208) and make your donation directly over the phone.

Just this once, the incessant ringing of bells is what tinnitus sufferers are desperate to hear.

BRITISH TINNITUS ASSOCIATION

Opposite
Client: Army Officer
Agency: Collett
Dickenson Pearce
Art Director: John Foster
Year: 1987

Next spread
Client: Army Officer
Agency: Collett
Dickenson Pearce
Art Director: John Foster
Year: 1988

This was written at the height of the 1980s financial boom, when the Army was losing its graduate recruits to the fat cats in the City. The brief was to make the life of a broker sound as dull as possible, even if you were on a couple of hundred grand a year. The opening is perhaps a bit heavy-handed, but the copy bows out neatly enough.

An Army Officer recruitment ad having some fun at the expense of life in an advertising agency. In hindsight, I'm not quite sure about the headline. The word "Whose" when applied to an inanimate box of soap powder jars somewhat. Or am I being too damned fussy? Answers on a postcard please.

Wanted.
Men unwilling to fight
the Battle of Waterloo.

Every morning they pour into London. Over a million of them.

The Divisions from Dorking. The Brigades from Basingstoke. The massed Regiments from Reigate.

And every night, as regular as clockwork, they pour out again.

Commemorating the 1815 battle with yet another battle for the 18.15.

A quite appalling thought?

That didn't prevent 15,000 or so graduates and sixth formers from being conscripted into their ranks this year.

The very best of luck to them.

But frankly, it's the conscientious objectors that interest us.

Young men who rebel at the idea of dashing for the 7.43 every day for forty years.

Who simply refuse to be cooped up behind some desk for the rest of their natural careers.

Who, in their heart of hearts, believe they are cut out to face greater challenges than anything E.C.2 can throw at them.

If those last three paragraphs have struck a chord with you, then consider the following one very carefully.

A career as an Army Officer could be the most rewarding and stimulating you could ever choose.

Not that you'll have to hang around for the rewarding and stimulating bits to start happening.

Quite the opposite, in fact.

Within nine months of joining as an Officer Cadet at Sandhurst, you could be in command of your own platoon of thirty trained men.

Finding out pretty quickly what the art of 'man management' is really all about.

Tackling learning curves steep enough to need an ice axe and crampons.

And don't be at all surprised if we need you to pack your kit in a hurry.

Germany, Canada and Northern Ireland are most certainly on the cards.

As are assignments in the Army's very own Southern Region: places like Australia, Brunei, Cyprus and Belize.

And when you get out there?

All we can say is you'll face challenges rather more demanding than placing Eurobond orders from a comfy office chair.

To find out more about a career as an Army Officer, fill out the coupon, or phone 0800 555 555.

If we like the look of each other, you could be joining us within a matter of months.

Trains to Sandhurst, ironically enough, leave Waterloo thirty minutes past the hour.

But you'll only need a single ticket. Not a season.

For more information about a career as an Army Officer, please phone 0800 555 555 at any time (call free of charge). Or post this coupon.

Full name_____

Address_____

_____Postcode_____

Date of birth_____Nationality_____

Send to Major John Floyd, Freepost
Army Officer Entry, Dept. A091,
P.O. Box 720, Maldon, Essex CM9 7XB.

Army Officer

Whose destiny wou

There's many a young man that dreams wistfully of a glamorous, exciting, go-getting career in advertising.

And do you know where you'll find most of them?

Dreaming wistfully behind a desk in some advertising agency.

For them, it seems, life as a Junior Account Executive isn't quite all it's cracked up to be.

Glamorous? How does wading through a 350-page research report on the laundry habits of typical C_1C_2 consumers grab you?

Exciting? Not unless pressing the 'collate' button on the office photocopier sets your heart beating a little faster.

Go-getting? Well, a tray of coffees for the client, maybe.

And at the end of the day (as they say in agencies), what will the sterling efforts of the bright young graduates have achieved?

21% prompted brand recall in Gateshead?

At this point we'd ask you to consider the following rather carefully.

To what use would you rather put your powers of intelligence, initiative and leadership?

Persuading the nation's housewives to switch from one make of soap powder to another?

Or safeguarding the way of life that offers them a freedom of choice in the first place?

A DETERGENT ON TEST IN TYNE-TEES?

As an Army Officer, that is ultimately what your job would be all about.

And don't worry, you'll get more than your fair share of 'man management' along the way.

For example, just a year after commencing training at Sandhurst, you'll find yourself in charge of your own platoon of thirty men.

(A year after joining an advertising agency, you might find yourself in charge of minuting a meeting.)

Can you imagine what the command of thirty trained soldiers actually involves?

It means you have to get to know your

l you rather shape?

A DETERRENT ON EXERCISE WITH NATO?

Battle manoeuvres with NATO in Germany. Night-time parachute training in the Mojave Desert. Learning jungle warfare techniques in Belize.

This is all bread-and-butter stuff to your average Lieutenant with eighteen months' experience.

And if you've got a bright idea for an expedition involving your own men, the Army will back you to the hilt.

That's exactly how a recent Trans-Australian camel trek saw the light of day.

Not to mention a diving sortie to photograph deep water wrecks off the coast of Ascension Island.

To learn more about a career as an Army Officer, post the coupon or phone 0800 555 555 free of charge.

If you've got what it takes to win a place at Sandhurst, we're pretty confident you'll want to swap that packet of Wiz.

men more thoroughly than your own family.

It means you have to earn their respect. Motivate them. Share their problems. Lay down the law, if necessary.

It's a process that will do a lot more to develop your self-confidence and resilience than anything you've ever done before.

And then what, exactly?

Well that, of course, depends on the type of regiment you've chosen to join.

But it's a safe bet that whatever you and your men will be called to do will be about as predictable as next year's Grand National.

Opposite
Client: Albany Life
Agency: Lowe Howard-
Spink, Campbell-Ewald
Limited
Art Director: Andy Lawson
Year: 1983

Next spread
Client: Plymouth Gin
Agency: Lowe
Howard-Spink
Year: 1985

Pages 268–269
Client: Tampax
Agency: Colma & Partners
Art Director: David Owen
Year: 1981

Tony Brignull and Alfredo Marcantonio had already shown the kind of writing that was possible on this account — it does help when you've got a stand-ard to aim for. Looking at the ad afresh, I think we should have done some-thing about the rather awkward type run-round at the bottom of the left-hand column.

A rare instance of long copy that was a real joy to write. Once I had fixed the snooty, Jeevesian tone of voice in my head, the words came relatively easily. Alan Waldie, the art director, did a wonder-ful job, even getting the type set in hot metal.

Working on an account for Tampax, I'm afraid we had to get all the joke ads out of our system first. One featured a dumb-struck girl in a bikini sitting at the bottom of an empty swim-ming pool, with the head-line "I didn't know they were that absorbent". The ad that eventually ran was, as you can see, rather more delicately wrought.

Are you making plans for your wife's death?

Come on now, own up. The thought hasn't so much as crossed your mind, has it?

All along, you've blithely assumed that you'll be the first to go.

That your wife will be the one who will need the financial looking-after.

That yours is the life that should be insured, not hers.

Noble and worthy sentiments indeed. But, if we may say so, short sighted ones, too.

There's no guaranteeing that your wife will outlive you. (According to statistics, little more than a 60% chance in fact).

So have you ever thought what would happen to you if the unthinkable happened to her?

Not in the dim distant future.

But tomorrow, Friday, 24th June 1983? Could you cope?

On the purely practical front, think of the cooking, the washing, the hours of housework

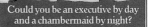

that you'd have to put in. More importantly, there's the children to consider.

Could you ever devote the sort of time to them they need and deserve?

The nightly bedtime stories? Helping them out with their maths homework? Teaching them what's what in the big wide world?

Heaven knows, you'd need help. Lots of it.

And like everything else nowadays, that sort of help doesn't come cheap.

According to a recent survey, the average mother of three ploughs through eighty hours of housework a week.

Eighty hours, mind.

At £2.50 an hour, that comes to a staggering £10,400 a year. Where on earth are you going to get hold of that sort of money?

Well, you could start at the bottom right hand corner of this page.

For as little as £15.00 a month, Albany Life can provide cover worth over £50,000 tax free.

If you prefer, we can even draw up a combined 'Husband and Wife' policy that pays out in the event of either of you dying.

If you'd like to discuss things further with us, post off the coupon straight away.

Planning for a wife's death may be no pleasant matter for a husband.

But for a father, it's a very necessary duty.

After hours of office work, could you face hours of housework?

Could you be an executive by day and a chambermaid by night?

Could you afford £2,000 a year for a family cook?

Who'll play nursemaid if the kids fall ill?

To learn more about our plans, send this coupon to Peter Kelly, Albany Life Assurance, FREEPOST, Potters Bar EN6 1BR.

Name _____
Address _____
_____ Tel: _____
Name of your Life Assurance Broker, if any:

Albany Life
A member of the American General Corporation group.

076

*Figure quoted is net of premium relief at 15% and applies to a woman aged 25 next birthday.

THE SELECTION AND MAINTENANCE OF A STOUT PAIR OF SHOES.

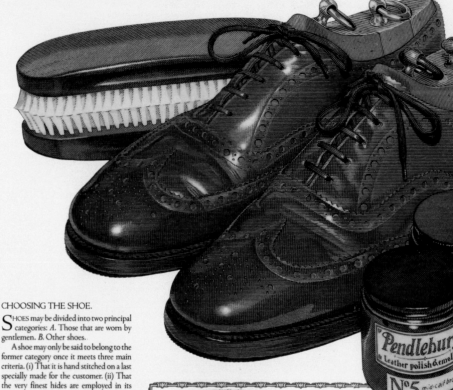

CHOOSING THE SHOE.

SHOES may be divided into two principal categories: *A*. Those that are worn by gentlemen. *B*. Other shoes.

A shoe may only be said to belong to the former category once it meets three main criteria. (i) That it is hand stitched on a last specially made for the customer. (ii) That the very finest hides are employed in its construction (Russian Calf, Grain Hide, Doe-Skin and Antelope are entirely adequate.) (iii) That its design (usually following the Oxford or Derby pattern) makes absolutely no concessions whatsoever to the fashions of the day.

Footwear that is mass-produced from *imitation leather*, or that employs *composition soles*, or that is conceived in *modish designs and colours* does not merit our further attention.

A CAVEAT REGARDING HEEL-HEIGHT.

THE prescribed height for the shoe heel is 1¼". Any shoe that attempts, via the artifice of a built-up heel, to increase the apparent height of its owner, will merely succeed in *reducing his stature as a gentleman*.

THE CORRECT METHOD OF LACING.

IT is of paramount importance that the laces of a good shoe be threaded in exact accordance with the scheme illustrated opposite. This is known as the McPherson's Loop.

By threading the off-side lace directly through to the near-side rear hole, an equal pressure is thereby exerted across the shoe's upper when the laces are pulled tight.

It should be borne in mind that external criss-cross lacing is a practice normally confined to the *sporting plimsoll*; if found on any other shoe, it is fairly certain that such footwear falls into category *B*. previously referred to.

CLEANING THE SHOE.

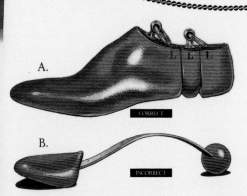

As in 1. remove all traces of peat bog, sphagnum moss etc. with a good quality damp rag. If the shoe is very wet, then air it naturally in a warm place (never in front of a fire). When barely damp, insert the tree.

2. Apply sparingly a coat of finest grade wax polish, using a special curry brush to ensure complete penetration into the *welt-recesses*. Although older shoes will need more polish, never apply in excess as this often *clogs the brogueing*.

3. Wait approximately ten minutes whilst the wax is thoroughly absorbed into the leather. Then polish briskly with a brush made from the very best goat hair.

4. Finally, finish off with a freshly-laundered duster to attain maximum brilliance.

N.B. On no account submit any shoe to the indignity of the *automatic electric polisher*. These machines, often to be found lurking at railway termini and in lesser hotels, are notorious for their complete lack of discrimination as to the hue of polish applied. Furthermore, they have been known on occasion to impart a *deep-gloss lustre* to a *gentleman's turn-up*.

THE IMPORTANCE OF THE TREE.

The consistent use of a proper shoe tree is amongst the foremost desiderata for correct shoe maintenance. Trees of the best pedigree are hand-fashioned by the original last maker from either Mahogany or seasoned Beech. They invariably conform to the three-piece wedged design as illustrated in 'A'.

At all costs do not insert into a good shoe any implement that bears even a passing resemblance to 'B'. This may cause lasting damage to the shoe's shape, not to mention *the owner's prospects for social advancement*.

THE CORRECT PREPARATION OF A GIN AND TONIC.

Unless a bottle of Plymouth Gin is plainly in evidence at the drinks table, all further efforts to create the definitive gin and tonic should be abandoned forthwith.

As is generally accepted by those knowledgeable in such matters, Plymouth stands alone in possessing the requisite *dryness* and *vigour of nose* for this most refreshing of libations.

(This is due in no small part to the inordinate length of *drying time* lavished upon the juniper berries and sundry botanicals employed in its manufacture.)

Plymouth should always be served in a large 8oz lead crystal tumbler, with a proprietary brand of tonic, thinly-sliced lemon or lime and generous quantities of freshly broken ice.

It should also be noted that the suggestion *'ice and a slice, squire?'* is a fairly reliable indicator that the gin you are being offered is not Plymouth, but another distillation of somewhat dubious provenance.

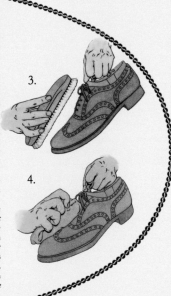

PLYMOUTH GIN IS NOT THE ONLY WAY TO TELL A GENTLEMAN.

She's going through the most difficult period of her life.

Her first one.

Suddenly, her mind is jammed full of new questions, new worries.

And who's really to blame her?

Even with all the lessons and frank talking they gave her at school, she never knew quite what to expect.

Which is why a mother's expert help and advice can be more important now than it's ever been.

Especially when it come to choosing the best kind of sanitary protection.

In our book, that means Tampax Slender tampons.

Slender are so slim and neat, even the youngest girls can use them with complete confidence.

Yet thanks to a special cotton material that we've developed, they're every bit as absorbent as our Regular size.

As you'd expect, there's an applicator to make insertion nice and easy for beginners.

Yesterday, Cathy was a girl of 13.

While our special three-way expansion ensures a perfect fit in length and breadth, as well as width.

This not only helps withdrawal.

But also results in a tampon so comfortable, so secure, you don't even feel it's there.

So who needs all the fuss and bother of bulky, old-fashioned towels?

Certainly not a ballet-dancing, tennis-playing schoolgirl like Cathy.

Nor your daughter for that matter.

Just to prove our point, we'd like her to try out Slender for herself.

Simply write to the address below, and we'll send her a free sample, together with an explanatory booklet all about periods.

After all, when you're coping with being a 13 year old woman, don't you need all the help you can get? **TAMPAX**. SLENDER

Tampax Limited, Slender Information.
W.O.D. Dunsbury Way, Havant, Hampshire PO9 5DG.
(Offer also available in the Republic of Ireland.)

Today, she's a 13 year old woman.

Lionel Hunt

In 1960, six months after leaving school, Lionel Hunt joined Pritchard Wood in Knightsbridge as a dispatch boy.

In 1961 he emigrated to Australia to be a cowboy. After a brief stint on a sewer-pipe laying gang, he joined an agency in Tasmania as a copywriter. In 1972 — after jobs as account executive, copywriter and creative director — he co-founded The Campaign Palace with Gordon Trembath. He was chairman and group creative director until 1998.

Lionel has won many awards including Gold and Silver at Cannes, The New York One Show and Australian award. Three times voted Creative Director of the Year in Australia, he was chosen Advertising Man of the Year in 1984 and is in both the award and Australian Awards Halls of Fame. He started agency Lowe Hunt in 1999.

Copywriting for print ads isn't about writing copy. It's about creating a picture that powerfully communicates the proposition. Most of the world's best ads are a combination of pictures and words. Some are just a picture. Even all-type ads create a picture of their own.

The best example I can give you of this is the ad Rob Tomnay and I did for Bluegrass jeans. I'm cheating here because it was actually a poster but imagine it as a double-page spread print ad. It doesn't even contain one complete word but it speaks volumes about the jeans.

All of which has led me to the conclusion that the most important part of being a good copywriter is working with a great art director.

In my case I was very lucky to have started our agency with Gordon Trembath who was the best art director in Australia in 1972 and still would be one of the best if he hadn't retired at the grand old age of 40. (They're also smarter than writers.)

What this meant for me was that it didn't matter what rubbish I wrote as Gordon would always make it look fabulous. So on those rare occasions when what I wrote wasn't half bad, the ad was virtually guaranteed great results and loads of awards.

There are, I know, some great copywriters who sit alone at their typewriters and come up with their ads in isolation but for me this would be a miserable experience, like going to prison.

So lesson one is to beg, borrow or steal the best art director you can find. It'll make your ads much better, your life a bit more fun, and your lunches so much more enjoyable. And if you're really lucky they'll think up most of your ideas and headlines for you which is like having your cake and eating it too.

Gordon worked on the Woman's Day "How to kill a baby" ad with me. I remember distinctly that we only had half a day to do it and that, before lunch, the line was "How to kill a baby seal slowly". At lunch, somewhere into the second bottle of Chardonnay I said "I know! How to kill a baby!"

Gordon looked at me as if I'd gone insane then had another glass himself, took a deep breath and said "let's go and sell it."

There are two important lessons buried in here. The first is that you should go to lunch every day with your art director no matter how busy you are. In fact, the busier you are the more important for you to go because it's the only place you can get any work done. The only interruptions come from people who want to put nice things in your mouth which is a pleasant change from the office.

The second is to have courage. All good ads are hard to sell and you need a steely resolve to get the good stuff through. I suppose it's better for your health if this courage is natural, rather than Dutch courage, but no one's perfect.

I have found that when you are up against an impossible deadline (like now) then it's vital to use up lots of that precious time and play several games of table tennis. Excuse me while I go off for a quick hit.

That's better. All the stress has gone, the adrenalin is pumping, I am flushed with success and now feel I can do anything. Which is exactly how Campaign Palace Sydney creative director, Ron Mather and I came up with the Ansett Airlines Hostess ad.

We had a morning to come up with the launch ad for the "new" airline and then go off and present it to Rupert Murdoch, one of the owners. This was a reasonably terrifying prospect and I remember worrying about the presentation of an ad that didn't exist. The more we thought about the presentation, the less we could think of anything for the ad.

Three games later and we had it but it was touch and go. So don't present your own work. It won't give you enough time to do the ad, play your games, and have your lunch.

But this absolutely requires that you surround yourself with the most brilliantly effective account directors in the business. As I have said to somewhat lesser suits on occasion "If the creative team takes the brief, develops the strategy, does the ad, sells it, and produces it, where does that leave you exactly?"

The hostess ad caused a huge controversy with talk-back radio running hot with disgruntled ex-hostesses ("old-boilers", Sir Reginald Ansett publicly called them) and church groups so it was a huge success. So much so that we were able to spoof it two days later for a TV station client who was running an airline sit-com. Killing two old birds with one stone, as it were.

The medical insurance ad for Underwriting and Insurance Ltd won a silver in Australia for the most outstanding copy in a consumer advertisement. As far as I remember, I copied most of it out of the client's own brochure. Another important lesson. If the headline (and picture) isn't riveting it doesn't matter what the body copy says. I'll bet my bottom dollar that most of the judges didn't read more than the first few lines of the body copy they so richly awarded but assumed from the headline, picture and layout that it was probably pretty good. Consumers sometimes do the same.

Next spread
Client: Underwriting
and Insurance
Agency: The Campaign
Palace Melbourne
Art Director: Ron Mather
Year: 1982

Pages 276–277
Client: Ansett
Agency: The Campaign
Palace Melbourne
Art Director: Ron Mather
Year: 1980

The headline coincidentally is dead straight, isn't it? It always pays to remember that if there is a compelling proposition you shouldn't bury it in so-called creativity. In this case the straight headline works with the picture to confront the over-50's worst fears about getting insurance.

The only other thing I've got to say is make sure you spend most of the day laughing. This is meant to be a fun business, not some kind of grim science, like embalming for example. In fact, our motto at The Palace is the same today as it's always been. Do great ads, and have a laugh.

So there you have it. Always work with a great art director. Always take him out to lunch. Be brave. Take up table tennis. Don't sell your own work. Surround yourself with brilliant account directors. Concentrate on your headlines before your body copy. Don't bury the proposition. And have a laugh. Yes, I think that about covers it.

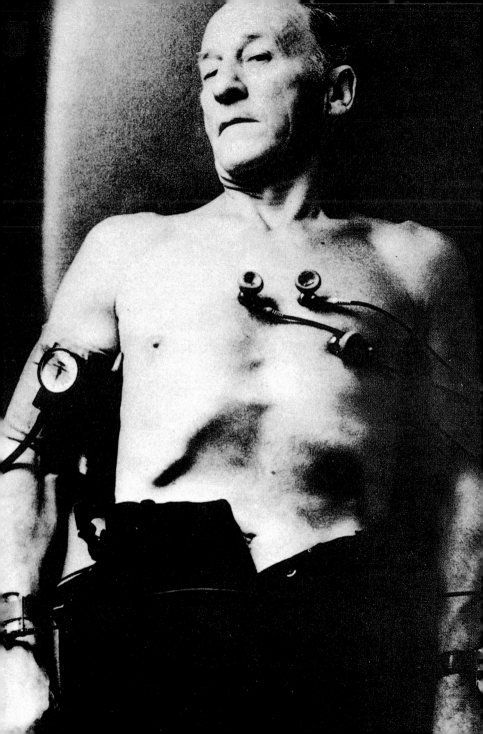

How to insure your life without a medical if you're over 50.

Trying to buy life insurance is a bit like trying to get a bank loan. The more you need it, the harder it is to get. In your fifties and sixties when you feel you most want life insurance, you find that nobody seems to want to give it to you.

You find yourself up against a probing medical examination, or at the very least, a barrage of questions on the state of your health.

As a result many older people are so certain they can't qualify that, not surprisingly, they don't even bother to apply.

Which often results in bitter hardship for those they care about most. You may think this is all very unfair. We do. So we've done something about it.

THE GOLDEN YEARS PLAN

The Golden Years Plan provides lifetime cover for people now aged 50 to 70 without medical examination and regardless of their state of health.

It offers the protection of life assurance to people who might otherwise be denied it.

HERE'S HOW IT WORKS.

The Golden Years Plan is offered in units. The amount of cover it provides is based upon your age at the time the policy is issued. The table below shows the cover provided at each age.

TABLE OF BENEFITS & PREMIUMS

Age when you buy Policy	No units bought — monthly cost			
	1 unit	2 units	3 units	4 units
	$9.50	$19.00	$28.50	$38.00
	Sum assured (excl. bonus) bought			
	$	$	$	$
50-52	1487	3104	4721	6337
53-55	1318	2750	4182	5615
56-58	1169	2440	3711	4982
59-61	1040	2171	3302	4432
62-64	930	1941	2952	3963
65-67	836	1745	2654	3563
68-70	755	1575	2395	3216

To ensure that everyone now between 50 and 70 can get this policy, Underwriting & Insurance Limited have developed special benefits for the first two years.

Should death occur from natural causes during the first two years your beneficiary will receive every cent of premium you have paid plus interest at 6% per annum compound.

Should death be the result of an accident at any time during the first two years the full amount of the sum assured plus any bonus allotted will be paid.

After the first two years the full benefit of the sum assured plus all bonuses allotted is paid in the event of the death of the Life Assured from any cause whatsoever.

NO MEDICAL EXAMINATION IS REQUIRED.

To apply for the Golden Years Plan you do not require a medical examination nor do we ask you any questions about your state of health.

Simply fill in the application form and send it to Underwriting & Insurance Limited.

THERE ARE NO SALESMEN.

Remember, this advertisement is our only approach to you. No salesman will contact you, but should you require any advice, simply ring our office on 51 1471 and our staff will be very happy to assist you.

THE GOLDEN YEARS PLAN LETS YOU INSURE HUSBAND OR WIFE.

You are able to insure your marriage partner by a simple cross proposal. Simply fill in clearly the name of the person to be insured and sign the form as indicated.

YOUR POLICY IS GUARANTEED RENEWABLE.

As long as your premiums are fully paid within the normal 30 days grace period, your policy cannot be cancelled by us, nor can we refuse to renew it. The sum assured does not decrease. In fact it increases as we add bonuses each year.

A 30 DAYS INSPECTION PERIOD WITH EVERY POLICY.

The Golden Years Plan is offered by Underwriting & Insurance Limited, a wholly owned subsidiary of C.E Heath & Co.,who are one of the largest non-marine syndicate managers at Lloyd's of London.

You are further protected by a money back guarantee as follows:

The Golden Years Plan gives you a 30 day Inspection Period. When you receive your Policy Document, please read it carefully. If, for any reason, you are not completely satisfied with the policy, you may return it to us within 30 days of receipt and your money will be refunded. This offer is guaranteed by Underwriting & Insurance Limited, 578 St. Kilda Road, Melbourne, 3004.

HOW TO JOIN THE GOLDEN YEARS PLAN.

1. Complete the Application Form in full, date and sign.
2. Cut along the dotted line.
3. Place in envelope together with your cheque, money order or postal note for the first month's premium only, made payable to Underwriting & Insurance Limited.

CLOSING DATE THURS. APRIL 12.

APPLICATION FOR GOLDEN YEARS PLAN LIFE ASSURANCE

Underwriting & Insurance Limited Head Office 578 St Kilda Rd. Melbourne 3004

Full name of person to be insured

Residential address _____

State _____ Postcode _____
Sex _____ Date of birth _____
Place of birth _____
Name of Policy Owner or Proposer

I hereby propose for the Golden Years Plan. I would like to pay future premiums | I require
☐ Monthly | ☐ 1 unit
☐ Quarterly | ☐ 2 units
☐ Half Yearly | ☐ 3 units
☐ Annually | ☐ 4 units
I enclose premium payment for $ _____ being the first month's premium

I understand that if for any reason I am not satisfied with the policy I may return it within 30 days of receipt and a full refund will be made to me

Signature of Proposer _____
Dated _____

If the hostess was out of uniform would you know which airline you were flying with?

Until recently probably not.

But from next June you won't be in any doubt at all.

Ansett will be offering you a real choice of the planes you fly in, the times you depart, and the services you get both in the air and on the ground.

In June we start taking delivery of our new fleet of 12 Boeing 737's and new generation 727's and start pensioning off our DC9's.

This means we'll soon be offering you Boeing comfort and reliability on all our jet routes.

Just as important, more planes will mean far greater frequency. And no more identical schedules.

You'll be far more likely to find a departure time that suits you, rather than one that just suits the airline.

And you'll check-in faster, get on and off quicker, and get your baggage sooner.

We'll also be offering major service benefits that we can't reveal now for reasons that will be obvious to readers who are also in a highly competitive situation. But don't wait until next June to try the new Ansett. Our competitive philosophy is showing up right now in lots of little ways that already make flying with us just that much better.

But you ain't seen nothing yet. **ANSETT**

Client: Bluegrass
Agency: The Campaign
Palace Sydney
Art Director: Rob Tomnay
Year: 1979

Hardly a word, but
volumes spoken.

Opposite
Client: Woman's Day
Agency: The Campaign
Palace Sydney
Art Director: Gordon
Trembath
Year: 1981

Circulation up 10%
and Gold in New York
One Show.

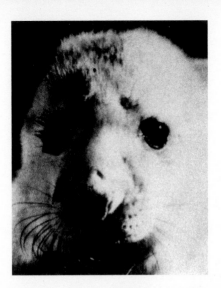

How to kill a baby.

It's easy. All you do is walk up to it. It won't run away.

Then, as it looks up at you trustingly, mistaking you for its mother, you smash in its skull with a baseball bat.

That's what happens to baby seals in Canada every year in a bloody ritual that lasts six weeks.

In Japan they do it a different way. They herd dolphins into the shallows, wait for the tide to leave them stranded, then go through the same grisly process.

Then there's the whales. You know what happens to them.

Doing it is dead easy if your mind is warped enough. Stopping it is a whole lot harder, but there is something you can do.

In this week's Woman's Day we're running a thought provoking article on what's happening to these beautiful creatures.

We're also running a simple competition that you and your children can enter. All you have to do is tell us in less than twenty words what the seals, the dolphins or the whales would say to us if they could speak.

There are cash prizes, but far more importantly, for every entry in the competition Woman's Day will donate 10 cents to Greenpeace to help their work in bringing this ghastly business to a halt.

Look for this week's Woman's Day. It's the one with the baby seal on the cover, seconds before it dies.

Woman's Day.

Leon Jaume

Leon Jaume did the copywriting course at Watford and with the help of some kind and skilled mentors, most influentially Tony Brignull and Dave Trott, has had a job as a copywriter ever since.

He joined WCRS soon after it started in 1979 and is now on his third stint at the agency. In between he has also worked at BMP, FCO and Ogilvy & Mather but has spent most of his life at WCRS where he remains and is called executive creative director. But that's because he is now quite old. He is also executive creative director at Engine.

He's still a copywriter and happy to be so.

Copywriters are taught early on that no one chooses to read their words. But things are actually a bit worse than that.

People do choose to read, and pay to read, someone else's. You're not simply a rival, you're a gate-crasher, an interloper.

You're stumbling on stage and grabbing the mic from the headlining act; you're barging onto a table for two while a first date gets under way.

You're a bad man. Or, it goes without saying, a bad woman.

And the person who can best help you win over the audience that doesn't want you there in the first place isn't another copywriter, it's your biggest adversary: the journalist.

Observe his methods. A good columnist knows his role in his readers' lives. Each time you write copy you have a role. What is it — friend, hustler, sage, wit, teacher, seducer, alarmist, expert? When you know your role you have your voice. Then you can tell your story.

It doesn't matter whether you write a few terse sentences or a grandiloquent saga, it should have a narrative. You're not making a list, you're telling a story. Even if it's in the form of a list.

And don't be ponderous or precious. Your ads should feel immediate and fresh. Train yourself to write faster. Journalists' disdain for advertising is well founded on the basis that half a dozen entire newspapers have usually been written and read in the time it takes a copywriter to burnish a few words.

Don't fossilise your ads and constantly revisit them. Do what your readers do. Throw them away and leave your mind open for the next one.

Where appropriate, have fun. Words written with joyful relish are more likely to be read that way.

And, despite the years of tradition, don't feel obliged to end with a pun or a witty flourish. Sometimes, just finish.

Opposite
Client: BMW
Agency: Wight Collins
Rutherford Scott
Year: 1981

Next spread
Client: Air Mauritius
Agency: Mavity Gilmore
Jaume
Year: 1987

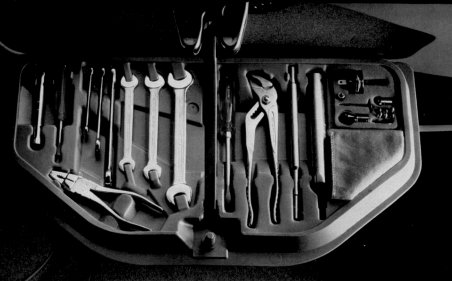

ONE FEATURE ON A BMW WHICH MIGHT BE MORE USEFUL ON OTHER CARS.

On other cars the toolkit is little more than a rolled-up afterthought stuffed behind the spare wheel.

There are no such loose ends on a BMW.

The BMW toolset is fitted into a recess in the bootlid and folds down in front of you with the twist of a clip.

This precision in design is reflected in BMW's pedigree on the racetrack.

You don't race to 31 World and European Championships by making cars in a hurry.

So, significantly, every BMW is assembled at a third of the speed of conventional mass-produced cars. Which allows time to build quality right through the car, rather than veneer a second-rate construction.

Just sitting in a BMW you feel this aura of excellence surround you.

Everything, from the ergonomic cockpit to the satisfying thunk of a closing door, reflects this philosophy of precision.

And the attention to detail continues even after a BMW leaves the factory.

For BMW dealers are so thorough that, in a recent Autocar longterm test, a BMW was the only one out of the 20 cars to score the top "six star" rating for its servicing.

All of which begs the question, why fit so comprehensive a set of tools into a machine that's been so meticulously built and maintained?

Well, you never know, it might come in handy for those odd jobs around the house.

THE ULTIMATE DRIVING MACHINE

THE IMAGINATION is indeed a persuasive force.

Particularly after a wearisome day baking quietly on a Mauritian beach within earshot of one of

to make a return trip inevitable.

You will have stayed at a hotel, nestling discreetly beneath the palms, with an average of two miles of white sand to itself and

Look, a plane.

our uniquely attentive barmen.

Frankly, you see, of all the rarities in this magical land, the Air Mauritius jumbo jet is the least common.

It is outnumbered by both its winged compatriots, the Mauritian kestrel, the world's rarest bird, and the golden bat of Rodriguez, likewise the most scarce of its species.

And to make sightings less likely still, you will soon be looking for the new Boeing 767: it is smaller and flies further than the jumbo, allowing us to whisk you from Europe faster than any other airline.

Our more astute visitors realise with increasing gloom towards the end of their stay that this means they will get home more quickly too.

But by then you will have tasted enough of our rare delights

three staff to attend to each guest.

You will, perhaps, have caught the world's largest blue marlin off Le Morne, or won money at the oldest race course in the southern hemisphere.

You may have savoured a lunch of palm heart creole style, requiring the sacrifice of an entire tree for your pleasure.

You may even have unearthed gold ingots and chunks of raw diamond left by forgetful 18th century buccaneers. But will you really have seen a plane?

Come, come.

If you would like to know more about holidays in Mauritius and how to get there, you can contact us at the Mauritius Government Tourist Office, 49 Conduit Street, London W1R 9FB. Telephone: 01-437 7508. (24 hours.)

Published by the Mauritius Government Tourist Office, Port Louis, Mauritius.

Eric
Kallman

Eric Kallman began his career at TBWA/Chiat/Day, New York penning the highly-lauded rebirth of the Skittles "Taste the Rainbow" campaign that helped the agency become one of the most creatively awarded in the world.

He moved on to Wieden+ Kennedy Portland where he and his partner Craig Allen created "The Man Your Man Could Smell Like" for Old Spice, the Old Spice Response Campaign and the Terry Crews campaign.

In 2011 Eric was the founding executive creative director of Barton F. Graf, helping to lead it to a spot on the Creativity A-list in each of its first three years. In 2014 Eric became executive creative director of Goodby, Silverstein & Partners in his hometown of San Francisco. In May of 2016 he co-founded Erich & Kallman with former Crispin Porter+Bogusky president Steven Erich.

In 2012, Kallman was honored as the third most awarded copywriter in D&AD history.

There are a bajillion ways to approach giving advice on how to write good ads. Here's one way to go:

First, you should "Seinfeld it" (aka "Larry David it") which means write down every conceivable entertaining observation and insight that you can think of based on the product or service that you're selling. In your best whiny Seinfeld voice write "What's the deal with (insert category/product/service here)" and keep writing. Don't worry about it sounding like Seinfeld, it won't. It will sound like you.

Second, you should "Will Ferrell it". This means writing down every conceivable fun, weird, imaginative and exciting thing that you can think of that has nothing to do with what you're selling. Then, work backwards and connect it somehow. Don't worry about it sounding like Will Ferrell, it won't. It will sound like you.

Now, put everything you've written on the wall. By "Seinfelding it" you've covered every idea you can think of working directly out of the product itself, and by "Will Ferrell-ing it" you've covered every idea you can think of that comes from the unique, outer reaches of you and connects back to the product. You've worked starting from two opposite poles, and many of your ideas are sure to overlap and fill in the middle.

Next comes the part where I used to advise that you share all of the ideas with someone you trust. It might be a strategist or an account person or a friend who's not even in advertising. But after starting a couple of agencies, now I think differently about it.

The next thing you should do is show your client. Show them all of it. Explain to them honestly the things you think are strong ideas, and the things you think might not be. They will like and trust you more because of it. Then, listen to them. They know their brand, their company and their culture better then you. You'll end up liking and trusting them more too. (Maybe for the first time!)

You'll know exactly what to do next after that. And the work won't just be special to you and everyone at your agency, it will be special to the people at the company you made it for.

In conclusion, did I just advise that you think of all of the good ideas that you can, put them on a wall and then talk them through with your client? Yes. Are there any short cuts, tips or tricks that lead to really amazing work? No. Sorry. But the more you do it the better you'll get, I promise.

Or, you can just think of a new lame way to align the brand you're working on with a social cause and win a Lion. You're choice!

Good luck!

Client: Skittles
Title: Touch
Agency: TBWA\Chiat\Day,
New York
Year: 2007

Everything a cursed man
touches turns into Skittles.

Client: Skittles
Title: Beard
Agency: TBWA\Chiat\Day,
New York
Year: 2006

An office. A woman is
interviewing a man with
a long beard. The beard
can operate like a trunk.

Woman (reading the
man's CV): Good. Good.
You're in Nansfield?

The man uses his beard
to feed himself a Skittle.

Man: Mm-hmm.

Woman: I have a cousin
from Nansfield.

Man: That's nice.

The man eats another
Skittle.

Woman: Your résumé
looks good, but we're
looking for someone with
more experience.

The man uses his beard
to feed the woman a
Skittle and strokes the side
of her face.

Man: Experience. (laughs)
Ohhh, funny. (throws a
Skittle into his mouth)

Male voice-over: Share
the rainbow. Taste the
rainbow.

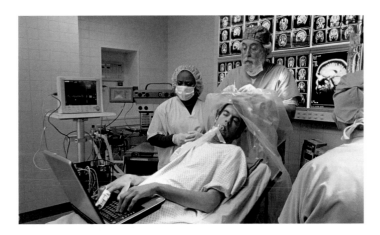

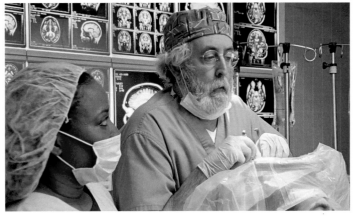

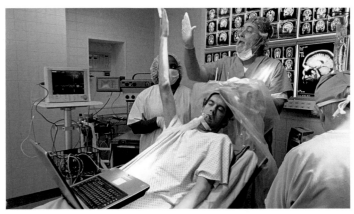

Client: Old Spice
Title: The Man Your Man
Could Smell Like
Agency: Wieden+Kennedy
Portland
Year: 2010

Isaiah Mustafa talks to
women from a bathroom,
then a boat, then on a
horse.

Opposite
Client: Kayak.com
Title: Brain Surgeon
Agency: Barton F. Graf
Year: 2013

A surgeon uses his patient
to search for travel deals
during a brain surgery.

Janet Kestin

Janet Kestin is co-founder of Swim, a creative leadership consultancy tapped by top agencies, design, media, and PR firms.

As former co-chief creative officer of Ogilvy Toronto, Janet and long-time creative partner Nancy Vonk led their office to global recognition for work like Dove's campaign for Real Beauty. They have won creative awards including Cannes Grand Prix, One Show and D&AD Pencils.

Advertising Women of the Year twice, they were among *Advertising Age* magazine's 100 Most Influential Women in Advertising in 2012.

Their HarperCollins release, *Darling, You Can't Do Both (And Other Noise To Ignore On Your Way Up)*, is described by Fast Company co-founder Alan Webber as "a guide to breaking the rules that stunt careers and wreak havoc at home. The how-to follow-up to *Lean In*."

It's 1995. My bible has just arrived in the mail. I put my hand on the cover, and wish for it to confer its magical powers on me. Because more than anything I want to write like those guys. David Abbott. Steve Henry. Those guys. But I'm not a guy and try as I might, I didn't and don't write like them. I do it my way and you'll do it yours, so as you read this, I strongly urge you to take to heart the words of the great Robbie Robertson of The Band, "Take what you need and leave the rest."

For me, every brief lives in the space between possibility and panic. What an opportunity! What if I blow it?

I poke it with a sharp stick a few times to see where I need to go, then run as far away as possible, coming back only when lost. It's a map you don't want to stick to too closely or you'll miss the adventure that comes from doing your own spadework.

When my career-long other half, my art director partner, Nancy Vonk and I got our first Dove brief, we were told that Dove is milder on skin than soap and that litmus paper could prove it. Hello, Grade 11 science experiment! We tested every soap on the market. Spent time in labs with scientists. Showed ourselves that litmus paper knew what it was talking about. And turned it into a TV spot with no voiceover or commentary (shocking!), exposing the competitors' names (double shocking!), and trusting women to judge what they were seeing for themselves. A world of words on a brief could never have gotten us there.

That's why it's better to hang out in pickle plants with little ladies in hairnets than to read about the 32 spices in the pickle brine. Why it's mesmerizing to watch a hundred robots turn sheet metal into sports cars from the shop floor. Why you want to offer yourself up as a test subject to R&D folks making body wash.

And then imagine yourself into the skin of the woman they're making it for. Who is she really? (I promise you she's not a 'female, age 18–54, with 2.4 children and a husband who earns $43,000 a year'.)

How do you have a good conversation with her? Or with the mechanic buying engine oil for his garage? Should you lead with your funny bone? Everyone likes funny, right? What about empathy or surprise? Sadness, curiosity, fear, pride. So many emotions, yet we feel this pressure to reduce it all to funny or witty or ironic, to the 'hip, young dude' voice beloved of ad people. One of the joys of what we do is that we can put ourselves into what we create. Be human. Does that mean you should have a style and be known for it? Some of the best copywriters do; I don't. I choose to write like whoever is talking — with a subtle hint of me.

I fill unlined pages with every fact, thought, scrap and phrase, jam random ideas into corners and empty spaces, circled for future attention, draw arrows from one line to another. I make an earnest attempt to dump everything out of my head in an uninterrupted stream of consciousness, till — oh no — I look back and see an ugly little sentence fragment. I brake hard. Tinker just a little. Resistance is futile. I edit as I scribble knowing that it halts the flow and suffocates the possibilities. Even though I've written 500 times on the black board: Write now, edit later. Write now, edit later. Write now, edit later.

I write a zillion openers, because I can't shake the belief that the right first line is the starter pistol that will propel me to the end of the race. So far, I've started this piece over a dozen different ways, worked each version through to THE END, only to find that, like a snake eating its own tail, I've written myself into a new beginning. Here are three:

1. I knew nothing about advertising when I started and pretty much feel like I know nothing about it again. (Too explanatory.)

8. There are 13 things I've done as a writer that you probably shouldn't, except #2, #6 and #11. (Too conventional.)

13. There was an old Indian craftsman who carved beautiful elephants from large, hunks of timber. Asked how he did it, he simply replied: "I just cut away what doesn't look like an elephant." (Too much borrowed interest. And the opposite of what I do.)

Once the words are down, the argument made or the silence deafening, I listen for the rhythm, for the beats of a line or a script, or the syllables in a chosen word. I think subconscious rhythm draws people in. Paradoxically, I often see before I hear.

Which may be a form of self-defense, because here's the truth of it: writing makes me anxious.

I don't like to write. I like to have written. That feels amazing, like Friday night.

Opposite
Client: Fleischmann's
margarine
Agency: Ogilvy Toronto
Art Director: Nancy Vonk
Year: 1995

Consider intelligence, and the role it

plays in choosing a margarine. Picking

up a mono-flavoured brand takes no

thought whatever. But four?

You've just bought all 4 varieties of Fleischmann's margarine. Can this be far behind?

You are wise to have Fleischmann's

Salt Free, Lactose Free on hand. It's

Won't you look clever when you are not fazed by a sudden visit from your lactose-intolerant boss.

particularly perfect when someone

Your kids won't try anything but Corn

Oil? You're covered. And your husband,

the patriotic squash junkie, will love Canola

because it tastes terrific

and is grown right here in Canada.

You know all the Fleischmann's

Your critical, Italian mother is pacified by your perfect Pasta Primavera and realizes that you are indeed a visionary.

choices are kosher and non-hydrogenated, so

Four margarines in the house. Sure sign of a higher I.Q., or a really big refrigerator?

with a special diet drops by.

Let someone else make

You accommodate the different tastes of everyone in the family, proving your genius yet again.

Bucatini alla Puttanesca

with any old thing. You smartly choose Olive Oil

for that certain je ne sais quoi, or 'qualche cosa'.

you don't miss a beat when Martha drops by.

There you have it. Four mouth-

watering varieties, and endless reasons

You are prepared, even if your recurring nightmare comes true and Martha does, in fact, drop by.

to want them. Not that much

fridge room? With your brains you'll find a way.

Fleischmann's Corn Oil — Fleischmann's Olive Oil — Fleischmann's Canola Oil — Fleischmann's Salt Free Lactose Free

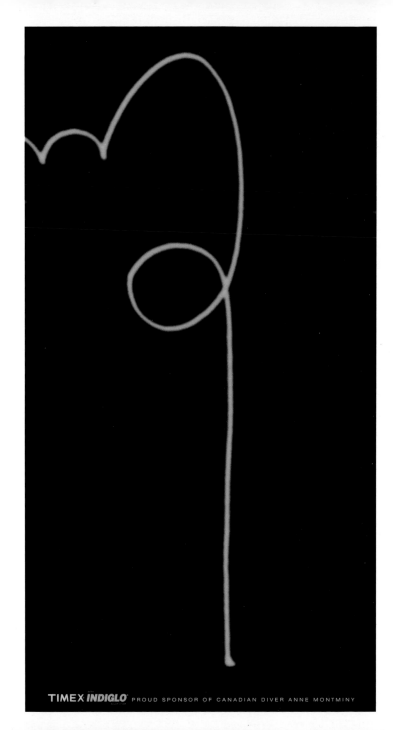

TIMEX INDIGLO PROUD SPONSOR OF CANADIAN DIVER ANNE MONTMINY

There must be something in the chocolate.

Laura Secord
1913

Laura Secord
1950

Laura Secord
1992

What makes ours the best chocolate you can give or get? It could be the hazelnuts from Rome. It might be the ripe cherries. Some would say the toasted coconut. Or maybe it's simply that Laura Secord chocolate is always fresh. Whatever it is, it's working. Look what it's done for Laura.

Laura Secord
IT DOESN'T GET ANY FRESHER

Client: Laura Secord
chocolates
Agency: Ogilvy Toronto
Art Director: Nancy Vonk
Year: 1994

Canadian heroine in the
war of 1812, warns the
British of an impending
American attack, and
winds up as the face of
a chocolate company
whose product is clearly
the fountain of youth.

Opposite
Client: Timex Indiglo
Agency: Ogilvy Toronto
Art Director: Nancy Vonk
Year: 1997

Timex invents the glow-
in-the dark sports watch.
Timex sponsors Olympic
athletes. Two briefs
become one campaign
when one wonders what it
would look like if athletes
practiced in the dark.

Next spread
Client: Dove
Agency: Ogilvy Toronto
Art Director: Nancy Vonk
Year: 1992

You know the story.

Do you really ne
household cleane

Undoubtedly not. Yet high alkalinity is an important part of why most soaps dry your skin. Let us explain.

Mr. Clean*, measures 10.8, rather more alkaline.

Because your skin is slightly acidic (pH 5.5), its balance

household cleaner
pH:10.8

Ivory™
pH:10.1

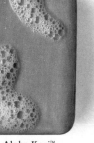

Alpha Keri™
pH:10.8

Jergens® Mild
pH:9.5

Look at the comparison on this page. There is a household cleaner at one end, distilled water at the other. In between are some familiar soaps with small numbers underneath. These are pH numbers and tell you the alkalinity of each. The distilled water, on the far right has a pH of 7, which is neutral. Ratings below pH7 mean a substance is acidic, above pH7 it is alkaline. The household cleaner on the left, in this case

mild   harsher

is disturbed by things that are strongly alkaline. Most soaps are made with lye, a highly alkaline substance. Alkali damages the "acid mantle" or protective layer that helps the skin hold in moisture. This is why soap is so drying.

Dove® has a superior formulation that makes it different from other soaps. You'll notice that it has the same pH as distilled water, just a little higher than that

the alkalinity of a
o wash your face?

of your skin. The remaining bars on this page, perhaps

yours is one of them, are closer in pH to the household

than Dove. Whether yours is natural, expensive, even

"pure" it will change the colour of litmus paper. Remem-

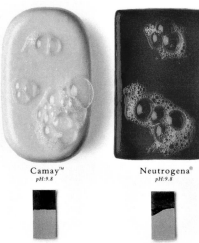

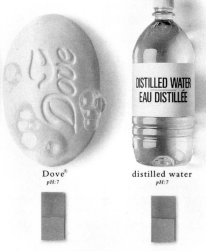

Camay™	Neutrogena®	Dove®	distilled water
pH:9.8	pH:9.8	pH:7	pH:7

cleaner. (Of course, we're not saying that washing your

face with soap is the same as using a household cleaner,

simply that most soaps are highly alkaline, therefore,

> **Can your soap pass the litmus test?** Lather up your soap. Rinse hands thoroughly. Lather up Dove. Press separate litmus papers against each. Compare. For free litmus paper write: Litmus Paper, P.O. Box 490, Sta. 'A', Scarborough, Ontario M1K 5C3.

incompatible with the balance of

your skin.)

How does your soap measure up

to Dove? It may surprise you to know

that almost any soap is more alkaline

ber, litmus measures alkalinity. As the comparison shows,

the more alkaline the soap, the darker the paper becomes

– the darker, the harsher.

So while the question of alkalinity may never have

entered your mind, you may find yourself deciding you

don't want it on your face.

Zahra was typical of our moms, whose schedule was work-work-family-wor-fami-rk. They weren't driven by special circumstances. There was no new business pitch or emergency presentation; it was just their commitment and impossible standards. And let's not forget guilt, because guilt is the operating system of most working moms. So, they almost always put themselves last. *Sure, I can put off that hair appointment one more week. So what if I haven't talked to my best friend since May? She understands. Yes, I should book that doctor's appointment, but it's hard to take time off work during the week. Yes, I can come to that meeting at school. Of course, I can get that extra bit of work done sooner.* They're busy every second, yet they have no lives.

Time to give our heads a shake

"No way." I didn't believe Dr. Elaine Chin, chief medical officer of the Executive Health Centre in Toronto, when she told me that male executives are more than twice as likely to get regular checkups as their female counterparts. "The more successful the woman, the worse she looks after herself." I'd always thought women were better about things like doctors and dentists. How often have we heard women say, "My husband would need his arm to be hanging by a thread before he'd go to the doctor"? I was always pressuring my husband to go to the doctor, without thinking about all of my own cancelled doctor's appointments, and before I knew it a year and a half had gone by. Guilty as charged. Dr. Chin said that between always being on for work, running to PTA meetings, driving kids

Darling, You Can't Do Both (And Other Noise To Ignore On Your Way Up)
Co-author: Nancy Vonk
Year: 2014

A career guide for women in business, commissioned by HarperCollins after a speech we gave on our life in advertising as women and moms.

Opposite
Client: Planta Dei Natural Pharmaceuticals
Agency: Ogilvy Toronto
Art Director: Nancy Vonk
Year: 1996

Night night. Sleep tight. Don't let the phenotributylin dibenhexylate bite.

{ *Instead of synthetic chemicals, our sleep aid uses valerian and lemon balm for a more natural sleep with no druggy feeling next morning.* }

How many syllables does it take to get a good night's sleep? Valerian doesn't interfere with the dream (REM) phase of your sleep. With Planta Dei Sedative Sleep Aid you sleep more naturally and wake up refreshed. All this, with no known side effects.

While many herbal options haven't been proven as medicines, Sedative Sleep Aid has drug status; it meets the standards of Health Canada. It's in your drugstore with conventional sleep aids. Try Planta Dei and call it a night.

Planta Dei Sedative Sleep Aid. Scientifically proven plant medicine.

Mike Lescarbeau

Mike Lescarbeau began his career in Minneapolis in 1983 at an agency that later on became Fallon. He moved to Boston's Hill Holliday then to London's Leagas Delaney in 1990. In 1992, he rejoined Fallon as a partner and creative director, and created famous campaigns for Lee Jeans, BMW, Jim Beam Brands and other clients, winning both the Grand Effie and Cannes Gold Lion.

In 2000, Mike co-founded One and All, a company with an unprecedented collaborative model that invited clients into the creative process. The company won the 4As' prestigious O'Toole Award in its first year and created groundbreaking campaigns for Summit Brewing Company, Target Pharmacy and the Red Wing Shoe Company.

In 2007, Mike became president and chief creative officer of Carmichael Lynch where he is currently executive chairman.

The ads on these pages were written in the Nineties, a very long time ago in the advertising business. When the publishers invited me to update my remarks for a new edition of *The Copy Book*, I was inevitably compelled to reflect on how much copywriting has changed. Would anyone be so presumptuous as to write a thousand words about a map today? Could you really expect someone to read long, long copy explaining how a jacket is made?

It's worth noting that people asked those same questions when we were making the ads you see here. Our answer was that you didn't need to worry about people reading copy if the words were interesting enough. But that was then. Fact is, I can't remember the last time I suggested a long-copy print ad approach to a creative team. There are just too many other ways to tell a brand's story now, inside and outside the discipline of advertising.

A lot of people lament the passing of a certain craftsmanship in copywriting. I think the craft is as strong as ever. It's just a different craft, and in many ways, a more honest one. After all, a copywriter now finds himself part of a much larger team, one that might require any number of writing tasks, across a daunting array of media old and new.

As I watch our agency's talented people tackle a client's problem, I admire their ability not just to craft a sentence or a headline, but to maintain the integrity of a simple, powerful idea throughout a whole raft of branded activities. So does that mean writing has become less important? No. Because, ironically, I've noticed that whatever form our best work takes, each great execution still owes its existence to an example of inspired writing. Sometimes that writing is in an ad, but just as often today, it's the brief itself.

Pages 304–307
Client: Timberland
Agency: Leagas Delaney
Year: 1991

Ads I got to write from a campaign conceived by London legends Tim Delaney and Steve Dunn. Timberland wisely emphasized its genuine outdoor heritage, despite the brand's UK target being young women in the dance clubs.

Pages 308–309
Client: Booker's Bourbon
Agency: Fallon McElligott
Year: 1994

TIMBERLAND GIVES YOU BACK THE COAT FOUR MILLION YEARS OF EVOLUTION TOOK AWAY.

There was a time when Man could venture into the wilderness clad in nothing but the coat God gave him.

But that was quite a while ago.

Sometime during the Lower Paleolithic Era, Homo Erectus became a creature of the great indoors. The thick hair that once covered his entire body was gone, and in its place came a man-made imitation.

Hampered by a brain the size of a walnut, man's earliest attempts at outdoor clothing were, needless to say, somewhat primitive.

Fortunately, however, our species has

wear, a practice that's all but extinct today. On other Timberland coats, we overstitch many seams to prevent wind and rain from penetrating the tiny holes left behind by our sewing needles.

The result is outerwear that leaves Man as well adapted to the outdoors as he's been in millions of years.

Our sturdy coats are just one example of the Timberland Clothing range, albeit a good one, since   everything we

That we pre-stretch our leathers on a special geometric last to keep them from cracking with time.

And that seams on many Timberland boots are sealed twice with latex, because that's the only method sure to keep the water out.

The truth is, here at Timberland, we wouldn't really know how to go about things any other way.

We've even gone as far as to find a machine that can test our waterproof leathers better than we ever could by hand. It's called a

At a company called Timberland, in Hampton, New Hampshire, we design outerwear whose natural practicality rivals the coats our animal relatives were born with. Coats that provide shelter from howling wind, pelting rain and mornings as cold as an ice age.

Witness our Timberland leather coats.

They're made from the best hides we can find, and believe us, we spend a lot of time looking. We insist upon cowhides from the open range, to avoid ugly nicks from barbed wire fences. Which means we often have to travel as far as other continents in order to find a supply that meets our standards.

We use two styles of leather on our outerwear at Timberland, Split Suede, and in the coat you see here, Weatherguard Newbuck.

Each is given a thorough dunking in waterproofing agents before getting a special finish to protect its suppleness and colour.

But we make more than leather coats that will help to keep you dry in the rain.

In other Timberland outerwear, we use a material that keeps you free of perspiration. To let these coats 'breathe' (just like the ones Mother Nature used to make) we include a layer of Gore-Tex. This man-made fabric, with over nine billion pores per square inch, allows moisture to escape from your body, but remains waterproof.

Of course, we wouldn't take all this trouble finding perfect materials only to turn around and make a coat that doesn't last.

To make doubly certain a Timberland Trenchcoat holds together, we double stitch the seams that will be exposed to the heaviest

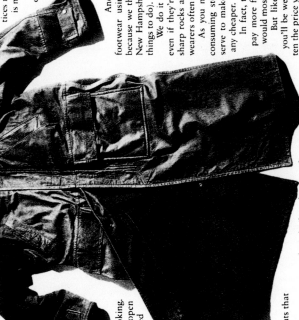

make is built to last you for aeons.

Using workhorses like canvas, cotton, wool and denim, Timberland puts together sweaters, shirts and trousers, even the duffle bags to carry them in. And since practical clothing doesn't ever seem to go out of fashion, you'll be able to wear them season after season.

Naturally, if you own a pair of Timberland boots or shoes, you're already familiar with the way we do things.

You may know, for example, that we impregnate the leather of all Timberland footwear with silicone to give it a longer life and to keep your feet dry no matter what.

But while we admit that our practices may seem a little obsessive, there is method to our madness.

We use solid brass eyelets in our boots, not because they look better, but because they don't rust when they get wet.

We use self oiling raw-hide laces for the simple reason that they don't get soaked with water and rot.

And we certainly don't construct our footwear using double knot pearl stitching because we think it's fun. (Even in Hampton, New Hampshire, there are more entertaining things to do).

We do it so that the seams won't unravel, even if they're accidentally cut open on the sharp rocks and thick brush that Timberland wearers often find themselves in.

As you might suspect, all of these time consuming steps in constructing them don't serve to make Timberland boots or clothing any cheaper.

In fact, the chances are very good you'll pay more for a Timberland coat than you would most others.

But like everything Timberland makes, you'll be wearing it long after you've forgotten the price you paid.

Which even someone with a shelf-like forehead and one continuous eyebrow can tell you is a very good thing.

In fact, even mankind's most distant ancestors would certainly have preferred a Timberland coat to their own hairy variety.

Ours, after all, have pockets.

Timberland (UK) Limited, Unit Four, St. Anthony's Way, Feltham, Middlesex. TW14 0NH. Telephone enquiries, please ring 081 890 6116.

IN ONE AMERICAN STATE, THE PENALTY FOR EXPOSING YOURSELF IS DEATH.

In the winter of 1968, Mount Washington in New Hampshire was the unlucky recipient of 566 inches of snowfall. Or to put it another way, that's just a little over forty-seven feet.

Snowstorms with winds in excess of a hundred miles an hour are not uncommon. Which makes the wind-chill

As for our Weatherguard Newbuck leather, it's given a unique chrome-tan finish so it stays supple throughout its life.

Partial as Timberland is to leathers like

Starting with stalwarts like wool, denim, canvas and cotton, Timberland makes a range that's always at home in the wild. Sweaters, trousers, jackets and shirts, even the duffle bags to carry them in.

Each item designed to withstand the twin tests of weather and time.

exposed flesh freezes instantly.

Some of the old folks in the state can recall the time in '34, when the Mountain was the site of the strongest wind gust ever recorded on earth: 231 mph.

They can recite articles from the local paper, The Littleton Courier, about hikers freezing to death up there in the middle of summer.

And they'll tell you, in no uncertain terms, that it's less important to dress according to the latest fashion than it is to dress according to the latest weather report.

It is this almost inbred respect for nature's wrath that compels the people at Timberland in Hampton, New Hampshire to design their outdoor clothing the way they do.

This clothing is ideal for people who venture outdoors regardless of the forecast and who pride themselves on being ready for the worst.

Take, for example, our Timberland leather coats. The leather is the best you can find, because it's the best you can find.

To get hides that meet our standards, we travel the world looking for sources of supply. A search made more difficult by our insistence on hides from animals raised on the open range. While that may sound pernickety, you'll never see scarring from barbed wire on a Timberland coat.

But we're not just concerned about how our hides are treated while they're raised. We also give them special treatment once we get them back to our workshops.

All the leathers used by Timberland get a dunking in chemical agents for water repellency. Then, to keep them looking new in any kind of weather, we give them special finishes that will never wear off.

When we use Split Suede, for instance, we give it a light-resistant finish to avoid fading. So it's not only rainproof, but sunproof, as well.

Newbuck and Split Suede, we realise that man cannot live by leather alone.

Which is why in some Timberland outerwear we use Gore-Tex, a man-made fabric with over nine billion pores per square inch. These microscopic openings are too small to let water in, yet large enough for perspiration molecules to get out.

Once we have the right materials in place, we start sewing coats that will last year after year after year.

On the coat you see here, we double stitch the seams that will be exposed to the heaviest wear. We run a pull cord through the waist of the coat to keep cold air from creeping up underneath. And we fit zippers of solid brass, so they'll never rust.

Since people who wear Timberland coats often venture off the beaten path, we've also taken special care that the pockets won't get torn in heavy brush. Each one is closed up with a thick leather cover and secured by buttons made from brass and bone.

And to make sure you never end up looking for those buttons in the woods (worse than looking for a needle in a haystack), we use heavy cord thread and reinforce each one on the backside with quarter-inch guards.

The finished product is a coat that will protect you from cold, wet and, on one of its more hospitable days, perhaps even the Mountain itself.

But it's not just outerwear that Timberland makes to last. Our clothing range also includes the kind of things you might wear when the temperature soars to above freezing.

hold together.

What you may not know is why they do.

We tape seal the seams of some of our boots with latex to make sure water can't get through to your feet.

We impregnate our shoe and boot leather with silicone, to give it a longer life. We sew in doubleknot pearl stitching that won't come undone even if it's accidentally cut. We use self oiling laces that won't rot, and solid brass eyelets that won't rust.

The list, like the winters up on Mount Washington, goes on and on.

Suffice to say that at Timberland, making outdoor clothing and boots is not just a way of life. It's a way of living.

Timberland (UK) Limited, Unit Four, St. Anthony's Way, Feltham, Middlesex. TW14 0NH. Telephone 081 890 6116.

Timberland

"I know bourbon gets better with age, because the older I get, the more I like it."

~ Booker Noe

Considering the special pride he takes in his favorite whiskey, it's not surprising that Booker has put his own name on the label. Nor should it come as any shock that he personally approves

BOOKER NOE grew to love BOURBON in his home state of Kentucky.

every batch of Booker's Bourbon before he allows it to be sent along to you. Fact is, only someone of Booker's experience can determine whether a straight-from-the-barrel bourbon is at the very peak of its flavor.

BOOKER NOE *will never forget* THE FIRST TIME HE sampled *the legendary bourbon* from his grandfather Jim Beam's distillery.

Even as he tells the story today, his face twists into a grimace, his head shakes slowly back and forth and his big hand swats at the air in front of him.

"I didn't like it at all," he says, without apologies.

Now, if that confession sounds a bit strange coming from a man who's devoted his life to making fine whiskey, there is a perfectly reasonable explanation.

Booker Noe, perhaps better than anyone else, under-

Kentucky home of Jim Beam Bourbon, Booker has come to cherish the subtle flavors found in the world's finest whiskey. And he's discovered he's especially fond of bourbon in its

"LIKE MOST PEOPLE, learning to love a fine bourbon took me a certain amount of time. But as the years have gone by, I've decided there is just nothing better than the taste of whiskey aged in charred white oak to the peak of its flavor. It's uncut, unfiltered and straight from the barrel. This is the bourbon I've chosen to put my name on."

purest form, taken straight from the barrel, at its natural proof.

It is this bourbon, Booker Noe believes, with all of its rich, oaky body intact, that is the very best of the best.

Until recently, uncut, unfiltered bourbon like this was the domain of the Master Distiller alone. And while he's no doubt appreciated having the privilege, Booker has always wished that other people, people who truly love fine spirits, could taste this whiskey for themselves.

Which is why Booker Noe recently began bottling his unique bourbon and making it available to the few connoisseurs who can appreciate it.

anywhere from six to eight years like the aging process. And since every barrel of whiskey ages differently, each batch of Booker's has a different proof, which can measure anywhere between 121 and 127.

Once selected, the bourbon is painstakingly hand-sealed in a hand-labeled bottle and marked with a tag showing its unique proof and age.

With any luck, you'll find Booker's Bourbon at your local liquor retailer. But since, by its nature, this is not a mass produced bourbon, you may have to look further. If you should find Booker's impossible to locate,

BOOKER'S BOURBON comes straight from the barrel, UNCUT and UNFILTERED.

we suggest you call the toll-free number listed at the bottom of the page, and see about obtaining your Booker's Bourbon that way.

Regardless how you obtain it, Booker Noe believes you'll find his bourbon well worth the time and effort you spend searching.

Especially if, like Booker himself, the years have done for your taste what they do for a bourbon's.

Bob Levenson

Bob Levenson has been called "the writer's writer", and "the best print copywriter ever".

Bob's relationship with Bill Bernbach began in 1959, when Bill hired him at Doyle Dane Bernbach. In the 26 years that followed, Bob won every major award that the advertising business could offer. In 1972 he was elected to the prestigious Copywriter's Hall of Fame. He rose through the ranks to become chairman of Doyle Dane Bernbach International and the agency's worldwide creative director.

The business relationship between the two men grew into a firm friendship that lasted until Bill's death in 1982. In his first book, titled *Bill Bernbach's Book*, Bob notes: "This is a book by one man about what another man's book might have been if either of them had ever written a book before."

Answers nobody wanted to questions nobody asked.

"I know every trick in the book" does not apply to advertising copy. There are no tricks and there can be no book. Including this one. Too bad. There are, however, three ingredients for a decent piece of advertising prose:

1. You must know what you're talking about.

In order to be informative — never mind persuasive — you need to know how the car is put together, how the chicken is taken apart, what the surfactant does, what to expect in the foreign country, in what way is the oil refinery "refined", etc., etc. In the absence of such knowledge, you will be doomed to rely more and more on adjectives; always a mistake.

2. You must remember who is doing the talking.

We use words like image, character, tone, texture, even personality, almost interchangeably. But whatever we choose to call it, it must be recognisable, distinctive and consistent. This is even more important than friendly, approachable or accessible. The writer who attempts to put the agency's mark on the client's copy or — God forbid — his own mark should pay with his job. And his severance should be that of his writing hand.

3. You must know who you're talking to.
(Or, better still, to whom you're talking.)
This can be knotty in the extreme. "Males, 18 to 34" or "Households above £30,000 pa" are categories worse than useless; they are destructive. You may actually have to enter the Hades of the focus group. (Purchase a round-trip ticket, with no advance reservations required.)

The very best tactic is to create your own customer or prospect. Keep your creation a secret and real life need never touch you.

Keep in mind, at the same time, that your prospect (even of your own creation) is likely to be smarter than you are and much warier. He is, after all, not in advertising; you are.

One final thing: being a copywriter is hard enough, hiring one is worse. "We need more (fewer) (better) (cheaper) (livelier) talent" has been heard in agency hallways since before agencies had hallways. Talent might just have something to do with writing ability. But I'm not sure. Many people have a way with words; often that's all they have.

Now that it doesn't matter any more, I'd look for a teacher-turned-salesman (or a salesman-turned-teacher) and take my chances.

Opposite
Client: Doyle Dane
Bernbach
Agency: Doyle Dane
Bernbach
Year: 1969

Next spread
Client: Volkswagen
Agency: Doyle Dane
Bernbach
Year: 1964

DO THIS OR DIE.

Is this ad some kind of trick?

No. But it could have been.

And at exactly that point rests a do or die decision for American business.

We in advertising, together with our clients, have all the power and skill to trick people. Or so we think.

But we're wrong. We can't fool *any* of the people *any* of the time.

There is indeed a twelve-year-old mentality in this country; every six-year-old has one.

We are a nation of smart people.

And most smart people ignore most advertising because most advertising ignores smart people.

Instead we talk to each other.

We debate endlessly about the medium and the message. Nonsense. In advertising, the message *itself* is the message.

A blank page and a blank television screen are one and the same.

And above all, the messages we put on those pages and on those television screens must be the truth. For if we play tricks with the truth, we die.

Now. The other side of the coin.

Telling the truth about a product demands a product that's worth telling the truth *about*.

Sadly, so many products aren't.

So many products don't do anything better. Or anything different. So many don't work quite right. Or don't last. Or simply don't matter.

If we also play this trick, we also die. Because advertising only helps a bad product fail faster.

No donkey chases the carrot forever. He catches on. And quits.

That's the lesson to remember.

Unless we do, we die.

Unless we change, the tidal wave of consumer indifference will wallop into the mountain of advertising and manufacturing drivel.

That day we die.

We'll die in *our* marketplace. On *our* shelves. In *our* gleaming packages of empty promises.

Not with a bang. Not with a whimper. But by our own skilled hands.

DOYLE DANE BERNBACH INC.

33 years later, he got the bug.

We're glad that most people don't wait 33 years to buy their first Volkswagen.

But Albert Gillis did, and maybe he had the right idea all along.

He didn't buy a new car for 33 years because he didn't happen to need one.

He and his 1929 Model A Ford did just fine by each other.

He always did his own repairs and even jacked it up at night to save the tires.

When he needed a new car last year, he went out and bought a Volkswagen.

"I heard they hold up," he explained . Does he like the VW?

Mr. Gillis is 78, a Justice of the Peace, and not given to hasty decisions.

"Your inspectors sure do a good job of inspecting," was as far as he would go.

But he did mention that he and Mrs. Gillis took a trip for their 54th anniversary.

They drove 6,750 miles and spent $62 on gas and 55¢ on oil.

"I didn't think they were supposed to burn oil," he said.

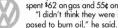

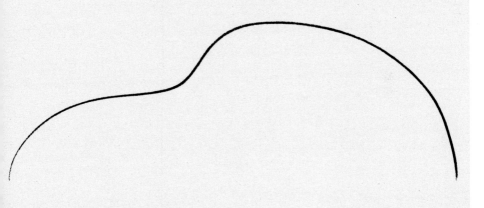

How much longer can we hand you this line?

Forever, we hope.

Because we don't ever intend to change the Volkswagen's shape.

We play by our own set of rules.

The only reason we change the VW is to make it work even better.

The money we don't spend on outside changes we do spend inside the car.

This system gives us an immense advantage: Time.

We have time to improve parts and still keep most of them interchangeable.

(Which is why it's so easy to get VW parts and why VW mechanics don't wake up screaming)

We have time to put an immense ammount of hand work into each VW, and to finish each one like a $6,000 machine.

And this system has also kept the price almost the same over the years.

Some cars keep changing and stay the same.

Volkswagens stay the same and keep changing.

James Lowther

After reading History at Oxford and learning to dag sheep in Australia, James Lowther decided to put the combined skills to work in advertising. After spells in Hobson Bates and Wasey Campbell Ewald, he joined Saatchi & Saatchi in 1977, where he eventually became joint creative director and deputy chairman.

As a copywriter, he has been responsible for award-winning campaigns for Castlemaine XXXX, Intercity, Schweppes, The Health Education Council, the COI, Cunard, and M&C Saatchi itself. He has an ad in *The 100 Greatest Advertisements* and a slogan in the *Oxford Dictionary of Quotations*.

In 1995 he left Saatchi & Saatchi to be a founder and joint creative director of M&C Saatchi.

He was chairman of the agency from 2000 to 2005 then became founding partner.

1. Rule no. 1 no rules

Everything I am about to say is stuff that has helped me write good ads. But at the end of the day, you could ignore all of it and do a great ad. More great ads are done by breaking rules than by following them.

2. Leave the office

Before you even open your pad, open five other things. Your ears, your eyes and your mind.

You'll never be a good writer of anything if you just sit in your office and stare at your desk. Your raw material isn't in the office or in Groucho's for that matter. It's out on the streets. Look at pictures. Listen to music. Go to films. See plays. And more importantly look at people. They're those funny things with two legs we're meant to be writing about, remember.

It sounds obvious but it's amazing how many people in our incestuous little business just spend their spare time with other people in this incestuous little business.

Get out. And observe.

For instance, the Castlemaine XXXX campaign would never have happened if my parents hadn't sent me to Australia to make a man of me. This it conspicuously failed to do. But it did teach me how to get bitten by a wild cockatoo, how to cheat at poker, and fifteen years later how to write a XXXX ad.

3. Chuck out the brief

Don't always accept the planner's brief. It's sometimes just a form of words that manages to get into one sentence all the contradictory things that the client and the account team wanted to say. As a result it can be about as informative as the communiqué after a dodgy EC summit. In my experience the best planners are often creative people.

4. Relax

I know this sounds odd in the pressurised world of fast lead times. We are all under pressure. We just shouldn't behave as if we are.

Sit back and sniff around the problem.

Have fun. Tell stories or jokes around the subject. That way you might come at the problem from an unexpected angle. (The script with which we launched xxxx was based on a revolting joke about a man who got a snakebite on his willy.) If you get that stuck, walk away from it for a while. It's amazing how much clearer it is when you revisit it.

5. Fish for birds

In the 19th century, the American writer Washington Irving visited the magnificent Alhambra Palace in Granada where the local birds had become so accustomed to being shot at by the locals that they had become very adept at avoiding this particular Valhalla.

One enterprising urchin had a wonderful idea. He got fishing nets and cast them off the battlements. The birds circling the battlements were caught hopping by this unfamiliar angle of attack and were trapped for the pot in their hundreds.

So next time you're tempted to go down the old familiar path, why not try fishing for birds and you'll probably get lions. Big gold ones.

6. Do the opposite

Here's a way of fishing for birds that may be worth a try.

Think of what everybody does in the category of product you're advertising and do the opposite.

Why do all our car ads look the same? Why do all our washing powder ads look the same?

Why not do a car ad like a washing powder ad? Or vice versa?

It may not work but it just might.

7. Don't just write

Just because you're called a copywriter, don't just think about writing.

The best copywriters are often highly visual. After all, a newspaper ad is just a blank sheet of paper on which you can do anything you want. As long as it makes a point.

The press ad I'm proudest of — the "headlights" ad — happened when I was looking at a photograph of a car in mist and I put my fingers over the headlights. After that, it didn't need a John Milton to come up with the headline.

John Hegarty once said to me that communication through the written word was being replaced with communication through images.

He said the Celtic civilisation never wrote down stories because they could make them more memorable by passing them down orally or visually. It's a great argument until I asked John where the Celtic civilisation was today.

Still I take his point.

8. Craft it

When I first thought about this piece, I was going to write the word "care" a thousand times and leave it at that.

Because that is what distinguishes good copywriters from average ones.

The best copywriters are not always the ones with the highest ability but the ones with the highest standards.

Who know that a 90% good ad is not enough. And who will keep going until it's 100% right.

When I did the Intercity press ads, Alex Taylor's brilliant layout was done in such a way that meant not only that every ad had just nine lines of copy but also every line had to have between 20–24 letters. I did also point out that Shakespeare did not labour under such typographical tyranny, but I gave it a go.

It was incredibly hard work and took twice as long as a long piece of copy. But it was worth it.

9. Fight for it

People don't like great ideas. They're original. Which means they're unfamiliar and therefore frightening.

This explains why mediocre advertisements sail through without touching the sides, whereas people always find a million and one reasons why a great idea should never run.

The best teams just never give up. One art director I had, subsequently a respected (and feared) creative director in London, used to jam recalcitrant account executives between our door and the wall.

The less drastic, though probably more successful method is to take the account team and client along with you. Explain why you're doing what you've done.

Why you've rejected other approaches. Charm them. Have drinks with them. Remind them over and over again of your thinking.

And if that fails, then you hit them.

10. Addendum

Since I first wrote the above, something has happened. People don't seem to care much about copy.

Teams often don't say which one is the copywriter. That's great if it means both can write. Not so great if neither can.

Words are important. Someone's got to care about them. Spell them right. Craft them into sentences. And get them set in a way that shows you want people to read them. Not just to fill in a space at the bottom of the ad.

Want to be a copywriter? Well you could do worse than learn to write copy.

Opposite
Client: Ministry of
Transport
Agency: Wasey
Campbell-Ewald
Year: 1974

Our second attempt at this
subject, after the client
turned down our first
effort, which we thought
was brilliant (two head-
lights made into a pair of
glasses). Just shows the
client isn't always wrong.
My art director was
Steve Grime. This ad was
chosen by John Webster
to go into *The 100 Greatest
Advertisements*.

TO MAKE THIS CAR DISAPPEAR, PUT YOUR FINGERS OVER ITS HEADLIGHTS.

Block out the headlights above, and you'll get a good idea of how other drivers see you. if you don't use your headlights on gloomy days.

The fact is they can hardly see you at all. And if you can't be seen, somebody can very easily get hurt.

This is one reason the law says you <u>must</u> put on your headlights when the daylight's poor. You can be fined up to £100 if you don't turn them on in conditions of daytime fog, falling snow, heavy rain or general bad light.

So remember the law. Remember the finger test. And be the bright one.

On gloomy days, put on your headlights.

See and <u>be seen.</u>

IN POOR DAYLIGHT, BE SEEN. YOU MUST USE HEADLIGHTS.

Issued by the Department of the Environment, the Scottish Development Department and the Welsh Office.

AUSSIES WOULDN'T GIVE A XXXX FOR ANYTHING ELSE.

Above
Client: Allied Breweries,
Castlemaine XXXX
Agency: Saatchi & Saatchi
Year: 1986

I guess the copywriting
bit here is the line, which
is now in the *Oxford
Dictionary of Quotations*.
It's a bit short and rude but
then I had plenty of time
to make it that way.

Opposite
Client: The Health
Education Council
Agency: Saatchi & Saatchi
Year: 1975

This was the first ad I did
when I was hired by
Saatchi & Saatchi. I was
nervous because it was a
bit edgy. I needn't have
been. Jeremy Sinclair and
Charles immediately said
they loved it. No other
agency in London at that
time would have said that.
I guess that's why
Saatchi's was great. Alan
Midgely, himself no
shrinking violet, laid it out
with a big thick screechy
Magic Marker.

Next spread
Client: Intercity
Agency: Saatchi & Saatchi
Year: 1992

I've described the process
of these ads in my blurb.
Enough to say, I loved having the time to do them
and hope they show that
craftsmanship can pay off.
Brilliant photographs by
Michael Kenna didn't
exactly hinder them either.

Pages 326–327
Client: Habitat
Agency: Saatchi & Saatchi
Year: 1991

Habitat had started great.
Then it wasn't. Now the
client wanted us to say it
was great again. We took a
DPS in the *Times* and used
it as a bloody great poster.
The client rejected it
because he took the line
literally, so we made a
video of people in the street
saying they got it and
rushed it around to their
board meeting the same
day. (We used to do stuff
like that.) The result was not
at all revolting... a hatful of
awards for the campaign.

If you drink too much there's one part that every beer can reach.

Your health isn't the only thing which suffers if you over-drink. A night of heavy drinking can make it impossible for you to make love.

And even if you think your drinking isn't affecting you, have you ever wondered how it might be affecting your partner?

Put it this way. How would you like to be made love to by a drunk?

The Health Education Council. **Everybody likes a drink. Nobody likes a drunk.**

Dedham Church, Essex, as seen from the 07.48 Ipswich to Liverpool Street.

At 100 mph, this is the only Constable you'll find alongside you. No contraflows, no speed traps, no road works. The only thing that will arrest you on a train is the beautiful landscape outside your window.

INTERCITY

English landscape art. A private view. In First Class you can ponder, work, eat, take coffee, or simply enjoy the fact that you have the best private seat for one of the best shows on earth; the English Countryside.

INTERCITY

HABI
REVO

This weekend, come along and see how Habitat has

AT IS

LTING

d. You have nothing to lose but your preconceptions.

Vicki Maguire

A promising career in fashion design was cut short when Vicki Maguire discovered she couldn't draw. Encouraged by her mentor Paul Smith to write her ideas down instead, she soon found her way into the world of advertising.

Vicki has spent over 15 years developing campaigns for various agencies before joining Grey London where she is now co-chief creative officer.

She has won more than 35 awards for her British Heart Foundation 'Hands only CPR' Vinnie Jones campaign — which has now saved over 50 lives and counting. The Angina Monologues, also for the BHF, earned her a British Comedy Award.

Vicki has been named Women of Tomorrow by the IPA, was voted one of the 10 Most Influential Women in Advertising by Business Insider, and in 2016 she became the first ever female chair of the Creative Circle Awards.

I learnt to write by listening.
To Grandmaster Flash
To Churchill
To Alan Bennet
To Dorothy Parker
To John Cooper Clarke
To The Ramones, to The Sugar Hill Gang, to The Goons
To *Vogue* Editors, to market traders
To the bloggers and the liars and the charmers and the fakers
To rogues and rappers
To Opera, x Factor and Sesame Street
To arguments
To fights
To break ups
And make ups.
All on the No 8 to Bow bus.

I learnt to write by listening to Paul Smith.
"Vicki you can't draw, write your ideas down instead."

My tip. Keep your mind and your notebook open to real life.

Opposite
Client: British Heart Foundation
Agency: Grey London
Year: 2011

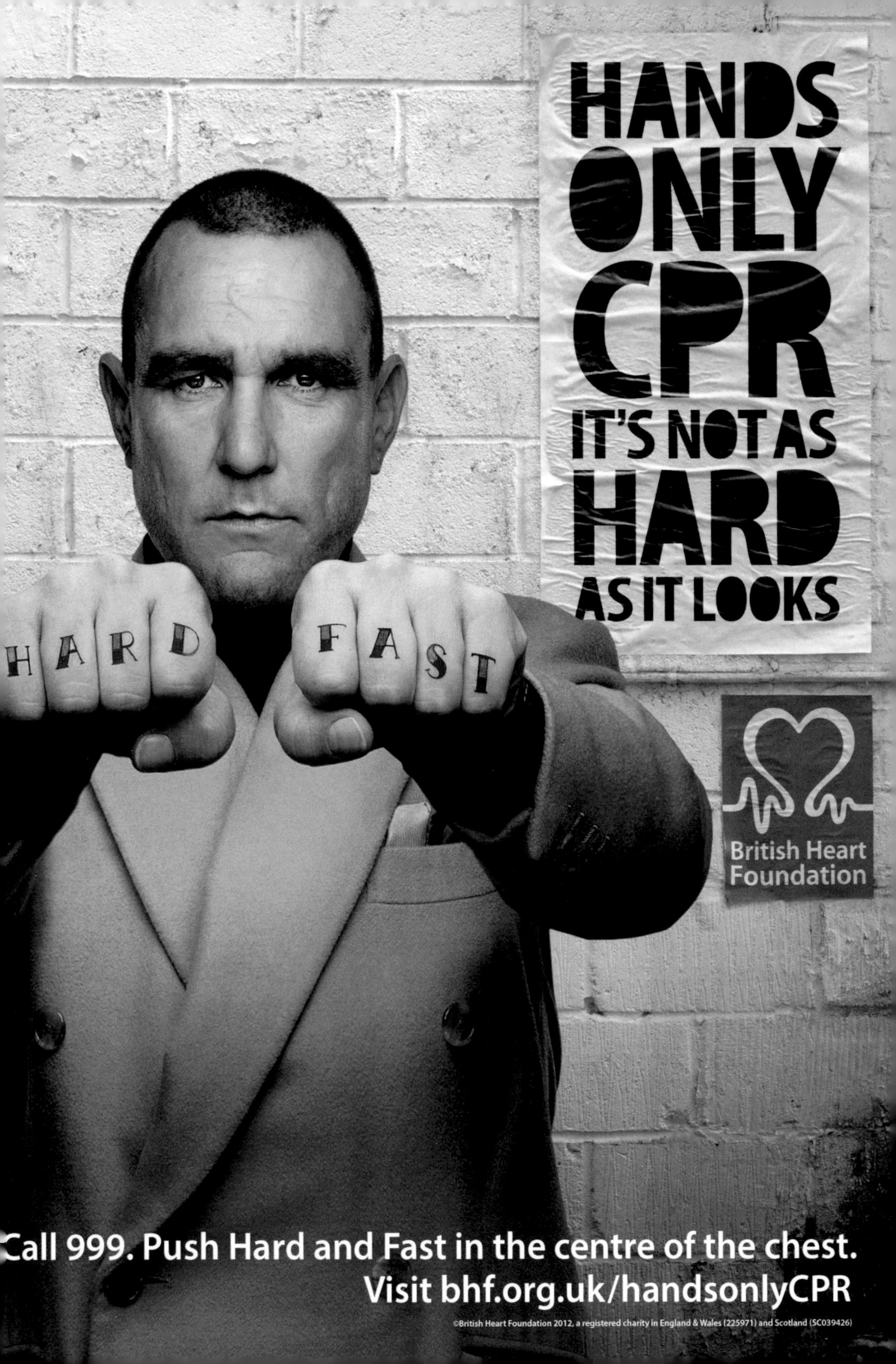

HANDS
ONLY
CPR
IT'S NOT AS
HARD
AS IT LOOKS

HARD FAST

British Heart
Foundation

Call 999. Push Hard and Fast in the centre of the chest.
Visit bhf.org.uk/handsonlyCPR

©British Heart Foundation 2012, a registered charity in England & Wales (225971) and Scotland (SC039426)

Client: Lurpak
Agency: Wieden+Kennedy
London
Year: 2008

Opposite
Client: Nike Women
Agency: Wieden+Kennedy
London
Year: 2008

NO I DON'T KNOW WHAT HAPPENED
IN EASTENDERS LAST NIGHT
HERE I AM
nikehereiam.com
PERRI SHAKES-DRAYTON
400m hurdler, UK

Alfredo Marcantonio

Alfredo Marcantonio, better known as Marc, began his career as a client at Volkswagen. He left to become a copywriter at French Gold Abbott and later Collett Dickenson Pearce, then the most creative agency in the world.

In 1981 he helped CDP bosses Frank Lowe and Geoff Howard-Spink to found Lowes. In 1987 he joined Wight Collins Rutherford Scott, but left to run BBDO, until its merger with AMV reunited him with David Abbott.

By 1998 he was vice chairman of AMV BBDO in London and creative vice president of BBDO Milan. More recently, following a stint as creative director of Leagas Delaney Italy, he has run MPH with creative services guru Steve Hobbs.

Marc has been involved in some of Britain's most iconic advertising. He is a co-author of *Remember those great Volkswagen ads?* and also wrote *Well-written and red*, a tribute to the *Economist* poster campaign.

I write copy the way my grandmother made minestrone soup. I throw in every interesting ingredient that I can find and slowly reduce them down. When you start off you have this rather thin, unpalatable solution but with constant stirring you should end up with something quite substantial.

Where do you get the ingredients? Well, there's that clutch of headlines you couldn't sell your art director when you did the ad. Then there are your notes from the factory visit. (You don't take notes? Well, body copy is a good reason to start.) Next, search the client's old ads for anything interesting or persuasive. And the competition's. (The most awful ads can harbour the most interesting facts.)

After that, read all the brochures, technical sheets, independent tests and press cuttings you can. Even the annual report can contain a few gems. These will all provide you with rational reasons for purchase. You have to look to the customer rather than the client to find emotional ones. What is the target audience like? What is important to them? How do they view the product, the manufacturer, the marketplace? What role does it play in their lives? Write to their hearts as well as their heads. That's where most decisions are taken. When you're all written out, review your findings, rejecting the weak points and re-writing the strong.

Self-praise is no commendation. (If I say I am the best copywriter in Britain, you wouldn't listen, if Dan Wieden said so, you might be fooled into believing it.) Also, raw statistics are more convincing than polished opinions. (A car that does 68 MPG sells better than one that's "outstandingly economical".) Beware of adjectives. They don't always do what you think. (You're all concerned about kitchen cleanliness but would you fancy a snack bar called "The Hygienic Café"?)

Don't be ashamed of mimicking the style of your hero copywriters at first. In my early days my best efforts all read a bit like Bob Levenson on a very bad day. (Tim Delaney thinks they still do.)

An ad is like a door-to-door salesman. It is an intrusion in people's lives. The headline may have got you onto the threshold but it's up to your sales patter to keep you there. Put the most surprising, most persuasive or most intriguing fact first. (My opening line about soup is about as interesting as this article is going to get.)

As with any form of creative writing, you will need to develop a tone of voice. A way of talking that's chosen not to reflect the agency, or the category but the product or service being advertised. Should you sound like some *éminence grise* talking from a distant podium? Or the bloke in the next seat on the railway train? I've heard tell that Bill Bernbach once suggested to a young writer that he make his copy more conversational by writing it as though it was a letter to an Uncle he had met, but rarely saw.

For me, copywriting is closer to speechwriting. It's not simply about informing, entertaining or amusing the audience. It is about winning them over to a product or a point of view. In his book, *Our Masters' Voices*, Max Atkinson analyses the devices that orators have used since ancient times. The seasoned copywriter will recognise almost all of them.

Perhaps the most useful is the "list of three". From God the Father, the Son and the Holy Ghost, through Hip, Hip Hooray to the archetypal Englishman, Scotsman and Irishman, a list of three words, three phrases or three sentences has some magical power. Time and time again, I have found that two facts or phrases are inadequate but four are unwieldy. It's a Marcantonio family tradition that stretches way back to 44 BC: "Friends, Romans, Countrymen, lend me your ears." 1900 years later Abe Lincoln announced: "Government of the people, by the people, for the people." And rather more recently Winston Churchill declared: "Never in the field of human conflict was so much owed, by so many, to so few."

You can't stump up a list of three? Fear not. Neither could many of the great orators. Turn to their other great weapon, the contrasting pair. This groups two items that are as different as chalk and cheese. (That's one to start with.) "Famous names at unheard of prices", "The big network for small phones". There can't be a writer on the planet that hasn't used this device in a headline or body copy.

Why does it work? I think it's engaging; the first word or phrase sets off in one direction but the second takes the reader back in a completely opposite one. William Shakespeare wrote perhaps the most famous contrasting pair on Earth: "To be, or not to be." While Neil Armstrong delivered the most famous on the Moon: "That's one small step for man, one giant leap for mankind." Dr Martin Luther King often made moving use of the genre: "I have a dream that one day my four children will not be judged by the colour of their skin, but by the content of their character." In the best examples the number of words and even syllables, in each of the two phrases matches perfectly, a symmetry that adds to both impact and memorability.

Next spread
Client: BMW
Agency: WCRS Matthews
Marcantonio
Year: 1989

The tone of voice here was set by Robin Wight. His BMW press ads were clean and efficient, just like the cars. Every one of them was true to John Salmon's credo "great advertising dramatises an intrinsic truth about a product". We used to find the "truths" on an annual factory visit. I spied some trays and jars of coloured liquids with bits and pieces soaking in them and asked what on earth they were. Lesson 1: visit the client's premises.

Alliteration is another powerful weapon in the writer's arsenal. Look at Dr King's use of alliteration with the words "colour" and "content". I find alliteration enormously rewarding, both to write and read. And it can be combined with the two previous devices to great effect. Add it to the list of three and you have Julius Caesar's "Veni, vidi, vici." Add it to the contrasting pair and you have the phrase one British politician used to describe her party's concern for the poor rather than the rich: "We are more about Bermondsey than Burgundy".

So there you are. You have written and re-written the facts until only the strong survive. You have woven them into a persuasive argument that will win over the hearts and minds of all fair-minded folk. You have developed a tone of voice that exactly matches the personality of the product. It's end-line time.

There are a number of ways to sign off. One is the final telling fact that completes the sale. Another is the call to action. Most popular of all there's the light, witty line that relates back to the headline in some way. (Hint: you know those rejected headlines I mentioned at the beginning? One of them might be just the job.)

Dun writin'? Right, now sit back and read the whole thing aloud. Yes, aloud. Preferably in the tone of voice you've written it in. Failing that, do what I do and impersonate the voice-over from the "Jones and Krempler" Volkswagen commercial. Am I mad? Quite possibly, but I've heard David Abbott doing it too.

WHAT A PART GOES INTO
BEFORE IT GOES INTO A BMW

The very liquids that keep a car going can cause many a car part to break down.

Petroleum has the power to soften some plastics.

Hydraulic fluid has an unhealthy appetite for certain forms of rubber compound.

While anti-freeze solutions can interfere with electrical contacts.

So, no sooner do BMW's engineers perfect a part, than BMW's lab technicians try to destroy it.

Components are immersed in any suspect substance they're likely to come into contact with. As well as a few they're unlikely to meet.

Critical items like the ABS braking sensor face even sterner tests.

Generously coated hydraulic fluid, detergent in an oven for 24 hours, a

If the sensor is still i repeated for 16 hours at 1

All being well, it is th and collision test. Not on

...uch testing not only helps BMW design parts ...mponents, it helps them develop the materials ...e made from.

...he alloy wheels now fitted to many BMW cars ...ase in point.

...hey are constructed from a metal that is created ...W's own formula.

A formula they continuously monitor and test.

Ten wheels from each delivery are hammered with an iron pendulum.

It simulates the effect of hitting a kerb at 20mph. And if the wheels aren't up to it, the whole consignment is consigned to the scrap heap.

If they do survive, each wheel is given an X-ray

before being passed fit for the production line.

There is a principle behind all these procedures.

Creating parts that perform outstandingly well creates a car that performs outstandingly well.

And for BMW, that is the true acid test.

THE ULTIMATE DRIVING MACHINE

35C5J) TAKE UNLEADED FUEL WITH NO MODIFICATION REQUIRED. FOR A 3, 5, 6 OR 7 SERIES INFORMATION FILE, PLEASE WRITE TO: BMW INFORMATION SERVICE, PO BOX 46, HOUNSLOW, MIDDLESEX, OR TEL: 01-897 6665 (LITERATURE REQUESTS ONLY), FOR TAX FREE SALES, TEL: 01-629 9277.

Opposite
Client: Albany Life
Agency: Lowe
Howard-Spink
Year: 1981

Next spread
Client: Ciga Hotels
Agency: BBDO
Year: 1990

Pages 342–343
Client: Meridiana
Agency: AMV BBDO
Year: 1991

The tone of voice for Albany Life was set by the Maestro, Tony Brignull. Art director David Christensen and I had the idea and the image early on, but I kept writing joky headlines that Frank Lowe wisely turned down. Lesson 2: if you have a funny picture, write a straight line. If you have a straight picture write a funny one.

This was written before the rise of the "boutique" hotel. Europe's great cities were being colonised by Hilton, Sheraton and Marriott with a view to offering the lucrative international business market the same standard of service wherever they were, all the way down to the cupboards and carpet. Lesson 3: look at a client's past, not just his present.

This was a doddle. I had flown to Florence many times myself, only to end up in Pisa. The city centre airport could only handle smaller aircraft, so you were forced to land 40 or 50 miles away. Da Vinci is also one of my heroes. I think the opening line is probably the best sentence I have ever written. Lesson 4: be lucky.

Will you be as fortunate finding a second career?

Heaven knows, you are going to need a second career more than this gentleman.

Compulsory retirement at 55 is on its way.

No matter how long your service, no matter how high your position, you could be out of a job, come your 55th birthday.

The company car will disappear.

The expense account will disappear.

The private health insurance will disappear.

Sadly, your mortgage won't. You may well find yourself repaying that until you are 60 or 65.

Civil servants should be alright. They have indexed-linked pensions, courtesy of the poor old taxpayer.

Members of trade unions should make out too. They often have an army of negotiators to battle on their behalf.

No, it's the private sector businessman who will be in trouble.

His retirement age is going down, but his life expectancy is on the up and up. Today's 40 year olds can expect to reach 80. You could easily be faced with 25 years in retirement.

How will you manage?

That fixed company pension that looked oh-so-generous ten years ago, won't be worth much in another ten year's time, never mind twenty or thirty.

State pensions aren't famous for keeping up with inflation either.

Of course, with the two added together, you may just have enough to survive.

But is that all you want to do?

Survive?

Wouldn't you prefer to do something positive with the second half of your adult life?

Albany Life and the Inland Revenue can help you.

Start salting away a regular sum each month. £15, £50, whatever you can spare.

We will bump up your contributions by claiming back from the taxman every last penny of tax relief we can.

We will then invest the total amount on your behalf.

We receive what is arguably the best investment advice there is. We retain Warburg Investment Management Ltd., a subsidiary of S. G. Warburg & Co Ltd., the merchant bank.

Start saving in your thirties or forties and you will amass a considerable sum, well before your 55th birthday.

When you are pensioned off, you will have a wad of tax-free money to cushion the blow.

Enough to set up shop in some sleepy Devon village.

Enough to pursue some half-forgotten craft, like working with cane or stained glass.

Enough to buy you a stake in some successful small business near your home.

Whatever you decide to do, you'll be better off mentally as well as financially. People vegetate if they have nothing but the garden to occupy their minds.

There is no reason why you shouldn't be active and working at 73, like Mr. Reagan here.

Though hopefully you won't have to carry the worries of the world on your shoulders.

To learn more about our plans send this coupon to Peter Kelly, Albany Life Assurance, FREEPOST, Potters Bar EN6 1BR.

Name

Address

Tel:

Name of your Life Assurance Broker, if any

Albany Life

CIGA HOTELS

Will the muse visit you during your stay at the Gritti Palace in Venice? You will certainly enjoy the same sources of inspiration as Mr Hemingway.

The Grand Canal still laps the hotel entrance as it has for five hundred years.

Titian's 16th century portrait of Doge Andrea Gritti continues to grace the hotel's walls.

ERNEST HEMINGWAY WROTE A NOVEL HERE. PERHAPS YOU MAY BE MOVED TO WRITE A MEMO OR TWO?

And the view from your window, across to the church of La Salute, is the same one that greeted the American author on his arrival in October 1949.

The Gritti Palace became not only the place where he wrote, but also the place that he wrote about, in "Across the river and into the trees".

In truth, other Ciga Hotels have proved equally inspiring. And neither satellite communications nor air conditioning have robbed them of their historic charm.

In Asolo, amid the hills of the Veneto, you will find the Villa Cipriani. Once the home of Robert and Elisabeth Browning.

But perhaps the most literary of our hotels is the Meurice, which borders the Tuileries in Paris.

For more than thirty years, its renowned restaurant served as headquarters to France's most noted literary circle.

An era immortalised in Fargue's "Les Piétons de Paris". And commemorated by the portrait of its Patron, Florence Gould, which presides over diners to this day.

If you are a person more attracted by the beauty of a traditional building than the sterility of a tower block, consider a Ciga Hotel next time you travel.

There are currently 36 to choose from, with room rates much the same as ordinary five star hotels.

To obtain a brochure describing them all, simply fax your letterhead or business card to Milan (02) 76009131. Alternatively, telephone Milan (02) 626622.

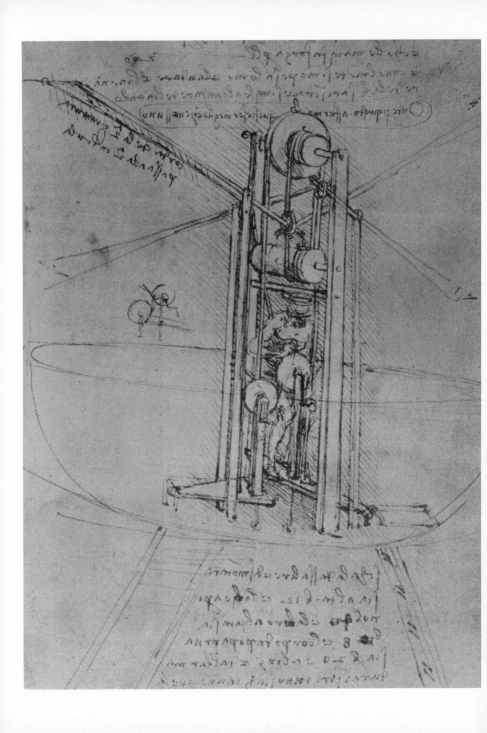

Florence, birthplace of air travel. It's taken 500 years to organise a direct flight.

No sooner did man walk upon the Earth than he began to dream of flying above it.

A fantasy that was given form by Leonardo Da Vinci, almost five centuries ago.

The Glider. The Helicopter. The Parachute. All were born on the drawing board of this

Florentine Maestro. But, aeronautical visionary though he was, Leonardo could never

Direct daily flights leaving London at 10 am and Florence at 8.05am.

have predicted the trials of reaching his native city by air. Ask any of the major

international airlines to take you to Florence and

they will promptly take you to Pisa. A pleasant enough city,

but a good hour or two's drive from the joys of the Uffizi. Thanks to Meridiana

you'll soon be able to take a less roundabout route. Starting September 1st, Meridiana

will fly you direct from London's Gatwick to Florence's Amerigo Vespucci Airport.

And fly you there in style. Tourist passengers travel in Business Class comfort, while

those in Electa Club enjoy facilities that put many a First Class in the shade.

The spacious cabin has unique seats with winged headrests and the international

menus are created by some of Italy's finest chefs. To learn more about Meridiana

and its new scheduled service direct to Florence, call your travel agent. It's the ideal

airline for those who don't have a leaning towards Pisa.

Meridiana
Your Private Airline

Opposite
Client: Olympus
Agency: Collett
Dickenson Pearce
Year: 1979

Next spread
Client: The Economist
Intelligence Unit
Agency: AMV BBDO
Year: 1995

Pages 348–349
Client: Parker Pen Co.
Agency: Lowe
Howard-Spink
Year: 1986

Tony Benn and Denis
Healey were bitter rivals
for the leadership of the
UK Labour Party when a
paparazzo snapped Healey,
top right, taking a photograph of his adversary. He
was a keen photographer
and was testing a pre-
release example of the
Olympus XA. I spotted the
picture in my wife's *Daily
Mail*. Then I saw that the
Guardian's smudger had
asked Benn to return the
compliment. Frank Lowe
sold the ad to the client
within an hour and got it
into the papers within a
day. Lesson 5: look through
every paper, every day.

Way before WikiLeaks,
here was an information
service that told you the
truth, the whole truth and
nothing but the truth. A
noble cause that encour-
aged journalists, politi-
cians and academics
in oppressed nations to
risk not only their livelihoods, but also their lives.
Lesson 6: tell it like it is.

A wonderful client, a fabulous product and marvel-
lous art direction, once
more by Mr Christensen.
The lesson? Like BMW and
Ciga it was the result of a
walk around the client's
factory and a trawl
through his archives.

By kind permission of the Daily Mail.

By kind permission of The Guardian.

They obviously felt like shooting each other.

Who can blame them?

They've got their hands on an Olympus XA. Automatic exposure control and a coupled range-finder ensure a perfect seaside snap.

A great help, whether you are an accomplished photographer, like the gentleman on the right. Or a less experienced one, like the gentleman on the far left.

It's nice they're seeing eye to eye over something.

THE OLYMPUS XA.

For several of our o
one sentence ca

Physical harassment. Deportation. Imprisonment without trial.

In some countries, these are the rewards that await those who attempt to tell the truth.

Many governments consider that honesty is not the best policy. Indeed, some will go to any lengths to conceal their record.

The national press is censored. Foreign media are banned. The reasonable question becomes a treasonable offence.

Such secrecy makes life difficult for us, but not impossible.

At the Economist Intelligence Unit, we monitor the political economic and trading conditions of more than 180 countries.

We have built up a unique worldwide network of more than 50

rseas contributors,
lead to another.

ntelligence-gatherers, some of whom have risked their livelihoods,
ven their lives, to assist us.

Their findings are rigorously checked by our own regional
xperts, then edited into a range of EIU publications.

Telephone Jan Frost in our London office on (44.171) 830 1007
nd she will gladly send you details of them all.

Alternatively, you can visit our website at http://www.eiu.com

Whether you are a minister or manager, we can provide you
vith insights and analysis you are unlikely to discover elsewhere.

Unless, of course, you are prepared to jump
n an aeroplane and take a few risks yourself.

The Economist
Intelligence Unit

E·I·U

Little wonder they don't build cars like they used to. Building a pen is difficult enough.

Oh, the elegant lines of the 1925 Hispano Suiza. Oh, the elegant lines of the 1927 Parker Duofold.

The car may no longer be available but happily the pen is making a welcome return.

We have long yearned to recreate this favourite Parker design. And our approaching centenary has provided a suitable excuse.

Like today's top cars the Parker Duofold Centennial boasts working parts that are 'state-of-the-art.'

But unlike them, it boasts workmanship that is somewhat old fashioned.

Rather than mould the cap and barrel 'en masse,' we machine them as we did in the old days, from a solid block.

Rather than cut the nib from some modern metal, we stay true to gold.

Rather than slit the nib on some new fangled contraption, we still do the job by hand, using a blade no thicker than a human hair.

And just as Hispano Suiza road tested its cars thoroughly after manufacture, we put our pens through their paces.

Upon completion, each Duofold Centennial is examined by a white gloved inspector. If deemed perfect, it is filled, written with and cleaned before being released for sale.

It is an exhausting way to produce a pen. But, as with the Hispano Suiza, the looks and handling provide ample reward.

✦ PARKER

Ed
McCabe

Born in Chicago in 1938, Ed McCabe began his career in advertising by chance at the age of 15, in the mailroom of McCann Erickson.

In 1959, he moved to New York City and landed a job as copywriter at Benton & Bowles, then at Young & Rubicam. In 1964, he joined Carl Ally. In the following three years the agency's billings increased tenfold.

In 1967, Ed co-founded Scali, McCabe, Sloves. During the next nineteen years, he created enduring campaigns including many of Volvo's most memorable ads. In 1974, he was the youngest person to ever join the Copywriter's Hall of Fame.

Renowned for his ability to teach creative people, Ed has trained and inspired at least a dozen people who have gone on to found agencies of their own. He left Scali, McCabe, Sloves in 1986 to seek fresh challenges. In early 1991, he founded McCabe & Company.

Pencils, I work with pencils. Sometimes pens and paper or computers. Lacking one of those, I'll write with someone's lipstick or eyebrow pencil. *In extremis*, give me a twig and some dirt, a stone and a sidewalk, a fingernail and anything it can be scratched into.

I scrawl things on pieces torn from the shopping bags of unsuspecting old ladies I accost on the subway. I scribble on sodden cocktail napkins. Even on lavatory walls, then shoot a shot of it with my cellphone camera.

For years, I had a table in a restaurant in New York. I wrote some of my best ads and the body copy for them on tablecloths. Every morning, the cloth from the night before would arrive at the agency, oily with dinner drippings and blackened with notes. We'd copy the tablecloth, then send it back so they could launder it fresh and white, only to be assaulted by me yet again.

When I have an idea, wherever I have an idea, I write it down. This compulsion knows no bounds. I've written ads on the soles of my shoes. I've written on the skins of friends and lovers, on my own hands or feet, on the clothing of total strangers, cajoled them into following me to a source of paper, and then paid for the damage done.

But that behaviour only occurs in the later stages.

In the early stages — that is, while I'm doing my studying and my research and memorising, before I know what I'm doing inside out, and outside in — when I'm in that empty state of ignorant acquisition, you couldn't get me to pick up a pencil for love nor money.

I make it a practice to never do anything until I know everything. I've written six different openings to this particular piece and I've thought about it for weeks. If I'd approached this the same way I do advertising, I could have spared myself much unnecessary writing and deadline tension. But I started with this notion that writing copy was one thing and writing about writing copy was another. As always, I've come back to the realisation that communication is communication and the same rules apply. *Never* go "Ready, Fire, Aim". If you do, you'll always shoot yourself in the foot.

Consider the familiar cycle of "Ready, Aim, Fire". "Ready" takes a second, "Fire" takes a fraction of a second, but it's the "Aim" part that's most crucial, that can seem interminable, what with the squinting, focusing, steadying, and just when you think you've drawn the exact right bead, you waver and have to begin all over again.

And so it is with the making of advertising. When I write, it's with explosive passion and bravado. With a tinge of insanity even. But before I write, I'm painstaking, plodding, disciplined — and uncommitted. Passion has no place in the planning.

When I think, I don't work. And when I work, I never think. When you are ready to write, it should be automatic, fuelled by knowledge so comprehensive that the advertising almost writes itself.

This is not just because it makes sense to be in full possession of all the facts, or to examine a problem from every possible angle and aspect. As a writer, one simply has no choice. Only with absolute knowledge of a subject can you hope to transcend the banality of mere facts and experience the freedom of insight.

I was once quoted as having said, "I can teach a monkey to write an ad but I can't teach a monkey to think". I still believe that to be true.

Really, any fool can write an ad. With today's technology, you could even program a computer to write body copy. Just plug in all the product information, some consumer benefits, a few relevant behavioural hot buttons, the client mandatory, and presto. I'm convinced out would come a serviceable piece of copy. Truly, you could manufacture advertising. Equally true, it would look and sound and feel — phoney. It would lack something sublimely ordinary, something human. It would seem as though a monkey, a fool or a machine had written it.

To me, all advertising that is truly great reeks of honest humanity. Between every word you can smell the hot breath of the writer. Whether a result of wit, intelligence, insight or artfulness, great advertising invariably transmits itself to the receiver on a fragile human frequency.

What I do, what we all do, is not about describing what a product or service does.

It's about making real how the products or services we write about bring improvement, comfort, even a bit of magic to a single human life.

Opposite
Client: Goebel Beer
Agency: Carl Ally
Year: 1964

One of the best things about new Goebel Beer is that it doesn't taste anything like old Goebel Beer.

It finally got through to us that a lot of you people don't exactly think that Goebel is the best tasting beer around.

It took a lot of time and a lot of money but we've done something about it. We developed new Goebel Draft—the first *genuine* draft beer bottled in this area.

It's genuine draft because like all honest draft beer Goebel is not pasteurized. (The pasteurization of beer, incidentally, has nothing to do with purity. Bottled beer is pasteurized simply to keep it from spoiling in the bottle. We found a way to keep Goebel from spoiling without pasteurization, without refrigeration.)

We don't expect you to run out and buy a whole case of new Goebel Draft. Or even a six-pack. Try one bottle. That's all it'll take to convince you that new Goebel is the beer that other beers merely claim to be.

Then you can run out and buy a whole case.

P S While we were at it we even improved our regular beer It's available in quart bottles and cans

The Goebel Brewing Company, Detroit, Michigan

You can't eat atmosphere.

Horn & Hardart. It's not fancy. But it's good.

Above
Client: Horn & Hardart
Agency: Carl Ally

Written on shopping bag,
8.15 am, New York, 1965.

Opposite
Client: Perdue Farms
Agency: Scali,
McCabe,Sloves

Written on yellow pad,
11 pm, New York, 1972.

Next spread
Client: Citizens for
Clean Air
Agency: Carl Ally

Written on shirt cardboard,
7 am, New York, 1966.

MY CHICKENS EAT BETTER THAN YOU DO.

Frank Perdue

The problem with you is that you're allowed to eat whatever you want.

My Perdue chickens don't have the same freedom. They eat what I give them. And I only give them the best. Their diet consists mainly of pure yellow corn, soybean meal, marigold petals—you'd call it health food.

My chickens drink nothing but fresh, clear water from deep wells.

The reason I'm so finicky about what goes into my chickens is simple: a chicken is what it eats. And because they eat so well, Perdue chickens are always tender, juicy and delicious. And have a healthy golden-yellow glow that separates them from the rest.

If you want to start eating as good as my chickens, take a tip from me.

Eat my chickens.

Tomorrow morning when you get up, take a nice deep breath. It'll make you feel rotten.

It is said that taking a deep breath of fresh air is one of life's most satisfying experiences.

It can also be said that taking a deep breath of New York air is one of life's most revolting, if not absolutely sickening, experiences.

Because the air around New York is the foulest of any American city.

Even on a clear day, a condition which is fast becoming extinct in our "fair city," the air is still contaminated with poisons.

On an average day, you breathe in carbon monoxide, which as you know is quite lethal; sulfur dioxide which is capable of eroding stone; acrolein, a chemical that was used in tear gas in World War I; benzopyrene, which has produced cancer on the skin of mice; and outrageous quantities of just plain soot and dirt, which make your lungs black, instead of the healthy pink they're supposed to be.

At the very least, the unsavory elements in New York air can make you feel downright lousy. Polluted air makes your eyes smart, your chest hurt, your nose run, your head ache and your throat sore. It can make you wheeze, sneeze, cough and gasp. And because air pollution is responsible for many of those depressing "gray days," it may affect your mental well being. If you're a person who is easily depressed, prolonged exposure to polluted air certainly isn't doing you any good.

Of course, at its worst, air pollution can kill you. So far, the diseases believed to be caused, or worsened by polluted air are lung cancer, pulmonary emphysema, acute bronchitis, asthma and heart disease.

600 people are known to have died in New York during two intense periods of air pollution in 1953 and 1963. How many others have died as a result of air pollution over the years is anybody's guess.

Who is responsible for New York's air pollution problem? Practically everybody. Dirt, smoke and chemicals belche from apartment buildings, industrial plants, cars, busses, garbage dumps, anywhere things are burned.

But the purpose of this advertisement is not to put the finger on who's causing the problem. It's to get you outraged enough to help put a stop to it.

What can you, yourself, do about air pollution? Not much. But a million people up in arms can create quite a stink.

We want the names and addresses of a million New Yorkers who have had their fill of polluted air.

The names will be used as ammunition against those people who claim New Yorkers aren't concerned about air pollution.

If we can get a million names, no one can say New Yorkers won't pay the price for cleaner burning fuels, better enforcement of air pollution laws, and more efficient methods of waste disposal.

The cost of these things is low. A few dollars a year.

The cost of dirty air is higher. It can make you pay the ultimate price.

Box One Million
Citizens for Clean Air, Inc.
Grand Central Station, N.Y. 10017

IF YOU'D LIKE TO GET IN THE THICK OF THE FIGHT AGAINST AIR POLLUTION, SEND US A LETTER ALONG WITH YOUR CHECK FOR $2.00 (OR MORE) AND BECOME A MEMBER OF CITIZENS FOR CLEAN AIR, INC.

Opposite
Client: Volvo
Agency: Scali, McCabe,
Sloves

Written on tablecloth,
10 pm, New York, 1970.

Next spread
Client: Vespa
Agency: Carl Ally
Year: 1965

Written on tablecloth,
1 am, New York, 1965.

VOLVOS LAST A LONG TIME. ISN'T THAT BAD FOR BUSINESS?

To some manufacturers, building a product that lasts is the height of foolishness.

But it's an idea that's highly respected among enlightened consumers.

So instead of designing our cars to fall apart so that you'll have to buy another one, we design our cars not to.

That way you'll want to buy another one.

How well our cars last is best summed up by this fact: 9 out of every 10 Volvos registered here in the last eleven years are still on the road.

And in a world where people are becoming increasingly disenchanted with the cars they drive, our customers are coming back for more. The car most often traded in on a new Volvo is an old Volvo.

How's business?

Well, Volvo is the largest selling imported compact in America today. And this will be our best year ever.

The Volvo policy of enlightened foolishness is paying off.

Maybe your second car shouldn't be a car.

Don't laugh.

It makes a lot more sense to hop on a Vespa than it does to climb into a 4000-lb. automobile to go half a mile for a 4-oz. pack of cigarettes.

To begin with, a Vespa can be parked.

It'll give you between 125 and 150 miles to a gallon. Depending on how you drive. And using regular gas.

The Vespa is a reliable piece of machinery. Its engine has only three moving parts. There's not much that can break. (People have driven Vespas over 100,000 miles without major repairs.) And it's so simple to work on, a complete tune-up costs six dollars.

It's air-cooled. There's no water, no antifreeze.

The transmission is so well built that it's guaranteed for life.*

Vespa has unitized body construction. The whole thing is made from one piece. It's not bolted together. It can't rattle apart.

If you buy a Vespa your neighbors won't move out of the neighborhood. The Vespa is a motorscooter, not a motorcycle. There is no social stigma attached to driving one.

There are six Vespa models to choose from. You can buy one of them with the money you'd spend just to insure and fuel the average second car for a year. And you can count on getting most of that money back should you ever decide to sell your Vespa. It won't depreciate nearly as fast as a car.

You may laugh at the Vespa today. But tomorrow when you're stuck in traffic and one scoots by, remember this.

The laugh is on you.

Vescony, Inc., 949 Commonwealth Avenue, Boston, Massachusetts.
*Providing regular maintenance is performed in accordance with schedule outlined in the warranty. Warranty provides for replacement or repair lat importers' optionl of all transmission parts at no cost for either parts or labor. Overseas delivery available. ©1964 Vescony, Inc.

Vespa

A motorcycle it ain't.

What is it?

It's a Vespa. A motorscooter.

The difference between a Vespa motorscooter and a motorcycle is that your neighbors won't move out of the neighborhood when you drive home on a Vespa.

The Vespa is a piece of transportation that makes the kind of sense nobody can argue with.

The Vespa is quiet. It has an oversize muffler. You can drive it at night without making anybody mad.

It'll give you between 125 and 150 miles to a gallon. Depending on how you drive. And using regular gas.

It's one of the most reliable pieces of machinery ever made. The Vespa engine has only three moving parts. There's not much that can break. (People have driven Vespas over 100,000 miles without major repairs.) And it's so simple to work on, a complete tune-up costs six dollars.

It's air-cooled. There's no radiator. So there's no water to boil, no anti-freeze to buy.

The transmission is so well built that it's guaranteed for life.* It's direct drive. No chains to break, no driveshafts to grease.

Vespa has unitized body construction. The whole thing is made from one piece. It isn't bolted together. It can't rattle apart.

Of course, we don't want to give you the impression that it's all sense, but no go.

Just for kicks, a guy in Austin, Minn., entered his Vespa in a professional motorcycle ice race. He had never competed in anything before. But he ran away from everything in sight. The next year motorscooters were banned.

But then, as we said before, a motorcycle it ain't.

Vespa

Vescony, Inc., 949 Commonwealth Avenue, Boston, Massachusetts. Overseas delivery available.
*Providing regular maintenance is performed in accordance with schedule outlined in the warranty. Warranty provides for replacement or repair (at importers' option) of all transmission parts at no cost for either parts or labor. ©1964 Vescony, Inc.

Andy McLeod

Andy McLeod started working as a copywriter in 1988, having met his art director, Richard Flintham, at Hounslow college. They worked at Butterfield Day Devito Hockney and Duckworth Finn Grubb Waters before joining BMP DDB in 1995.

At BMP DDB they won many awards, including one D&AD Black Pencil and five D&AD Yellow Pencils, two One Show Golds and a Gold at Cannes. They started the Marmite Love it/Hate it campaign (Flintham loved Marmite, McLeod hated it).

In 1998, Andy co-founded (and became executive creative director of) Fallon London with Flintham and three others. Fallon quickly became one of London's most respected agencies. In 2007 Andy left Fallon to pursue a career as a director. He joined the production company Rattling Stick, where he is now an award-winning director.

I'm not a copywriter any more, so I don't write copy. Mind you, I never did write much anyway. I was always too busy trying to get people to read the headline.

I was never quite optimistic enough to expect them to read the long bit underneath as well. Let's face it, when flicking through this book, more people will read the headlines on the ads than will read the copy. And this is a book about copywriting, for copywriters. About as much of a shoe-in as you're ever going to get.

So I always tried to avoid writing lots of copy. The best piece of copy you can write is less than ten words long; it's a headline. And for me, a great headline is just the truth about a product expressed in an arresting way.

My favourite lines aren't clever at all. They just express a clever idea in a clear and concise way. There's nothing particularly clever, as a piece of writing, about "Use your vote, you know he'll use his". It's just a clear expression of a relevant truth. But I'm bloody proud of it.

When we started the Marmite "you either love it or hate it" campaign, we didn't think in terms of what would be a clever headline.

We thought about what the truth of the product was, and then we wrote it down. It might be a clever observation, but it's not a clever piece of writing. We were just expressing the truth that had somehow remained background, bringing it forward into the public eye.

"Skoda, no really, Skoda" just took what everyone thought they knew about Skoda cars, i.e. that they were rubbish, and applied it to what the truth was, i.e. that Skoda had just made a brilliant car.

So for me, smart writing is simple writing. It's about communication. The quicker the better. Which is why there might be a bit more white space on this page than on some of the others.

Client: Ministry of Sound
Agency: BMP
Year: 1997

Not a clever piece of writing as such, but the truth, succinctly told. Our payment for this campaign was a lifelong, get-in-free, access-all-areas gold card to the Ministry of Sound nightclub. We only made it down there once.

USE YOUR VOTE.
YOU KNOW HE'LL USE HIS.

Client: Skoda
Agency: Fallon
Year: 2000

Skoda cars were a joke.
And then they suddenly
made a great-looking,
award-winning small car.
Nobody could quite

believe it. Our launch
campaign played on that
disbelief. Bravest client
since our Marmite client
back at BMP DDB.

There's a waiting list for the new Skoda.

Fallon

Client: Skoda
Agency: Fallon
Year: 2000

Opposite
Client: Marmite
Agency: BMP DDB
Year: 1997

Again, there's nothing clever about this headline, but we felt pretty clever about having helped make the waiting list a reality.

Flintham and I would argue about anything if it meant better work came out of our office. So Marmite was made for us. He loved it, I hated it, and we knew we were on to something that could run and run. The ads we launched with maybe weren't as good as many that came after, but as a brand property it has stood the test of time.

Client: Sony
Agency: BMP DDB
Year: 1997

You're once,
Twice,
Three times a lady,
and I let the passengers off before getting on.

SONY

Stamina extra life batteries. No sudden jolts back to reality.

Client: Umbro
Agency: Fallon
Year: 2001

Opposite
Client: Timex
Agency: Fallon
Year: 2000

Umbro were a great client in the early days of Fallon London. Whilst the big sports brands were doing everything from roller skates to yoga mats, all Umbro did was football. We loved that.

Timex is one of those great egalitarian brands. No airs and graces, no high-faluting fashion credentials. Telling the time, and telling it how it is.

WE'VE HAD SOME
COMPLAINTS THAT
MONDAY WAS A
REALLY LONG DAY,
BUT WE'VE CHECKED
AND IT WASN'T.

TIMEX

Tim
Mellors

Tim Mellors is the vice chairman and global creative director of Grey Group. He is based in New York.

He's been a magazine journalist, a commercial film director, host of a BBC TV series and is a trained psychotherapist. He's been the creative director of Publicis, Saatchi & Saatchi, GGT and his own agency Mellors Reay.

He has been president of the jury at Cannes, president of D&AD and president of the Creative Circle.

Tim's awards include 15 Lions and five D&AD Pencils.

This is the only good bit of copy I think I've ever written.

Why? Well I don't see myself as much of a writer kind of writer. I'm not a craftsman, I love words when I speak them, they come jumbling out in an amazing way, but when I write them it's like threading a needle with garden gloves on.

So the Alexon piece appealed to me. It just came straight out of my brain, down my arm onto the Pentel and ended up fully formed on the paper.

Avedon's photograph of Iman, in the days before the Thin White Duke, is mesmeric (look at the eyes). Add Arden's brave — some would say reckless — art direction wrapping Alexon's finest round her head. Even Max Bygraves would have been inspired to write something good by such a concoction.

I don't believe any piece of ad copy I've ever read comes anywhere near the wit and perspicacity of Zoe Heller, or the cranky wisdom of Bernard Levin. And when you get right down to it, that's what we're up against, right there in the next column.

Like all creatives I'm insecure, praise-driven and full of self-doubt. So how do I have the temerity to offer up this bit of writing in this august publication? Charles Saatchi told me he loved it.

—

It's 23 years later. The information highway arrived, drove a bus through the middle of life as we knew it and is now already looking a bit patchy and as gridlocked as the M25.

So what possible relevance has copywriting got today, given the term seems as outdated as job vouchers, type mark-up or visualisers? I was surprised, therefore, to find myself grubbing around for a bit of writing I could stick in the book to keep up my dubious credentials as "one of the world's best advertising writers".

My ego told me in 1995, "Make sure you get a proof of every ad you wrote that got into D&AD. I'm sure that's what the others will be doing." (I was right.) But when I looked at the sheaf of work, I actually felt most of it was cobblers, so I chose one ad I personally liked, and thought still might appeal in twenty years time.

I did the same again this time. This is an ad I wrote for the Cannes interview I did with Yoko Ono. Again it doesn't fit the normal copywriting tenets or rules, but by whetting people's appetites and creating curiosity, it massively overfilled the Cannes auditorium.

I still don't think I'm much of a copywriter, but as a salesman, I'm bloody brilliant.

Opposite
Client: Grey Group
Agency: Grey Group
Photographer:
Albert Watson
Year: 2010

Next spread
Client: Alexon
Agency: Saatchi & Saatchi
Year: 1984

oh ... oh
YOKO

The Dakota, New York 11 May 2010

Tim Mellors (Worldwide Creative Director of Grey): So I saw this film of hundreds of bums. I think it was at the Arts Lab London in 1967. You made it didn't you?

Yoko Ono: Oh, "Bottoms." Yes, did you like it?

TM: Like it? I don't know if I liked it but I thought it was fascinating and memorable, like a dream. How many bottoms were there?

YO: 365...like the days of the year. (smiles)

TM: Around that time you did a show in Lisson Grove. Was that where you first met John Lennon?

YO: Yes, the Indica Gallery. I had set up a white ladder, he climbed it and looked with a magnifying glass at a tiny label on the ceiling. It said, "YES."

The conversation continues at Grey's 4th Annual Cannes Music Seminar

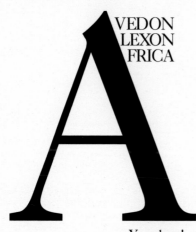

A VEDON
LEXON
FRICA

Yee hoo!, the old woman cries, as she butts the dancer gently in the belly. The dancer has been approved. The dancer is outstanding. The eye popping, limb contorting swirl of magic and colour that is the tribal dance of the Nomads of the Niger has reached its mesmeric climax. In a great white egg of a studio somewhere on New York's East Side, Richard Avedon the photographer who Truman Capote has called "The man with gifted eyes," breathes the tingling magic of the Wodaabe tribe into Alexon's African collection. Colours and primitive pattern woven into cloth, woven into clothes bring Alexon screeching into the now.

Barbara Nokes

After dropping out of school at 14, Barbara Nokes started her career as a secretary in London. In the next two decades she became a copywriter, married Stewart Charteris, was the first woman on the board of Doyle Dane Bernbach, worked at Collett Dickenson Pearce and Boase Massimi Pollitt, wrote about her Do-it-Yourself Divorce for *Cosmopolitan*, married Roger Nokes and gave birth to their daughter Daisy.

In the 80s and 90s, she became a founding partner of Bartle Bogle Hegarty, John Hegarty's copywriting other-half and his deputy creative director, then became creative director at Grey London, and gave birth to her son, Luke. She currently works as a creative advertising consultant.

Barbara has won major awards including D&AD, One Show, Campaign, Cannes Lions, Creative Circle and BTAA.

"They come in different ways, so many different ways," Mick Jagger declares with a melodramatic pleading in his voice, like he's being forced at knife-point to divulge some great private secret. Which, in a sense, he is — how he and Keith Richards write songs together. Not the old shopworn shorthand about the birth of "Satisfaction" or "Honky Tonk Women", but how they really do it from genesis to revelation.

These words open an article on the Rolling Stones by David Fricke published in a recent *Rolling Stone* magazine.

They seem an extraordinarily appropriate way to begin my section of D&AD's book on copywriting.

The point is, I suspect nobody really knows how they do it. We all have our ways of putting off that awful moment when, in the good old days, Mont Blanc or biro met a virgin sheet of A4.

Now, of course, it's the moment when chewed fingers meet PC. Call me old-fashioned, but I can't help wondering if the nature of copy will change now that it's created directly onto a screen. The nature of art direction has certainly changed since a Mac started to mean something other than a hamburger to the art directors among us. Before I start to write a piece of copy, I like to have a conversation with somebody who lives and breathes the product or service. For cars, that might be a client, it might be a motoring journalist. For nappies it could be with a mother, father or nanny. Or an expert in paper technology. For any manufactured article, the quality-control people at the factory are usually good value.

The point is, in my view, a copywriter can't have too much information at his or her fingertips. Copywriting is, after all, the art of saying a great deal in as few words as possible. (And, in that way, can be closer to poetry than prose.) So, I assemble my facts and figures. Then I might list the few ingredients instinct tells me will best make this particular cake. And then, and this is the important bit, I think myself under the skin and into the head of the person I'm addressing.

Empathy really is all. A child I know once demonstrated this brilliantly. He was a boy about eight and rather well-spoken. I overheard him playing in the next-door garden in the mixed inner-London street in which he lived. He was dropping his aitches and effing and blinding like there was no tomorrow. When asked why he was speaking this way he said, with devastating child's logic, "So David will understand me". Quite.

So, gather your facts and get under the skin of your target. Talk to them in their language, not the Queen's. What else? Be brief. I believe it was Pascal who added an apology to the bottom of a long letter, explaining that he hadn't had time to write a short one. Why take twenty words to say what you could say in five? Why decide on a long copy ad when a poster-in-the-press will do? For most people, and particularly women who work outside as well as inside the home, money isn't the most precious commodity these days; time is. We copywriters would do well to respect that.

For that reason, I make no excuses for including completely copy-free ads in these pages. And, indeed, actual posters. For a copywriter, communicating a headful of ideas via a handful of words is, in many ways, the ultimate challenge.

If I could proffer just one piece of advice it would be this: edit, edit, edit.

"I resign."

"You can't, you're the boss."

Everybody has bad days. Even bosses.

But when you're the boss of a small business, a bad day can get out of proportion.

In a big company, you'd probably be surrounded by experts in finance, sales, personnel, marketing, production and so on.

People you could talk to, argue with,

try your ideas on, blame, have lunch with, confide in and who would generally make you feel better.

But when you're the boss of a small business, you're on your own.

At ICFC we've learnt quite a lot about the growing pains of small businesses.

We've helped nearly 5,000 of them over the last 34 years.

And we've usually found that some friendly advice and somewhere between £5,000 and £2 million can brighten up the blackest day.

ICFC

The smaller business's biggest source of long-term money.

INDUSTRIAL AND COMMERCIAL FINANCE CORPORATION LIMITED. ABERDEEN 0224 53028. BIRMINGHAM 021-236 9531. BRIGHTON 0273 24391. BRISTOL 0272 29208L. CAMBRIDGE 0223 62126. CARDIFF 0222 34021. EDINBURGH 031-226 3885. GLASGOW 041-221 4456. LEEDS 0532 30511. LEICESTER 0533 26854. LIVERPOOL 051-236 2944. LONDON 01-928 7822. MANCHESTER 061-833 951l. NEWCASTLE 0632 615221. NOTTINGHAM 0602 47691. READING 0734 861943. SHEFFIELD 0742 66456l. SOUTHAMPTON 0703 32044.

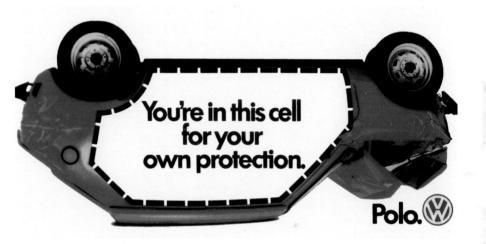

You're in this cell
for your
own protection.

Polo. VW

Client: Volkswagen
Agency: Doyle Dane
Bernbach
Art Director: Peter Harold
Year: 1980

Opposite
Client: ICFC
Agency: Doyle Dane
Bernbach
Art Director: Peter Harold
Year: 1975

Next spread
Client: Dr White's
Agency: Bartle Bogle
Hegarty
Art Director: John Hegarty
Year: 1986

Brief: present the Polo as
the best small hatchback
in the world. Recognition:
D&AD Yellow Pencil.

Brief: offer small business
owners a loan; be sympa-
thetic to current difficulties
(not hard as I wrote this
by candlelight during the
3-day week). D&AD Wood
Pencils in Press and Copy.

Brief: contemporise the
image of Dr White's while
maintaining the brand's
authority. Help make BBH
famous. Recognition:
D&AD Yellow Pencils in
Press and Copy.

Have you ever wondered how men would carry on if they had periods?

At the risk of sounding sexist, we must observe that men can be terrible babies when they're ill.

A cold so easily becomes 'flu.' A headache, 'migraine.' Indigestion, a 'suspected heart attack.'

If men had periods, the cry would go up for the 3-week month, never mind the 5-day week.

The fact is, it's women who have the periods. Month after month after month . . . for about 35 years.

And far from carrying on, women are busy, for the most part, soldiering on.

We like to think we're some help.

As the chart shows, there are Dr White's products designed to make your life a bit more bearable, whatever kind of periods you have to put up with.

And whatever your preferences might be.

Unlike most other manufacturers, we have no axe to grind in the tampons versus towels war: we make both.

And we make both exceptionally well.

Dr White's Contour tampons have rounded end applicators, so insertion doesn't make you catch your breath . . . or anything.

Dr White's Secrets are slim press-on towels, individually wrapped to spare your blushes.

And Dr White's Panty Pads have a leakproof backing to help keep your mind off your period.

After 106 years in the business, we aren't naive enough to imagine we could make your period a lot of laughs, exactly.

But we're certain we can make it less of a (dare we say it?) bl**dy nuisance.

WHICH DR WHITE'S TOWELS AND TAMPONS WILL SUIT YOU BEST?				
IF YOUR PERIOD IS:	>Light	>Medium	>Heavy	>Very Heavy
Looped Towel	Dr White's Size 1	Dr White's Size 1 or 2	Dr White's Size 2	Dr White's Size 2 or 3
Press-on Towel	Dr White's Panty Pads Regular	Dr White's Maxi or Panty Pads Super	Dr White's Maxi or Panty Pads Super	Dr White's Maxi
Slim Towel	Dr White's Secrets	Dr White's Secrets		
Press-on Mini Towel	Dr White's Fastidia			
Applicator Tampon	Dr White's Contour Regular	Dr White's Contour Super or Regular	Dr White's Contour Super or Super Plus	Dr White's Contour Super Plus
Pant Liner	Dr White's Alldays for light days, use with a tampon, just in case or to keep you fresh any day.			

Dr White's Towels and Tampons.
Help make your period less of a problem.

IF YOU'RE FINDING YOUR PERIOD A PROBLEM, PLEASE FEEL FREE TO WRITE TO SISTER MARION AT SMITH AND NEPHEW CONSUMER PRODUCTS LIMITED. ALUM ROCK ROAD, BIRMINGHAM 88 30Z.

Client: Creda
Agency: Doyle Dane
Bernbach
Art Director: Peter Harold
Year: 1981

Brief: communicate the
build quality and advanced
technology of Creda appli-
ances. Recognition: D&AD
Wood and Yellow Pencils.

GOLDEN SHRED GETS ITS TANG
FROM SEVILLE ORANGES.

SOME MARMALADES DON'T.

Client: Robertson's
Marmalade
Agency: Bartle Bogle
Hegarty
Art Director: John Hegarty
Year: 1984

Brief: emphasise the
quality and heritage
of Golden Shred. Help
make BBH famous.
Recognition: D&AD
Black and Yellow Pencils.

Chris
O'Shea

Chris O'Shea left school at 16 and went straight into advertising. He was at French Gold Abbott for six years then followed David Abbott to the fledgling AMV.

After five years he thought there must be more to life than advertising, resigned and became a truck driver for six months, realised there wasn't, and rejoined AMV. In 1984 he joined Lowe Howard-Spink as copy chief then executive creative director with his art director Ken Hoggins.

In 1989 they set up Chiat\Day's London office. In 1991 they founded Banks Hoggins O'Shea, where his long association with Waitrose began. Five years after the agency merged with FCB, Chris, Ken and Waitrose left to start HOW, which later became part of Miles Calcraft Briginshaw Duffy. He left in 2008 to do all those other things he wanted to do in life.

This probably won't be the best piece of copy you've ever read. But then again if it helps you write the best piece of copy you've ever written, I'm sure you won't complain.

I'll start with where I start.

If it's an ad that has the faintest whiff of an award about it, I go into the bathroom at home with an HB pencil, an A3 pad, 2 old annuals and lock the door.

The pencil and pad are because mankind, for all its genius, still hasn't come up with a quicker way of transferring thoughts from the brain to paper.

The old annuals are because I always begin by reading through dozens of good ads in order to fill my mind with quality writing. (This is based on the principle that you'll do more for your tennis game by partnering Roger Federer than the nerd in the next office.)

And the bathroom? Because I need solitude.

I begin by drawing a line from top to bottom of the pad two-thirds of the way across it.

The larger portion, on the left, is where I'll write the actual copy.

And the smaller is to serve as an "ideas repository" for later use — pleasing phrases, thoughts for the ending, interesting stylistic touches — that will dart into my sieve-like brain as I'm writing and, unless noted down, be lost forever.

Then I think about structure.

If there is any secret to writing copy it is, to my mind, simply a matter of setting down information in the correct order. If I can get this right, the argument will flow smoothly, moving logically from one point to the next.

Then I start writing. And stop. And start. And stop.

Is it just me, or is the opening paragraph never, ever easy? (I'll often write four or five different ones before deciding on the best route into an ad.)

All the while I have fixed in my mind a mental picture of who will read what I'm writing.

I don't mean "AB males aged 35–44 with a promiscuous attitude to white spirits." I mean I think of an actual person, be it a friend, neighbour or relation, who is in the target audience.

When I see that person in my mind, I know what will appeal to them.

That way I can write copy the way I believe all copy should be written: as a conversation between two human beings rather than an announcement from manufacturer to consumer.

As I'm writing I try to keep it simple.

This dictates that I write in "spoken" rather than "written" English.

(A fact which neatly avoids any criticism of this piece from all you eagle-eyed grammarians out there.)

The temptation is always to indulge in verbal gymnastics. It's taken me a long time to learn that, while they may impress your peers, they serve only to obscure communication. (An old but very good writer once told me, "You're paid to make clients' products look clever, not yourself.")

I also try to remember that I have more than the 26 letters of the alphabet at my disposal. I have colons, semi-colons, italics, dashes, question marks, brackets, strokes, even (yes!) exclamation marks. Used sparingly, they can add richness and texture.

And now the vexed question of length.

I love long copy.

Holding someone's attention for three minutes has to be better than whizzing through six sales points in 30 seconds.

It allows me to build, layer by layer, a well-reasoned argument that hopefully leads the reader to the inescapable conclusion that the product I'm telling him or her about is better than anyone else's.

That said, however, if it comes out too long for what
Ken Hoggins, my art director, has in mind, I cut it.
(Cutting invariably improves copy.)

But if it comes out too short, I don't add to it. Padding always
shows. (I just try to persuade Ken to set the type bigger.)

As I near the end of a piece I check the rhythm and cadence
by reading it again and again. Out loud. In a phoney
American accent.

(If you think that's crazy, don't call me, call David Abbott.
He gave me this tip.)

What next?

Oh yes. The really inspired / poignant / rib-ticklingly funny
last paragraph.

That's always a problem, isn't it?

Opposite
Client: Dell
Agency: Chiat\Day
London
Art Director: Ken Hoggins
Year: 1990

Next spread
Client: Cow & Gate
Agency: AMV
Art Director: Andy
Arghyrou
Year: 1984

This is an example of building, layer by layer, a well-reasoned argument. It's also a bit of a tongue-in-cheek corporate mini-drama. It was fun to write and, I hope, entertaining to read.

Having been given a brief, I like to have a 30-minute chat with the person who wrote it. It gives them the opportunity to extemporise and it gives me the chance to jot down ideas as they speak. You'd be amazed how many briefs get solved there and then. This one popped out fully formed in the first five minutes. (Though we did sit on it for a week — no point making it look too easy, is there?)

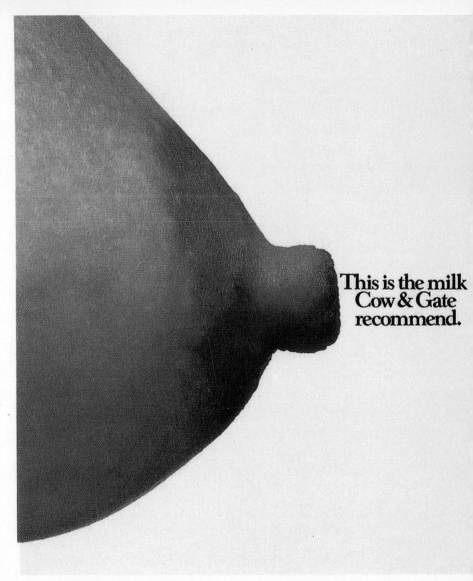

This is the milk Cow & Gate recommend.

We would be the first to say that a mother's own milk is the best food for her baby.

And the DHSS share our view.

For it was they who, in 1977, defined the composition of mature breast milk and then in 1980 proposed specific guidelines for the formulation of baby milks.

Not surprisingly, you'll find Cow & Gate Premium follows these guidelines to the letter.

Its major nutrient levels approach as closely as possible, the average

That's why ours resembles it so closely.

compositional values of mature breast milk.

Or to put it more simply, no other baby milk is closer to breast milk than Premium.

And this fact hasn't gone unnoticed amongst paediatricians and midwives.

Only one baby milk is now used in more hospitals than Cow & Gate Premium. And that, we're happy to report, is called "Breast Milk."

Cow & Gate The Babyfeeding Specialists.

Client: Cow & Gate
Agency: AMV
Art Director: Andy
Arghyrou
Year: 1983

This ad comes with a
tragic story. The D&AD
jury had nominated it for a
Silver — the famous Yellow
Pencil. At the awards
ceremony I saw the other
nominations and was
convinced ours would win.
It didn't. I got the hump
and left early. What I didn't
know was that 30 minutes
later it was announced
that it had won a Gold —
the even more famous
Black Pencil. And as the
spotlight criss-crossed
the Grosvenor House
searching for me, I was
sitting on the train home
sulking. Like I said, tragic.

Next spread
Client: Waitrose
Agency: HOW
Art Director: Ken Hoggins
Year: 2002

See? I can write short
copy. I'm very proud of
this Waitrose campaign,
which was originated by
Markham Smith and
Richard Dennison and
numbered over 50 differ-
ent executions. It shows
that supermarket price
ads (for this is what they
are) can be beautiful
rather than crass.

May we
liver and

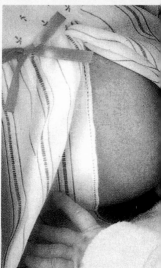

During the first few
months of life, breast milk
is the perfect baby food.

Then, at around 3 or 4
months, something a
little more substantial is
called, or even cried, for.

But liver and bacon?
Are we mad?

On the contrary. We're
one of the country's long-
est-established makers of
baby food.

Experience has taught
us that most mothers pre-
fer their babies to move
from the breast or bottle
to real grown-up food as
naturally and smoothly
as possible.

So our babymeals are
designed to help you do
just that.

**Learning to eat in
easy stages.**

Cow & Gate baby
meals aren't simply little
glass jars of babyfood.

They're a two-stage
training programme that
gently paves the way to
adult food.

Stage 1 meals are for
babies starting out on
solids, and still getting
much of their nourishment
from breast or baby milk.

Since your baby will
only be able to suck and
swallow, they're finely
sieved or puréed.

Then, about 3 months
later, it'll be time to move
onto our Stage 2 meals.

But more about that
later on.

The first step.

If you're still troubled
by the thought of a young
baby tucking into liver
and bacon, let us explain.

Sooner or later your
baby will have to get used
to adult food tastes.

And there's really no
reason why it shouldn't be
sooner rather than later.

That's why our Stage 1

range includes lots of
grown-up tastes.

There are cereals,
meats, vegetables,
puddings, fruits and e
artificial additive-free
yogurt desserts.

So during those fir
few months of weanin
your baby's palate will
in for quite an educati

After 2 or 3 month
it'll be complete. And
your baby will be rea

ecommend the
acon to follow?

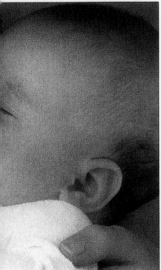

graduate to our Stage meals.

**Grown-up tastes.
Grown-up textures.**

The next stage is to develop your baby's ability chew.

For this reason, our age 2 meals are thicker, d have either meaty or uity pieces in them.

With a little practice ur baby will soon lise that food needs to be chewed before it can be swallowed.

(And knowing that babies don't like coping with too many changes at once, most of our Stage 2 meals are available in the same varieties as Stage 1.)

The 55 meal menu.

You wouldn't take too kindly to eating the same food day in day out.

And neither do babies.

That's one reason why we make 23 different Stage 1 varieties, 23 Stage 2 varieties and 9 yogurt desserts.

But it isn't the only reason.

Perhaps more importantly, your baby grows so fast in the early months that a varied and well-balanced diet is essential.

What's more, it should help you avoid trouble in the years to come.

By educating your baby's palate to accept all sorts of different tastes and textures you should forestall 'food fads' later on.

The best for your baby.

When it comes to feeding young babies, you can't be too careful.

That's something that we at Cow & Gate never, ever forget.

So we buy only the best foods.

All our suppliers must meet the rigorous standards we set.

Every item of food that comes in is checked by our inspectors.

Then our chemists carry out checks of their own.

And the same thing happens all through the cooking process.

In fact, over 20% of

our staff do nothing else.

**It tastes
like adult food . . .**

If you think all babymeals are bland and flavourless, you've obviously not tasted ours.

We've recently altered our recipes so our meals now taste much more akin to grown-up food.

The fact is, we've found that babies prefer them that way.

And so do mothers.

Because when the time comes to move onto adult food, the switch will be that much gentler because your baby will already be used to its taste.

. . . but it isn't adult food.

Compared to adult food, our babymeals have some very important differences.

We add a little extra vitamin C to some of our desserts to replace the amount lost in cooking.

But we don't add any salt whatsoever to any of our meals.

And none of them contain any artificial colourings, flavourings or preservatives.

But we do, however, make sure they supply protein, vitamins and minerals a growing baby needs.

Gently does it.

We hope we've shown you how our babymeals make the journey to adult food in short, gentle steps.

If you have any queries, have a word with your Health Visitor.

Or by all means write to us at Cow & Gate, Trowbridge, Wilts BA14 8YX.

But it's worth remembering that no two babies are the same.

While you can encourage progress, never force the pace.

And be prepared for some little dramas and setbacks on the way.

But don't lose heart.

If it's a Cow & Gate meal now, it shouldn't be too long before it's real home cooking with the rest of the family.

Two short steps to grown-up food.

Waitrose offers you a wider range of smoked salmon than any other supermarket - including one that's smoked over chippings from old whisky barrels for a richer fuller flavour. Find out more at www.waitrose.com

Waitrose

Speyside Scottish Smoked Salmon,
£4.99/140g (£3.57 per 100g).

Jagdish Ramakrishnan

Jagdish Ramakrishnan started his career in India with Lintas and spent four years in Bombay ad agencies before moving abroad. Most of his copywriting years have been in Singapore with Saatchi & Saatchi.

He also ran BBDO Singapore's creative department for a few years before moving to his current role in Ogilvy & Mather's regional office. He is a voracious reader, a passable guitar-player, a tree-spotter, an ethical vegan and a firm believer in rights for animals. In the past, he has conducted forest walks for the Nature Society and lectured on the sexual habits of tropical flora.

In 2001, he co-founded an animal protection organisation called ACRES, which runs a 24-hour wildlife rescue centre and campaigns against animal abuse in all its forms.

I have a tumour pulled out of my stomach one Wednesday.
The surgeon retrieves it like a stray golf ball
from a thicket of innards.
He shows the photo,
the seething mass of feral cells.
I ask, "How long has it been inside me?"

Now, looking at the knife's wake on my belly skin,
it strikes me.
Writing should come from the gut too,
hurting and scarring.
You can tell when it does. It doesn't sit still on the page.
It waits crouched, tight, set to pounce,
its verbs active, raw-sounding and hard-edged,
stripped of adverbs,
its sentences pulsing with rhythm, short here, long there,
detailed in some spots, broad in others, whole lines clotting
and clumping into paragraphs, flushing with purpose,
the boil of alphabets ready to burst
with a single thought,
a single idea,
an idea fit to leave its writer drained and its readers shaken.

Opposite
Client: AWARE
Agency: Saatchi &
Saatchi Singapore
Year: 2006

Next spread
Client: Greenpeace
Agency: Saatchi &
Saatchi Singapore
Year: 2005

Pages 402–403
Client: SPCA
Agency: Saatchi
& Saatchi Singapore
Year: 1997

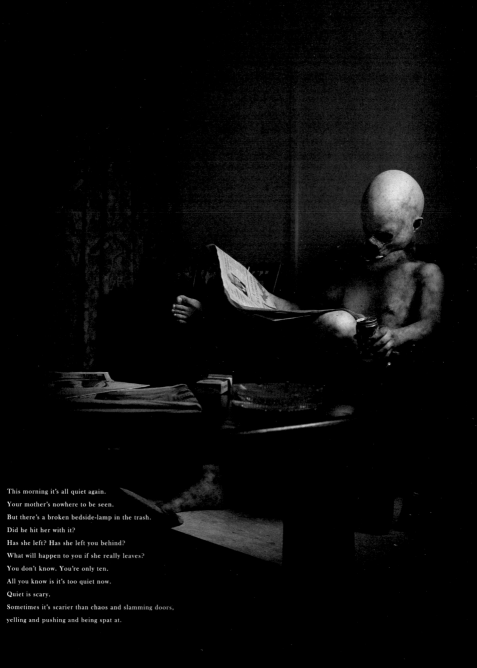

This morning it's all quiet again.

Your mother's nowhere to be seen.

But there's a broken bedside-lamp in the trash.

Did he hit her with it?

Has she left? Has she left you behind?

What will happen to you if she really leaves?

You don't know. You're only ten.

All you know is it's too quiet now.

Quiet is scary.

Sometimes it's scarier than chaos and slamming doors,

yelling and pushing and being spat at.

NO CHILD SHOULD HAVE TO LIVE WITH A MONSTER
To report instances of domestic violence, call **AWARE** at 6774 5935

It was a bit like a submarine.

A fat, blue submarine.

It must have weighed over a hundred *tonnes*.

And it had this small hole at the top that *shot out a spray* whenever it came to the surface.

Not that it came up often.

It usually stayed deep down, making *weird noises like* some drowning symphony orchestra.

Some said the noises were songs, but no one knew for sure.

Act before it's too late. www.greenpeace.org/supportus **GREENPEACE**

TED BUNDY. JEFFREY DAHMER. THE BOSTON STRANGLER.
HOW DO YOU THINK THEY GOT THEIR START?

From psychopaths and murderers to child abusers and wife beaters, almost all violent criminals have a history of animal abuse.

Ted Bundy's first victims weren't pretty, dark-haired co-eds. They were cats and dogs.

The Milwaukee Cannibal, Jeffrey Dahmer, was suspected of killing and eating over 17 people. But his murderous career actually began with the killing and torturing of animals.

Albert De Salvo, the Boston Strangler, didn't become a strangler overnight either. As a young man, he experimented with puppies and kittens. He trapped them in orange crates and shot arrows through the boxes.

Ed Kemper, David Berkowitz, James Oliver Huberty – even the teenager who brutally murdered two children in Kobe, Japan, this year was no exception – all of them graduated from abusing animals.

The FBI and law enforcement agencies in many countries recognise this connection.

In fact, the FBI's Behavioural Science Unit uses animal cruelty as one of the factors in assessing the 'threat potential' of dangerous criminals.

Sociologists, psychologists and people who counsel battered women recognise it too.

So why do violent people pick on animals?

Research shows that animal abusers usually grow up in troubled and violent families. Ironically, they may themselves be victims of abuse.

For some, the animals are merely scapegoats. Their anger is really directed against parents, neighbours or society as a whole.

For others, the violence is a means to get attention, to shock people or to terrorize them into submission. By strangling a cat, an abuser demonstrates his power. "This is what I can do. And there's nothing you can do to stop me."

It's also a way of saying "you're next." It is a warning.

But a warning that is frequently ignored by the only people who can help – the witnesses.

Tragically, almost 7 out of 10 cases of animal abuse go unreported. Neighbours look the other way and passers-by quicken their steps.

It is only when we hear of women being attacked on the streets or children murdered on the way home from school, that we begin to take notice. "Who could do such a terrible thing?" we wonder.

If you witness any act of animal cruelty, please call the SPCA or the police. Please remember that the animal may not be the only one in need of help.

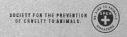

SOCIETY FOR THE PREVENTION
OF CRUELTY TO ANIMALS.

PEOPLE WHO ABUSE ANIMALS ARE CAUGHT SOONER OR LATER.
BUT NOT NECESSARILY FOR ABUSING ANIMALS.

 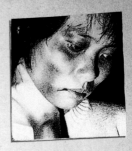

What is the difference between a boy who kicks a dog and a man who beats his wife?

Apparently, just a matter of time.

Studies conducted over the last three decades show that people who abuse animals invariably go on to abuse humans.

When the FBI analysed the lives of violent criminals and serial killers on death row, they found that almost all of them had tortured cats and dogs when they were young.

Other research shows consistent patterns of animal cruelty among people who commit child abuse or spouse abuse.

A survey of fifty-seven families under treatment for child abuse revealed that in 88% of the families, at least one person had abused animals.

People who counsel battered women report that up to 70% of the women with pets have had their dogs and cats beaten, choked, mutilated, tortured, dismembered, hanged or shot by their husbands.

What does an abuser gain by attacking helpless animals?

He gets revenge. He gets a feeling of power and control. And when he discovers he can get away with it, he gains the confidence to start attacking people.

And the violence doesn't just progress from animals to humans.

It is also passed on from generation to generation.

An abused child, in turn, becomes an abusive child. He vents his anger and frustration on dogs, cats and smaller children at school.

When he grows up, he becomes an abusive husband and an abusive parent. In the process, he produces another generation of violent children.

How do you stop this vicious cycle?

Organisations like the Humane Society International stress the importance of correcting abusers early.

Cruelty to animals, whether by a child or an adult, should never be ignored. It is a warning sign.

Not only is it a sign of a mentally disturbed individual, it is also a sign of a troubled family where child and spouse abuse may already be happening.

If you witness any act of animal cruelty, please call the SPCA or the police. Please remember that animals are never the only victims of animal abuse.

Tim
Riley

Tim Riley began his career at Boase Massimi Pollitt (now DDB London). After seven happy years he left to join Simons Palmer Denton Clemmow & Johnson, and then spent time at Leagas Delaney and Bartle Bogle Hegarty.

In 1996 he moved to AMV BBDO where he is currently creative partner and head of copy. Tim's work has won most of the major awards including three D&AD Yellow Pencils and a Cannes Gold Lion. He has also served as a member of the D&AD Executive Committee.

When *The Copy Book* was first published in 1995, Tim was the youngest contributor. He can no longer claim that distinction.

I've never been much good at long copy. This was proved to me again when I tried to write my piece for this book. So instead, here are some loosely-connected observations. I hope they help.

Nobody is interested in your ad.

It's easy to imagine, especially when you're leafing through a beautifully-produced volume like this one, that everybody is just as interested in ads as we are. They're not. Nobody opens a magazine, turns on the TV or goes online to look at the ads. Ads are, by and large, just background noise. And people are amazingly adept at screening them out. They've had years of practice. So your ad had better be fascinating. It's going to have to fight for its life.

You can say a lot with a little.

It's good discipline for a writer to work at a place that doesn't believe in writing. I spent three years at BBH, where less was most definitely more. "The best copy" John Hegarty would say, "is no copy." And: "If the French could inspire a revolution with just three words: "Liberté, Egalité, Fraternité", why should you need any more than that to sell a soap powder?"

I saw a documentary a few years ago about Alan Plater, the great TV writer, who made a similar point. The greatest, most profound line in all of drama, he said, is "To be or not to be". And what does it consist of? Five two-letter words and one three-letter word.

Steal from the greats

I always loved the Health Education ad that Charles Saatchi and Michael Coughlan wrote at Saatchis: "This is what happens when a fly lands on your food". It describes how flies have to vomit on food so that it's soft enough for them to eat. But it's done in plain, simple, unhysterical language, that somehow makes it all the more compelling. (Once you've read it, you'll never leave food uncovered again.) So when Peter Gausis and I got the *Guardian* H-Block brief, I tried to use the same spare style.

Later, when the *Economist* campaign was still just a couple of years old, I remember seeing a newspaper ad Richard Foster and John Horton had done. They'd swapped the trademark red background for green, and the headline read: "*The Economist* is full of surprises." That, I thought, is how to move a campaign on. When I got to BBH and I inherited the Boddingtons "Cream of Manchester" work Mike Wells and Tom Hudson had created, "Vanishing Cream" was my attempt to do something similar.

Work at the best place you can

Easier said than done, I know. But if you're lucky enough to have the option, always choose the best agency. Even if they're not offering you the most money. It's like they say on those property buying shows on Channel 4: better to buy the worst house in the best neighbourhood.

I was incredibly fortunate. My first job was at BMP, and this was the creative department: Frank Budgen, Bill Gallagher, Joanna Wenley, Patrick Collister, Sean Toal, Mitch Levy, Will Farquar, Ian Ducker, Kevin Neale, Mike Elliot, Alan Curson, Simon Hunt, Dennis Willison, Julian Dyer, Mike Durban and Landsley Henry. The creative directors were Alan Tilby and Paul Leeves. And tucked away in an office at one end of the corridor was John Webster.

If that line up didn't inspire you to do better work, nothing would. And, on the occasions when you got stuck (and there were plenty), they were around to help.

Visuals or words?

In the last few years, visual ads have dominated the print awards. Largely, I suspect, because the biggest awards schemes are international and visuals travel better. And that's fine. If a visual can do the job, great. But does that mean writers are becoming redundant? I don't think so.

First of all, I'm willing to bet that 90% of briefs can't be solved by purely visual solutions. Not only that, words can do things that visuals alone cannot. The maverick art director Gary Denham once said to me: "A picture is worth a thousand words. But you can only express that idea *with* words." Words are potent things.

If I had one criticism of visual ads, it's that they often seem to be interchangeable. A clever visual pun for a washing powder could work just as well for any number of other washing powders. A tone of voice, a personality — something all advertisers strive for, seems easier to achieve when you use words as well. Look at the stuff Dan Germain's written for Innocent. Or Richard Russell's work for Honda. Or those brilliant press ads Sam Cartmell wrote for Tesco.

And there's one other thing. The most awarded UK print campaign last year? Dixons. Long copy. Not a visual in sight.

Keep the faith.

Opposite
Client: Boddingtons
Agency: Bartle Bogle
Hegarty
Art Director: Mike Wells
Year: 1994

Next spread
Client: Imperial Cancer
Research Fund
Agency: AMV BBDO
Art Director: Rob Oliver
Year: 2000

VANISHING CREAM.

Boddingtons. The cream of Manchester. Brewed at the Strangeways Brewery since 1778.

Lawyer

Teac

At least one in every three people will contract cancer. It's a chilling statistic. But at the Imperial Cancer Research Fund,
believe there's good reason to be optimistic about the future. Recovery rates are improving every year, thanks in part to w
carried out by our doctors and scientists. 90% of men with testicular cancer are now treated successfully. Nearly 70% of child

Cancer

vive the most common form of childhood leukaemia. And deaths from cervical cancer have fallen by 50% in the last fifteen
rs. That's good. But we need to do better. We want to turn one in three into none in three. If you'd like to find out about the
rk we do, call 0845 601 1891 or visit www.imperialcancer.co.uk The Imperial Cancer Research Fund. Turning science into hope.

No.2

Your greatest ally in the struggle to stop smoking. A bowl of cornflakes.

Instead of your usual early morning cigarette, eat some breakfast.

It'll take your mind off the cravings and keep your blood sugar levels up.

So you'll be less likely to feel tired or grumpy later on and start craving again.

For information and support call 0800 169 0 169 or visit www.givingupsmoking.co.uk

Don't give up giving up.

No.4

The best way to stop smoking? Start drinking.

A glass of water can help you beat the cravings.

Try taking a small sip every now and then, as if you were taking puffs on a cigarette.

It works surprisingly well. (Though you may find you spend more time in the loo.)

For information and support call 0800 169 0 169 or visit www.givingupsmoking.co.uk

Don't give up giving up.

Client: NHS
Agency: AMV BBDO
Art Director: Rob Oliver
Year: 2000

NHS

No.5

How can a cigarette lighter help you give up cigarettes?

Here's one for everyone who likes a cigarette while they're driving.

There's an easy way to stop yourself smoking in the car. Throw the lighter away.

For information and support call 0800 169 0 169 or visit www.givingupsmoking.co.uk

Don't give up giving up.

NHS

No.8

Why a pen makes a good substitute for a cigarette.

Do you light up whenever you're on the phone?

Try keeping a pad and pen nearby and instead of smoking, doodle.

Just having something to do with your hands will help the craving go away.

For information and support call 0800 169 0 169 or visit www.givingupsmoking.co.uk

Don't give up giving up.

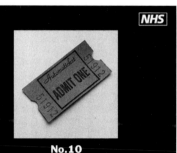

No.10

NHS

The easy way to go two hours without a cigarette.

When you're trying to give up, it helps to go to places where you're not allowed to smoke.

So why not spend an evening at the cinema?

For information and support call 0800 169 0 169 or visit www.givingupsmoking.co.uk

Don't give up giving up.

No.11

NHS

If you're trying to give up smoking, he's a good role model.

Next time you feel like a cigarette, try nibbling a carrot instead.

It helps take away the craving, and what's more, it's good for you as well.

That's all folks.

For information and support call 0800 169 0 169 or visit www.givingupsmoking.co.uk

Don't give up giving up.

Client: NHS
Agency: AMV BBDO
Art Director: Rob Oliver
Year: 2000

No.14

**Take your mind off smoking.
Start painting.**

Next time you get a craving, find something
else to do with your hands.

Like painting your nails, for instance.

You see? Giving up really does make you look
more attractive.

For information and support call 0800 169 0 169
or visit www.givingupsmoking.co.uk

Don't give up giving up.

No.16

**Stop smoking cigarettes.
Try bananas instead.**

If you usually have a cigarette with your mid-morning
tea or coffee, replace it with something else.

A biscuit, or better still, a piece of fruit.

For information and support call 0800 169 0 169
or visit www.givingupsmoking.co.uk

Don't give up giving up.

DURING THE H-BLOCK HUNGER STRIKE, IRA
PRISONERS WROTE THOUSANDS OF MESSAGES
ON CIGARETTE PAPERS LIKE THIS ONE. EACH
MESSAGE WAS SCREWED UP INTO A BALL,
HIDDEN IN A PRISONER'S ANUS, SLIPPED TO
A VISITOR, HIDDEN AGAIN IN THE VISITOR'S
MOUTH, THEN TAKEN TO IRA HEADQUARTERS.
NOW YOU CAN READ THESE MESSAGES - THE
INSIDE STORY OF THE HUNGER STRIKE.
'TEN MEN DEAD' BY DAVID BERESFORD
STARTS TOMORROW IN THE GUARDIAN

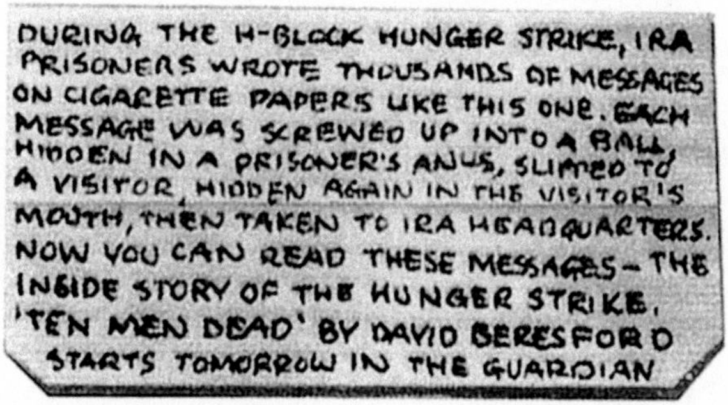

DURING THE H-BLOCK HUNGER STRIKE, IRA PRISONERS WROTE THOUSANDS OF MESSAGES ON CIGARETTE PAPERS LIKE THIS ONE. EACH MESSAGE WAS SCREWED UP INTO A BALL HIDDEN IN A PRISONER'S ANUS, SLIPPED TO A VISITOR, HIDDEN AGAIN IN THE VISITOR'S MOUTH, THEN TAKEN TO IRA HEADQUARTERS. NOW YOU CAN READ THESE MESSAGES — THE INSIDE STORY OF THE HUNGER STRIKE. 'TEN MEN DEAD' BY DAVID BERESFORD STARTS TOMORROW IN THE GUARDIAN

Client: The Guardian
Agency: BMP
Art Director: Peter Gausis
Year: 1987

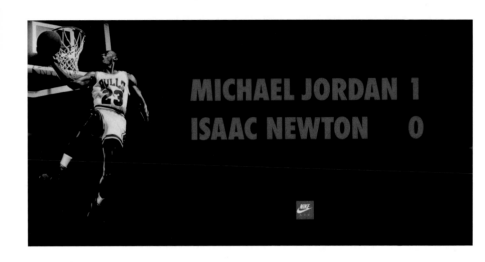

Above
Client: John Smith's
Agency: BMP
Art Director: Peter Gausis
Year: 1987

Top
Client: Nike
Agency: Simons Palmer
Art Director: Andy McKay
Year: 1992

Opposite
Client: D&AD
Agency: AMV BBDO
Art Directors: Nick Bell,
Carlos Mancebo
Year: 2010

Which awards are the most attractive?

The creative world is not exactly short of awards.

Dynamic sculptures cast in solid metal, hefty enough to break a bone should you drop one on your foot.

Translucent blocks that dapple the office walls with pretty coloured light when the sun hits them at the right angle.

Heroic, winged figures that resemble a collaboration between Albert Speer and Leni Riefenstahl.

And then there's another one. It's not much to look at.

Just a short, stubby piece of wood painted yellow.

The D&AD pencil.

You don't see as many of these. And therein lies the appeal.

Most awards schemes cheerfully hand out prizes in every category, every year.

Not D&AD.

Pencils only go to work that reaches the very highest standards.

But if D&AD juries weren't so mean, D&AD awards wouldn't mean as much.

A nomination alone is something to cherish. Just getting work into the book is an achievement in itself. Many would say it's better than winning at other awards shows.

After all, once your work is in the D&AD Annual, it will be gazed at, admired, pored over (and quite possibly ripped-off) by creative people from Milan to Minsk.

Entries are now being accepted for next year's awards.

The closing date is Wednesday 27th January 2010.

So whether you work in advertising or design or digital, it's time to start studying those categories.

Other awards may look more exciting.

But no other award is quite as attractive. dandad.org/awards

Awards 2010

Somebody mentions Jordan.
You think of a
Middle Eastern country with
a 3.3% growth rate.

The Economist

"Can I phone an Economist reader please Chris?"

Pros:

Sparkling conversation
Improved career prospects
Extreme wealth
Ennoblement
Immortality

Cons:

Slight risk of paper cuts

The Economist

Above
Client: The Economist
Agency: AMV BBDO
Art Director: Andy McKay
Year: 2002

Top
Client: The Economist
Agency: AMV BBDO
Co-writer: Gideon Todes
Art Director: Rob Oliver
Year: 1999

Opposite
Client: The Economist
Agency: AMV BBDO
Co-writer: Richard Foster
Year: 2007

Nigel Roberts

Nigel Roberts started out as a copywriter at Saatchi & Saatchi. Then he worked for a while for DMB&B, then Leagas Delaney. He became a creative director at TBWA, then Ogilvy, and then AMV BBDO, CHI & Partners and again Leagas Delaney. Over the last 30 years, he has had the chance to work for and with some amazing and brilliantly talented people. And a few right useless bastards.

To be honest, I never wanted to be a copywriter. I wanted to be an art director. Well, who wouldn't? As job titles go, it's a belter. Two words that sound like: "the person in a position of authority over the special stuff". Count me in.

Whereas copywriter. Hmmm. Not sure.

But I couldn't find a spare copywriter that I wanted to team up with. Then Greg Delaney suggested I swop over — find an art director instead, get a job and then swop back once I was "in". Made sense. So that's what I did. Except for the last bit.

Once I'd started being a copywriter, I quite liked it. I wouldn't say that I enjoyed actually doing the job itself. Because it was bloody difficult to do well. Still is. But what I loved was the satisfaction in the end result.

Art direction, however original and beautifully crafted, will always be at the mercy of everyone's subjective opinion. But you can't argue with a great headline. Take David Abbott's "Would you want to sit next to you at dinner?" for the *Economist*. If anyone can convince me that that isn't brilliant, I'll eat a planner.

Advertising should make you think. It should undermine a negative opinion or build on a positive one. Sometimes a great visual execution of a good strategy can do this on its own. Sure. But more often than not, the best way to really communicate with the consumer is with words. Good art direction taps them on the shoulder. Good copywriting does the talking.

Straightforward enough.

Well, you'd think so. But then why are we surrounded
by so much lazy, vacuous drivel?

Because that isn't advertising. It might pretend to be.
But it's just publicity.

Publicity informs, at best. But advertising, good
advertising, sells. It does everything that publicity does,
and a shed-load more.

When I have to write a headline, I start by writing about
fifty. I draw a dozen boxes on the blank page, then write a
headline in each. After I've filled four or five pages, I look
through them and pick out the best few. Hopefully, within
those, there's something I really like and think that the
client might buy. If not, then I keep going.

I refuse to write any body copy for an initial presentation.
If a headline needs the copy to be assessed, then it isn't
a good enough headline.

When the headline's approved, then I'll write the copy.

Usual rules — get all the relevant information that I can,
think about the structure of my argument, then shut
the door and get on with it. I try to find a first sentence that
forces the reader to continue to the next. And then try to
make each sentence keep them reading until I've told them
everything that I want them to know.

I try to remember who the reader is, and write the copy
as though I'm talking to them, not at them. And I use plain
English, usually. Because no one wants to be patronised
with words they don't use or understand. That would
be frustraneous.

But, unfortunately, the chances to write good copy have become rarer than a helpful comment in a research group.

Press, even more than posters and TV, is the King's old clothes. Especially press ads with copy.

Most of today's press ads are just mini-posters. Look at the awards annuals — the press sections and poster sections are indistinguishable.

Don't get me wrong — I love posters. Well, good ones. (The bad ones are corporate graffiti.) A poster has to work in seconds. And when it does, the purity of the idea is an enviable thing. But if a couple of seconds of your consumers' attention is all you expect of a press ad, then maybe you're wasting an opportunity.

"But we live in a time-starved visual age", some people are prone to say. "Crap", I'm prone to say. I'm writing this on my train home, and 94.53% of the people in this carriage are reading. There are more magazines in the shops than ever, and there's still nothing more authoritative than the day's newspaper. The Internet is filled with avidly-followed blogs. And everyone's emailing everyone.

Has anyone ever, ever said that the film was better than the book?

Who would you rather be stuck in a lift with, Marcel Marceau or Peter Ustinov? (Probably neither as they're both dead now, and that would be unpleasant. But anyway.)

Words are great. People still read. But they only read what they want to.

So I try to make sure that they want to read my ads.

Opposite
Client: Full Tilt Poker
Agency: CHI & Partners
Year: 2006

An online poker site featuring the best professional players in the world. I had to learn how to play the game before I could start writing the ads.

Next spread
Client: The Big Issue
Agency: TBWA
Year: 2001

Why would you buy *The Big Issue*? Because you should hope to God that you never need to sell *The Big Issue*.

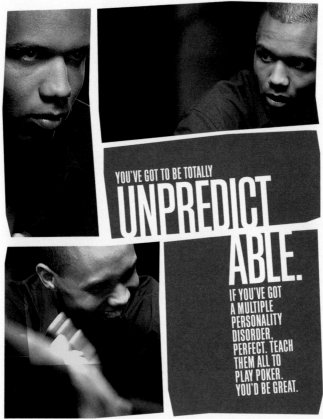

YOU'VE GOT TO BE TOTALLY

UNPREDICT ABLE.

IF YOU'VE GOT A MULTIPLE PERSONALITY DISORDER, PERFECT. TEACH THEM ALL TO PLAY POKER. YOU'D BE GREAT.

If cold, wet, hungry and scared is what thousands of
kids run away to, imagine what they run away from.

Tonight, kids will be wandering the streets, amongst pissheads, pushers, pickpockets, never a policeman when you need one, prostitutes, perverts and pimps. They'll scavenge for food and beg for money. Then they'll try and find a doorway that someone hasn't pissed or puked in, where they can wait for the morning. And that's their idea of being safe. Safer than houses. Because their house is where they were sexually abused, and threatened with what would happen if they ever dared tell anyone about 'their little secret'. Or their house was where they were beaten, not smacked. Punched. Beaten the crap out of. They're not stupid. They know that running away is no adventure. But they will never go home. One in three of them attempts suicide. Those that fail are in and out of care until they're old enough to stay out. It's how a lot of young people end up living rough. The Big Issue Foundation knows that helping them isn't merely about getting a roof over their heads. We also have to understand what's going on in their heads. So what is it that can make someone who trusts almost no one trust us? We never push. And we're not out to reach any targets. If anyone decides to sell The Big Issue it's because they need the cash, and The Big Issue is pretty much the only legal way they can earn it. When they collect the magazines, they become aware that The Big Issue Foundation offers support for drink and drug addictions, advice and training for jobs, and of course, help with accommodation. But there's no pressure on anyone to take it. If someone does want to change their life, then they have to do it themselves, but not by themselves.

The Big Issue is a social business. The Big Issue Foundation is a charity (No. 1049077). For information call 020 7526 3280.

Does anyone ever ask for your opinion? No, not you, that guy behind you.

The Economist

Above
Client: The Economist
Agency: AMV BBDO
Year: 2004

Opposite
Client: Waterstone's
Bookstores
Agency: TBWA
Year: 1999

Next spread
Client: Nissan
Agency: TBWA
Year: 2001

Pages 430–431
Client: The Prince's Trust
Agency: CHI & Partners
Year: 2006

For copywriters, the best brief ever. I just wish I'd had the chance to do more of them. Now they've stopped the campaign, no one does. Madness.

Waterstone's wanted a brand campaign to show that they really care about what they sell. When the marketing director changed, the ads all changed — just to cut price retail. Which suggested that they didn't give a toss.

Everyone knew that Nissans were cheap. But cheap doesn't mean anything until it means good value.

An incredible organisation. But most people had no idea what they do. Don't they make those posh biscuits?

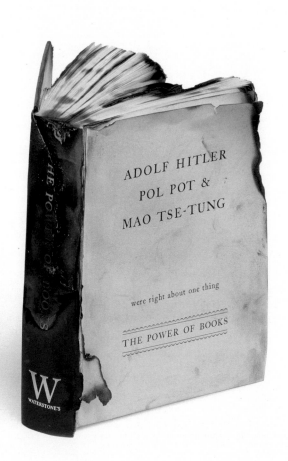

TOO FEW PEOPLE EXERCISE DUE CAUTION WHEN APPROACHING
CAR SHOWROOMS. FIRST, CHECK, AND DOUBLE CHECK THAT IT IS
A NISSAN SHOWROOM. IF NOT, THEN INDICATE, IN GOOD TIME, THAT
YOU WANT A CAR THAT, LIKE ALL NISSANS, HAS BEEN DESIGNED
WITH THE CONTROL PEDALS, DRIVER'S SEAT AND STEERING WHEEL
CORRECTLY ALIGNED SO AS TO MINIMISE UNNATURAL STRAIN ON
YOUR BODY. IF THIS ISN'T CLEAR, THEN PULL OUT AND PROCEED
TO YOUR NEAREST NISSAN DEALERSHIP. REMEMBER, 'CLUNK
CLICK EVERY TRIP' MEANT YOUR SEATBELT, NOT YOUR VERTEBRAE.

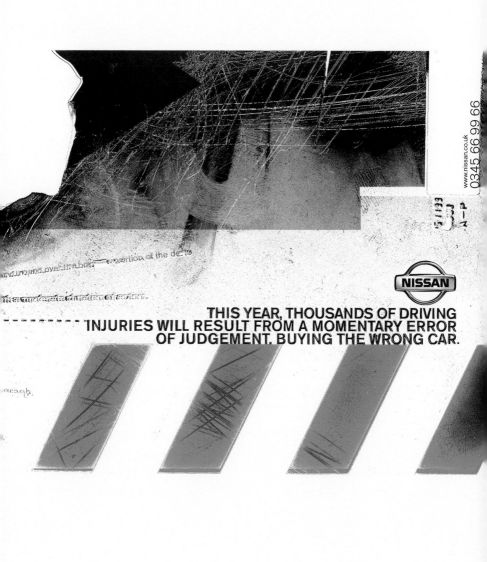

NISSAN

THIS YEAR, THOUSANDS OF DRIVING INJURIES WILL RESULT FROM A MOMENTARY ERROR OF JUDGEMENT. BUYING THE WRONG CAR.

Prince's Trust   Helping change young lives

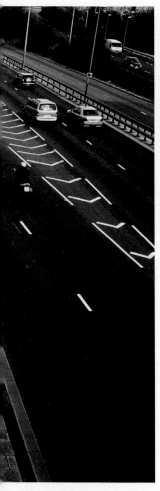

If nothing succeeds like success, then nothing fails like failure. Which is what a lot of young people think they are – failures. If they can't keep up at school, they're told they're failing. If they leave without any qualifications, then they've failed. They don't just 'not' get a job, they fail to get a job. And they don't get 'into' trouble, they fail to stay out of it.

At first, they blame everyone else – their teachers, parents, the kids they hang around with. Then they start blaming themselves. They're natural born failures, apparently. And if there's anything to feel positive about, they fail to see it. But we do see it. The Prince's Trust believes that every young person has potential. Whether they're falling behind at school, leaving care, finding it impossible to find employment or in trouble with the law, we believe, with the right support, every young person has the ability to change their life.

So we offer them support and training. We offer guidance and sometimes even financial assistance to set up their own business. We help them get the skills they need to make a new start. Most importantly, we help them get their self-confidence back. We help them realise their potential. For more information call 0800 842 842. Or visit princes-trust.org.uk

Every day we meet more young people who believe they'll never get anything right. They're wrong, ironically.

Client: Oddbins
Agency: TBWA
Year: 2000

Wine experts,
not wine snobs.

Andrew Rutherford

During thirty-something years in the advertising business, Andrew Rutherford worked in agencies of all shapes and sizes — from four people when he and the others started Wight Collins Rutherford Scott in 1979 to 36, Saatchis when he joined, to several hundred, Saatchis when he left. On the way he worked for the *Sunday Times* (great fun) to Lintas (well, different), and others. He has been called everything from trainee copywriter to world creative great Panjandrum.

He worked in Australia, the US, briefly, the Far East, even more briefly. He sat on the D&AD Executive Committee, and chaired the British Television Advertising awards jury. So it was fun for him, and it still is. But in all that time and in all those places, in truth, he did just one thing. Thought up ads, and wrote them. (OK, two things.) Sometimes good, mostly so-so, sometimes crummy. But it's what he does best, and it's certainly given him the most joy and dismay and satisfaction.

He bashed a knife loudly against a tin tray. Bang! Bang! Bang!… The din cut through the rowdy street market, and heads swivelled towards it.

"Ever tried to cut yer froat with a blunt knife?", he shouted, sawing at his jugular with mock frustration. An interested crowd started to gather round him.

Hint 1

Get attention. An invisible ad is not an effective ad.

"Better still, ladies. Ever tried to cut yer old man's froat with a blunt knife?" The laughter attracted more people. What was going on here? This might be fun.

Hint 2

Intrigue your reader. But not irrelevantly. Lead him or her in the right direction.

"I'll tell you wot is murder ladies. Have you ever tried to cut the rind off a rasher, or fillet a fish or string runner beans with a knife like this?" I started to lose interest, and was about to move off when I noticed that several of the women were nodding in recollection. He'd struck a chord. I stuck around.

Hint 3

Single out your target. Understand their problems, hopes and needs. Ignore everyone else.

He scornfully flung aside the knife, and produced his "little miracle" as he called it. It looked just like a knife to me, but apparently it was like no other knife we'd ever seen. He told us it was as sharp after six months of non-stop demonstrations as the day he'd discovered it. "Watch this", he said. And for the next few minutes with impressive dexterity, he sliced beans, sharpened a pencil, peeled an avocado, chopped a prawn… even shaved a slice from a stone.

Hint 4

Always demonstrate your product's superiority if you possibly can.

As he worked, he talked. He told us that the metal was discovered through space research, that micro-surgeons used specially fine scalpels made from it, and that this "little miracle" (he wouldn't call it a knife) was banned from general sale in some countries, because it was "too easy to cut yer old man's froat with it".

Hint 5

Facts are more persuasive than empty claims. (But a little humour can sugar the pill.)

He told us we were lucky to be standing there, because the only other place he knew where we'd find it "was at 'arrods, where it cost ten quid. No tell a lie, £9.99 — 'arrods give you back 1p back from a tenner".

Hint 6

Create a desire — a shortage perhaps.

Hint 7
Give the product credibility (Harrods, in this case).

However, he would save us the inconvenience of going all the way to Harrods. And better still he'd give us more than one penny back. In fact, he'd give us more than one pound back. How much? Five pound? No, he was daft, but it was his nipper's birthday party, he was in a hurry to get away… so just this once he'd give us eight pounds back from a ten pound note. Just £2 for this "little miracle", but he only had a few, so…

A sea of hands shot towards him wildly waving banknotes to catch his eye.

Hint 8
Clinch the sale. Make the buyer want to do something, and make him do it.

As I walked away clutching my little miracle I began to sense that I had a lot to learn about persuasive selling, and that any aspiring copywriter could do a lot worse than go into the streets and watch a real pro like this at work.

That was some time ago, and I hope the ads I've chosen to show you incorporate at least some of the wiles and wisdom I heard that day.

Opposite
Client: Jaffa
Agency: Saatchi & Saatchi
Year: 1972

Sadly, I've lost my favourite Jaffa ad. Under the headline: "A word on grapefruit to help you choose the perfect one" was a long copy ad, with sub-heads and exploded diagrams with captions. But every single word of the copy was "Jaffa". The argument that a single word can be more persuasive than a hundred is worth remembering when writing copy as when buying grapefruits. By the way, I like the Jaffa ad, above, as well.

You can tell a melon's perfect by squeezing it.

You can tell a pear's perfect by sniffing it.

You can tell a banana's perfect by peeling it.

You can tell a plum's perfect by pinching it.

You can tell an apple's perfect by shaking it.

You can tell a grapefruit's perfect just by reading it.

If it doesn't say Jaffa it's not a Jaffa.

Opposite
Client: Ball Partnership
Singapore
Agency: Ball Partnership
Singapore
Year: 1989

I wrote this with Neil
French in Singapore. I've
put it in because, well,
I like it, and because it
reiterates in print the
techniques the market
trader uses so effectively
hawking his knife.

Next spread
Client: The Health
Education Council
Agency: Saatchi & Saatchi
Year: 1971

I knew I'd written a pretty
fair ad when I went into
my office one lunch hour
to find half a dozen secre-
taries gathered round my
pin board engrossed.
I think my street trader
would approve. A headline
to catch attention — and
especially of the young
people it was aimed at.
Masses of information
(but not, I think, too much).
And a call to action.

WHAT MAKES THIS SUCH A GOOD ADVERTISEMENT?

1. You noticed it.

This is, after all, the First Rule of Advertising, isn't it? (See page 2 of the book).

2. You're reading it.

And, presumably, you're doing so because it may offer something useful, even if it's only information. (See page 3 of the book).

What book? Wait.

3. It's offering you something you've always wanted.

At this stage, you're finding out that, not only is it offering you an intangible morsel of useful information, but a book as well.

A book full of tips that could save you fortunes, or help you make millions.

Maybe.

4. It tells you how to get it.

The book is free

You'll notice we didn't put that piece of information in the headline. Neither did we print it in red, or in a starburst, or even in big letters.

This is because the fact that it is free is not the most important thing about it.

And also because we really only want to give it away to people who are serious about good advertisements.(See headline).

To get your free book, call Hong Kong 762 878, or Kuala Lumpur 298 4611, or Singapore 225 8088, or Bangkok 223 6848, or, in Australia, Sydney 957 4132.

And just ask.

5. It does not have a logo.

So, when you first glanced at the ad, you couldn't tell who placed it. So you had to read it. (See page 10 of the Book).

That's why this is such a good ad.

What are your chances of getting pregnant tonight?

120,000 unwanted babies are born in Britain every year. The more you know about contraception, the less chance you've got of having an unwanted baby. How much do you know?

Questions

1. How many children can a woman have?
2. If 'withdrawal' has been good enough for hundreds of years, what's wrong with it now?
3. Does swallowing a whole packet of the Pill bring on an abortion?
4. Do spermicides offer protection against VD?
5. How can one woman make another pregnant?
6. What does family planning advice in a clinic cost?
7. Which is the odd one out? The Margulies Spiral, Hall Stone Ring, Golden Square, Lippés Loop.
8. Would these be safe in June?
9. Can a virgin wear a loop?
10. Does a woman need to worry about contraception after she's had the menopause?
11. Who first practised birth control? The Ancient Egyptians, The Greeks, The Romans, The Elizabethans or The Victorians?
12. What's wrong with douching to prevent pregnancy?
13. How long should you leave a cap in place after intercourse?
14. What can a family planning clinic tell you that a friend can't?

Answers

1. A healthy woman could bear a baby every year. Perhaps 20 or 25 children. Could you bear the thought?
2. The Victorians practised 'withdrawal'. In those 60 years the population of Britain rose from 18,000,000 to 37,000,000. 'Withdrawal' is chancy because a man can release sperm before he reaches orgasm. So all the willpower needed and frustration caused by withdrawing can be wasted.
3. No.
4. Not at the moment. Spermicides kill sperms, not VD germs. However scientists are working on it.
5. Just by talking to her, and giving her bad advice. Too many women would rather listen to friends about contraception than go to a family planning clinic where help is friendly, private and, above all, accurate.
6. Before April 1st it will be free in some clinics, about a couple of pounds in others. After April 1st all advice, examinations and fitting will be free at National Health Clinics. And the contraceptives, themselves will be available on prescription (20p). Much cheaper than an unwanted baby.
7. They're all names of intra-uterine devices, except, Golden Square— a famous place in London.
8. Probably. The dates stamped on French Letter packets allow a certain margin of error—but you wouldn't be wise to bank on it.
9. No. The loop is for the woman who has already had intercourse—or, better still, had a baby. And very effective, too. But a virgin can't be fitted with a loop.
10. A woman can still have a baby two years after her last period. The more recently she's had children the greater the risk.
11. Even the Ancient Egyptians, 3000 years ago, concocted strange contraceptive creams. Obviously they weren't too keen to become mummies, either.
12. It doesn't work, and it can cause infection.
13. Six hours, at least. You can leave it in longer, but not less.
14. Your friend may tell you what's best for your friend. A doctor or clinic will tell you what's best for you. Women differ both emotionally and physically, and need different contraceptives.

15. After a woman has ovulated (that's when she's most fertile) her temperature rises. And three days after ovulation she's 'safe' to make love. So a thermometer can help discover the 'safe' period. Unfortunately a touch of 'flu, say, can also put your temperature up, which is confusing.

16. If you have comfortable periods before you have a loop fitted, you are unlikely to develop painful periods afterwards. If you do you should consult your clinic or doctor.

17. The so-called 'safe' period is the eight or nine days before a period. Unfortunately while you know when one period ends, it is impossible to be sure when the next will start. Periods can be regular for months and then suddenly vary. So to use the 'safe' period with security could restrict your lovemaking drastically.

18. Not necessarily. The loop and sterilisation are both inexpensive, and very effective. However, the very cheapest methods, 'withdrawal' and the 'safe' period are much less safe.

19. No. Nor does holding your breath during orgasm. Or jumping up and down after, or sneezing before, intercourse. There's more superstitious nonsense talked about birth control than anything else.

20. You might have to wait a little while. But seldom more than 20 or 30 minutes–and never as long as nine months.

21. It can make you slapdash about your contraceptive. And it can lower a girl's resistance. A few large tots on a Saturday night can mean a tiny tot nine months later.

22. No. Nor are you more likely to have twins.

23. No one, single or married, man or woman, should think they will be frowned on at a family planning clinic. These clinics are there to stop unwanted babies, and single girls seldom want babies.

24. You would feel very secure. This is an IUD, one of the safest contraceptives of all. It may not look very comfortable, but if you've already had a baby, you probably wouldn't feel it at all.

25. Yes. And he does. Sperms are only a tiny proportion of the fluid when a man has a climax. A vasectomy just stops the sperms reaching the fluid.

26. It's tragic to see the number of girls in their early teens who become pregnant every year. The most effective form of contraception for these young girls (or anyone else) is not to have sex. Failing that, one can only say the more a young person knows about contraception the better.

27. If you don't know, contact your local health department, your family doctor, look under 'Family Planning' in the telephone directory or Yellow Pages–or write to, The Health Education Council, 78 New Oxford Street, WC1A 1AH.

The Health Education Council

---

16. Will the loop make your periods more painful?
17. Is it safer to make love before a period or after a period?
18. Are the cheap forms of contraception always the least effective?
19. Does it help to stop babies if you stand during intercourse?
20. How long do you have to wait in a family planning clinic?

21. How can alcohol make you pregnant?
22. Do you become unusually fertile when you stop taking the Pill?
23. Do all the family planning clinics welcome single girls?

24. How would you feel with this inside you?
25. Can a man have a climax after a vasectomy?
26. Is there a special method of contraception for young girls?
27. Where is your nearest family planning clinic?

"I bet he drinks Carling Black Label."

Client: Carling Black Label
Agency: Wight Collins
Rutherford Scott
Year: 1985

This isn't an ad, of course,
but I'm proud of it because
all my son's friends think
it's great, and everyone
knows it, and that can't be
bad. Incidentally it started
life as "I bet he drinks a lot
of milk", but we didn't win
the pitch so it changed
drinks. Never throw away
a good idea. Never throw
away any idea, period.

LABOUR ISN'T WORKING.

UNEMPLOYMENT OFFICE

BRITAIN'S BETTER OFF WITH THE CONSERVATIVES.

Client: Conservative Party
Agency: Saatchi & Saatchi
Year: 1978

How can I defend this poster? I who have gone on record deploring the endless and often mindless use of puns and word-play in headlines? I said, and I still believe, that such tricks are the first resort (and usually the last) of the lazy. In my defence I would say that just occasionally a word-play works a treat. Also it's short. Three words is about right for a poster. Five at most.

John
Salmon

John Salmon started his career in advertising as a typographer at Erwin Wasey, London, and became a television writer when commercial TV started in the UK. He left England in 1957 to gain copywriting experience in Toronto and New York. He returned to England eight years later when offered a job as a copywriter in Doyle Dane Bernbach's newly opened London office.

He joined Collett Dickenson Pearce in 1967, and was made creative director two years later. He became group chairman responsible for the overall creative standards in London and the European network.

He retired from the agency in 1999.

Clearly, there are limits to the amount of copy anybody can be expected to read about anything. It varies according to the level of their interest in the subject and the amount that can usefully be said about whatever you're flogging. I believe it was Howard Gossage who first said, "People don't read copy, they read what interests them". Furthermore, I agree with David Ogilvy who said, "The more you tell, the more you sell."

However, first of all you have to attract attention and arouse interest. This is the job of the headline and picture rather than the body copy, and there is a good deal of research which shows that only a small proportion of those who are stopped by an advertisement go on to read more than half of the copy. The copywriter's job is to increase the proportion as much as possible.

Conventional wisdom suggests that the headline and picture should communicate the main message of the ad. But sometimes a curiosity headline (like "Lemon") will stop an extraordinarily large number of people and provoke an unusual level of interest in the copy.

Those who get engrossed in the copy are the readers most likely to be sold by the ad. It follows that the more people you can encourage to get into the copy and the more you can make them read, the more successful your ad is likely to be.

Writing the first sentence is as difficult as writing the headline. It has to expand the headline idea and lure the reader on to the next sentence. The first line of the Lemon ad is, "This Volkswagen missed the boat." According to anecdote, this was the original headline. True or not, there is a lesson here. Save all those headlines you write as you are struggling to come up with the greatest line of your career. Some may find a place in your copy.

You should write from the stand-point of the reader's self interest and base your copy on the benefits, tangible or emotional, offered by your product or service. Develop a tone of voice that will resonate with the particular people you are hoping to nobble. You'll find this easier if you go and talk to some of your potential or actual customers. They will become flesh and blood human beings, rather than anonymous "consumers".

One of my reservations about group discussions is that they provide digests of what the respondents say inflected by the researcher which tend to make personal contact with customers seem superfluous.

In direct conversation you will be able to discover how they relate to your product. You'll hear the language they use when they talk about it and the value they place on it. This is likely to be quite different from the terms used by the brand manager to whom the product is the most important thing in the world.

The ability to communicate product benefits to customers in language they find credible and sympathetic is one of the major values an agency offers its clients. Copy should read like a letter from a friend.

The look of the copy is important, too. A uniform mass of grey type may provide the rectangle of texture that your art director wants but it will deter many potential readers. Regardless of the length of your copy, there is no plausible reason for making it uninviting or hard to read.

Generally, use short words, short paragraphs. This will automatically break up the copy into bite-sized portions and make it impossible for the reader to stop.

On the other hand, short paragraphs can result in a lot of widows and this can make copy look bitty and uninviting. So co-operate with your art director and be ready to adjust your words in the interests of getting an attractive setting.

Sometimes the fear of making copy formidably long leads writers to condense their material too much. Impacted language with a lot of meaning packed into too few words is hard to digest and can be another reason for readers to give up.

Publications vary in the demands they make on readers, both typographically and in the difficulty of their prose. This is because they are addressed to groups with different levels of education and different levels of reading skill. Make your copy slightly less demanding than the editorial matter in both respects.

I always hang on to my copy until I have forgotten the act of writing it. When I look again I invariably want to alter or cut something. I go on doing this until the traffic man snatches it out of my hand.

Next spread
Client: London's
Metropolitan Police
Agency: Collett
Dickenson Pearce
Year: 1974

Pages 450–451
Client: Army Officer
Agency: Collett
Dickenson Pearce
Year: 1972

Copy is the core of advertising. Content matters more than form and an idea isn't an idea unless it can be expressed in words. That is not to say that the visual aspects of advertising aren't vitally important.

To my mind a synthesis of image and words which leaves the reader just enough to do is the ideal to aim for. For example, a picture of a Volkswagen and the word "Lemon". Here the reader is virtually compelled to solve the enigma of a paid advertisement which shows a picture of a product and describes it in a totally deprecating manner. The act of solving it makes him a participant before he has read a word of copy. By reading it he becomes involved.

It becomes his.

WHAT WOULD YOU DO IN THESE SITUATIONS?

You answer a call from a neighbour who is disturbed by a domestic shouting match. When you get there the flat is wrecked, a woman is stretched out on the floor and the neighbours are crowding in. What's your first move?

You answer a call to the scene of an accident. A car has run into a petrol tanker at a junction. The driver and passenger of the car are covered in blood and are very still. The tanker driver is in a state of shock. A heavy flow of traffic is moving past at a good clip. Petrol is spreading over the road. A man is lighting a cigarette. Over to you.

PANIC ☐ TICK HERE   **VOMIT** ☐ TICK HERE   **COPE** ☐ TICK HERE   **RUN** ☐ TICK HERE

RIGHT now you may be hesitant to claim that you know how to cope with situations like these.

But after only six months with us in the Metropolitan Police you could be handling even trickier problems with confidence.

How can we be so sure?

We're careful who we take on.

You have to be British, at least 5'8" tall, intelligent and fit before we'll consider you.

You also have to have a "good character", which means we can't take a chance on you if you've been in serious trouble with the police.

We will bring out the worst in you.

Then you go to Hendon for 16 weeks of intensive training.

Quite a bit of the time is spent in classrooms, learning about law; about police procedures and about the powers of a Police Constable.

You'll do social studies. And you'll learn how to give evidence in court.

And you get practical police training from instructors who are all very experienced police officers. They set up crime and traffic incidents that would make Chief Superintendent Barlow think twice. And then they act the part of awkward members of the public. If you've got a quick temper or a sarcastic tongue they'll find it.

You'll learn how to control yourself under stress. And you'll learn where the pitfalls are for a young Police Constable, and how to avoid them.

You'll go for one week on street duty with an experienced policeman.

Then if you pass your exam, you'll be posted to one of the Metropolitan Police divisions.

During the first few weeks at a police station, you'll go out on patrol with an experienced police officer.

Then you learn what it's really all about.

Very quickly you'll realise the difference between being at Hendon and being on the ground in London.

An instructor pretending to bleed to death isn't the same as someone actually doing so outside the local bank.

On the other hand, the criminals you meet may not be quite as awkward as some of the instructors acting the part.

Just like in any other occupation, you get to know when to apply the rules and when to use your common sense.

And then, all of a sudden you're on your own. And we guarantee that by then you won't panic, run, or vomit whatever you encounter. (Well, you won't vomit where anybody can see you anyway.)

But you are still on probation until you've been in the force for two years.

During which time you'll go on various courses. You'll learn the basics of criminal investigation and you'll probably learn to drive.

And you'll learn more every day you're on street duty.

When the two years are nearly up and you're through your exam, you're all set to apply for promotion or specialisation if that's what you've decided you want.

How far you go is up to you.

The never-ending variety of things that you have to deal with as a Police Constable will keep you involved and interested for years.

A lot of constables spend their whole time in the police on street duty. They feel, quite rightly, that this is where the main police work is done.

In fact, everybody who is in the police who isn't a constable on street duty is helping the constables on street duty to do their job.

You help prevent people injuring one another and robbing one another.

You help them overcome all kinds of difficulties that they can't, won't or don't know how to overcome themselves.

And you can only do so if you're there on the ground, in contact with the people. You can't do it from an office.

Nobody does it just for the money.

The pay isn't sensational. But it's a lot better than it looks at first glance. You start at a minimum of £1,433 a year for a 42 hour week during your probation. Then you get a rise every year for the first six years. Besides which police pay is reviewed regularly to keep it in line with the cost of living.

If you are married you get a free house or flat or a tax paid rent allowance of up to £15.53 per week to pay for your own accommodation. Obviously if you are single you get less.

Promotion is by examination.

Once you've proved yourself as a Police Officer, there's nothing to stop you going for promotion if you want to.

You simply have to pass the promotion exam. After five years service (less in

some cases) you become a Sergeant.

After another four years you may move up to Inspector.

If you do exceptionally well in your exam for Sergeant, you can apply to go to the National Police College, Bramshill, for a one year course.

A year after successfully finishing the course you'll almost certainly be an Inspector. (And this is possible before your 25th birthday.)

From an Inspector up wards promotion is by selection.

Along the way, you may decide you want to specialise. You may apply to go into the CID or the Traffic Division, the Mounted Branch or become a Dog Handler. You might fancy the River Police.

As a member of the Metropolitan Police you are automatically a member of all the many sports and social clubs run by the force. No matter what your favourite sports or hobbies are we cater for them. And our facilities are probably as good or better than you'll find anywhere.

Now, here's a challenge you've got to face right now.

The dreaded coupon.

Have you got what it takes to fill it in and send it to us?

We'd like to think we can depend on you.

LONDON'S 8,000,000 PEOPLE TAKE A LOT OF LOOKING AFTER. COME AND GIVE US A HAND.

How to beat the Army Officer Selection Board.

It's a fact that only about 20% of the candidates applying to the Army Officer Selection Board pass. In spite of what some disgruntled applicants may tell you however, the Board isn't bent on keeping people out.

Quite the opposite. While setting a necessarily high standard, the Board goes out of its way to help applicants show their stuff.

So we're only going an inch or two further by giving you a few tips that could improve your chances.

Are you a fit person?

First off, don't be in a hurry to present yourself to the Board if you can't run up stairs without blowing like a geyser. Get fit first.

While none of the tests used by the Board demand Olympic standards, they all call for considerable mental effort. And you can't

A typical command task.

One member of the group **A** has the problem explained to him by the Officer **B**. (Each member of the group has a turn at leading the group through a different problem.)

He then has a few minutes to figure out a solution before explaining it to his group and getting them to implement it.

The problem is to get the group and the heavy drum **C** from one side of the cross poles to the other.

If he wishes he can use the two wooden poles **D** and the length of rope **E**.

However if he uses them they must end up on the other side along with the drum. The group must pass through triangle **F**; nothing and no one may touch the ground between the start line **G** and the finish line **J**; nothing and no one may touch any part of the cross poles. Finally, no one may jump unless they are suspended over bar **H**.

Ten minutes is allowed for the completion of the command task.

How would you tackle it?

Take the task illustrated for instance. Study it now while you're calm and collected and doubtless a number of possible solutions will occur to you. You can probably imagine yourself giving crisp, explicit orders to your team and them moving across the obstacle with their equipment in a smooth flow of action.

It won't be like that if you're jack-knifed on the grass wheezing for breath. The Board will not have the chance to see how good you really are.

Another thing that will help you over the obstacles is an understanding of levers, pendulums and inclined planes. So if you're rusty brush up.

You don't need a plum in your mouth.

We'd hate anybody who has been to a public school to get the idea that the Board is prejudiced against them.

So if you went to Eton don't waste time hanging around the East End trying to pick up the accent. It will do you no good. And the converse is equally true if you happen to come from the East End.

The Board isn't interested in your style of speech. But it will be keenly interested in what you have to say.

During the time that you spend with the Selection Board you will be interviewed by a Major, a Lieutenant-Colonel, and a Brigadier: possibly by a Major-General and certainly by an Education Officer.

You had better have plenty of material.

Like most people, they enjoy chatting to somebody who has had a bit of experience.

Somebody who has been around and who has met different sorts of people.

They don't want to hear a rundown of the week's television programmes. And if this is the limit of your experience hold off your application until you've branched out a bit.

Buy a rucksack and start working your way around the country. Talk to the crew on your father's yacht. Anything to broaden your contacts.

Understandably, officers like talking to candidates about the Army. So it's worth considering joining the Cadet Force or the University Officer Training Corps. These outfits can give you access to the regiment or corps that interests you. All grist to the mill. You might even consider reading a few books on military subjects.

All the interviewers will be looking for evidence of a keen interest in the Army. And they are not easy to fool. If you aren't interested, really interested, please don't bother them.

One of their favourite questions is 'What will you do if you get turned down by the Board?' Think about it. What are you going to say?

If you can impress your fellow candidates you'll impress the Board.

Besides talking to members of the Board, you'll be talking to your fellow candidates. There will be a group discussion on current affairs which will be led by the group leader and watched by other members of the Board

So start reading the papers a bit more avidly than you do at the moment.

Later you'll be given a choice of subjects and a quarter of an hour to prepare a lecturette. You'll also have to present persuasive arguments in favour of your solution to a variety of problems.

So, if you have trouble talking to groups of people, take steps right away. Join a debating society or a drama club. Take a soap box to Speaker's Corner. It won't take you long to overcome the communication problem.

And if you haven't had any experience of organizing groups of people at school you should try your hand with a youth group.

Don't think from all this that the Board expects you to appear before them ready and prepared to take command of a regiment. It's just that we felt that you'll make a better showing if you have some idea of what you're in for.

Remember, the Board want to pass you. But to be worth training at Sandhurst you have to display the qualities (however latent) required of an Army Officer.

If you think you're ready to face the Army Officer Selection Board, and you're under 29, write to: Major K. S. Robson, Army Officer Entry, Dept. F1, Lansdowne House, Berkeley Square, London, W1X 6AA. Tell him about your educational qualifications and your life in general so far.

Army Officer

Paul Silverman

Paul Silverman was the chief creative officer of Mullen, Wenham, Massachusetts. He was a published fiction writer and journalist before joining Mullen in the mid-1970s when it was a three-person shop. The agency grew to employ over 160 people with a client list that included Timberland, Rolls-Royce, Campari and J&B Scotch. Over the years Paul's work won at Cannes and all major American shows. The *Wall Street Journal* gave him a full-page spotlight in its Legends of Advertising series.

Paul Silverman retired from Mullen in 2002 and went on to write over 100 short stories, many of which were published. He died in 2009 after a lifetime of achievement.

All written advertising derives from an ancient myth about an Arabian prince. In every piece of copywriting the consumer is Aladdin. The product is the genie in the lamp. This is the first of many pontifications about copywriting I'll try to cram into this short piece. Only after reading them all will you understand that success cannot be assured unless you learn, not Arabic, but Chinese.

What, after all, is a copywriter? An advocate, rather like a lawyer. Like lawyers, copywriters build persuasive cases for clients by selecting truths that are positive and omitting truths that are negative. This is different than lying. Lying is inelegant and foolish. It is not professionally challenging.

Being challenged is important, and this is why, if you want to perform at your copywriting best, you must let the clock tick until it sounds like a time bomb. In other words, insist on a deadline and wait until it gets pretty close. Deadlines are the legal amphetamines of professional writers.

In my opinion, a deadline breathing down your neck will be a far more effective stimulus than a jog around the park or an hour on the treadmill. A maxim of the Age is that physical exercise clears your mind and generates energy. I find it makes me calm and, therefore, stupid. The absurd conceptual fusions required in copywriting can best be achieved under tension and anxiety.

For related reasons I would urge that you avoid the so-called "brainstorming" session, in which a dozen people gather in a room, loudly free-associate ideas and paper the walls with meaningless truisms scrawled in magic marker. This is a 1950s advertising cliché and the refuge of mediocre minds. Good stuff usually comes out of two people who are so plugged into each other conceptually they can be a thousand miles apart and still complete each other's sentences.

To get an honest shot at the gold, make sure you find employment at one of the agencies (there are only a handful) skilled at consistently selling bold creative work. A lifetime of creating great copy at a timid agency will win you the reputation of being a timid copywriter, because all that will reach the public are your tenth-draft compromises.

Be sure to remember that clients are not literary critics. Usually they buy your passion, not your prose. Look them in the eye. Don't rely on the fax machine to sell your stuff.

Copywriting requires different skills than novel-writing. A good analogy is baseball, where you have two kinds of pitchers. Starting pitchers, who pace themselves to go the whole game. And relief pitchers, who jump in when there's a crisis and throw brilliantly for short bursts. A relief pitcher can't waste a pitch. And a copywriter can't waste a word.

It follows that effective ad-writing must move at higher speeds than normal writing. To make your writing move fast always assume a passive reader. Not someone leaning forward at his desk to devour every word, as if his job depended on it. But someone sitting back on a toilet seat, riffling and browsing, his mental engine at idle.

To break through such torpor will require a sledgehammer or a hell of a headline. Once you have it, avoid second starts. Consider the headline your first sentence.

Object to everything as you write it. Keep rewriting until you say yes. Build your ad on a series of yes responses.

Develop the ability to split your personality. Role-play, just like actors do. Visualise one reader and write to that one person. Stay on this track. Pay attention to paragraph transitions. They are the corners of your race track. Avoid the natural impulse to brake and hesitate. Puns, these days, are risky business. But brilliant puns work. Anything brilliant can break any rule.

Alas, we live in such a visual age that even the word "copywriter" sounds old-fashioned. Shaping copy on a Mac to fit a visual makes you feel less like an author than a designer of words. Which brings us to the role of the art director and/or type designer.

These days, even the Shakespeare of Madison Avenue would be defeated by lousy typography. Typography supplies colour and mood, much as the voice does in spoken language. This is old news in China, where the written language consists of thousands of characters, each of which was originally a picture. In this fact there is inscrutable guidance for copywriters of all nations, even those of the barbarian West.

Modern copywriting is cinematic, meaning that the double-page spread has evolved into a movie screen. Like an ancient Chinese scribe, your job is to write pictures. Use words as though they were frames of film in a camera, and shoot fast.

Next spread left
Client: Mass
Army-Navy Store
Agency: Mullen
Year: 1991

Sometimes you write a headline and look for a picture. In this ad, the picture suggested the headline.

Next spread right
Client: Timberland
Agency: Mullen
Year: 1990

Verbs, of course, always make faster pictures than adjectives.
a) A sharp, jagged cut in the paper was made by the knife.
b) The knife ripped through the paper.

Of course, scenes on film (moving or still) communicate faster than any words, even verbs. And since the best ad-writing involves compression (cut, cut, cut), one could argue that a copywriter's greatest act is to conceive of an unforgettable scene in which no words occur whatsoever.

As my allotted space runs out, I envision you, the reader, some years from now. You are in a red booth under a dragon-festooned lantern. You dine on bird's nest soup and Peking duck. The meal ends. The waiter brings you a fortune cookie. You crack it open and dig out the ancient message. "Wealth awaits the writer who truly values the art director over the dictionary".

WHEN YOU'RE ABOUT TO WET YOUR PANTS IT'S NICE ~ TO HAVE ~ WATERPROOF SHOES.

Gore-Tex® comes in handy when you're in stressful or stormy circumstances in the wilderness. Not only does it repel water but it breathes, so you stay comfortable. At Mass Army-Navy, Gore-Tex and other

MASS ARMY-NAVY STORE

waterproofing agents are featured in a wide range of waterproof footwear and outerwear. All, of course, carry non-threatening price tags. So all you have to worry about are the challenges of the outdoors.

1436 MASS AVENUE, CAMBRIDGE 497-1250 | 895 BOYLSTON STREET, BOSTON 267-1559

This shoe has 342 holes.
How do you make it waterproof?

Wherever you look in our footwear line, you find holes.

You find wingtips with scores of stylishly arranged perforations.

You find handsewns with scores of needle holes. Moccasins. Canoe moccasins. Boat shoes. Ultralights for easy walking. Lightweight comfort casuals for weightless walking.

Built by a lesser waterproofer, each of these styles has enough openings to admit a deluge.

But we're the Timberland company, and you have to understand where we got our start. Over twenty years ago, we were exclusively a boot manufacturer, and we were the first people to successfully produce fine leather sporting boots that were totally waterproof.

The lessons we learned then are why we're able, today, to build wingtips and handsewns you could go wading in.

Lesson one. Select only the cream of the world's leather crop, then spend the money to impregnate every pore with silicone at the same time the leather is

being tanned in the drum. (We leave the shortcuts to our competitors, the ones who merely brush the surface with silicone after the leather is tanned. And the consequences, unfortunately, we leave to their customers.)

Lesson two. Be inventive. It takes more than one technology to stop water.

For example, to build a waterproof wingtip, we take a page right out of the old Timberland bootmaker's manual. We bond the upper directly to the midsole, creating an impermeable seal around your foot.

Then we build a special umbrella under those stylish wing perforations. It's actually a "shoe within a shoe."

A bootie lining of our softest saddle glove leather, fully waterproofed with silicone. Guaranteed to stop a monsoon.

Handsewns require a different solution, but one that also harks back to our boot days, when we became an early collaborator of the W.L. Gore

Company, creators of waterproof, breathable Gore-Tex™ fabric.

To waterproof the needle holes of a handsewn moc, we use an exclusive technique in which Timberland saddle glove leather is laminated to a Gore-Tex bootie. Once we place this inside the moc, you have a shoe that's an open and shut success. Open to air and shut tight to water. Climate-controlled, in other words, both inside and out.

So even if it never leaves the canyons of Wall Street, every Timberland waterproof shoe owes its character to a world that will never see a sidewalk. The canyons, tundras and marshlands where our boots were born.

Which makes Timberland shoes more than waterproof.

They're water proven.

Boots, shoes, clothing,
wind, water, earth and sky.

Steve Simpson

Steve Simpson began his advertising career in Chicago with a now-defunct agency (you make the connection). He next spent six years at Hal Riney & Partners in San Francisco before joining Goodby, Silverstein & Partners in 1990, where he became partner and creative director. He was a member of the seven-partner management team during that firm's period of enviable business and creative growth.

In August 2010, Steve joined Ogilvy & Mather as chief creative officer for North America, with worldwide chief creative officer duties for IBM.

Steve's work has won every major industry award several times over. He has won the MPA Kelly Award, as well as its Copywriting award, twice. In 2003 his "Fresh TV" campaign for Chevys Mexican Restaurants was inducted into the Clio Hall of Fame.

A copywriter should have no style.

That is to say, you should not have your own style. You should, instead, have many many many styles.

You should be a mimic, a ventriloquist, a shape shifter, a turncoat, a changeling, an assassin, a seducer, a wise man, a fool, a lawyer, a wit, a pedlar, a courtier, a professor, a carnival barker, a clown. You are at once 14 years of age, an indeterminate 18–34 and finally a sleek prosperous 50.

You sell banking products in the morning, dog food at noon, and computer peripherals before the cocktail hour.

You speak, variously, the language of the housewife, the working mother, the depressive, the IT manager (sometimes these last two are the same), the teenager with pimples, the investment banker, the investment banker's victim, the six- year-old keening for breakfast cereal, the 60-year-old pining for deep but not permanent sleep, the dandy, the regular Joe, the fellow rogue who just happens to drink exactly your brand of liquor.

You are a budget Cyrano, a rented hack, a ghost. You should not be famous, any more than a spy should be famous.

And should you ever want to apply your own personal, finely tuned prose style — Pah! The last thing you should ever do is let your own style — if you have one — creep in. If someone says that a piece/an ad "looks like something you wrote", consider it a failure.

Your job, your real job, is to tell a story in the voice of the brand. And, really, you can't expect whole companies of people — whole multinational corporations even — to start speaking just like *Steve Simpson* just because *Steve Simpson* has alighted on their business. You have to learn the company, learn their business, how they speak, where they come from, what they are about and what they want to be about. Then you have to put their straight story and their plain prose into better.

Like all people who make pronouncements and offer advice, I fail to live up to either. As evidence, I offer some work of my own on the following pages. The brands and audiences could not be more different; even so, one spots the same tricks perpetrated by the same hand. Pure indulgence. My honest plea is, do better.

Next spread
Client: Hewlett-Packard
Agency: Goodby,
Silverstein & Partners
Year: 2005

Pages 462–463
Client: Norwegian
Cruise Line
Agency: Goodby,
Silverstein & Partners
Year: 1994

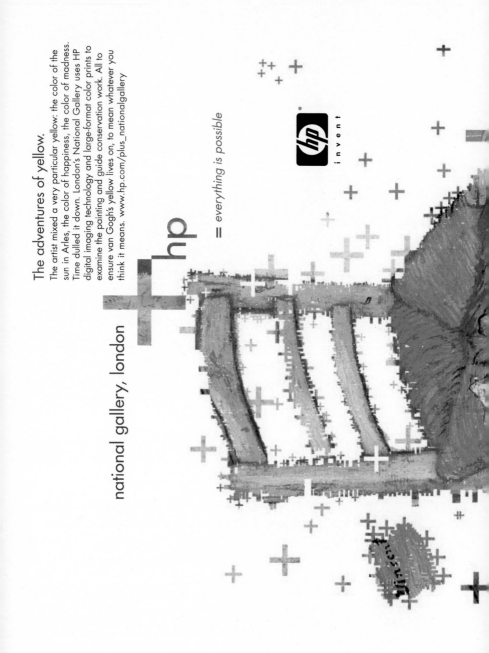

The adventures of yellow.

The artist mixed a very particular yellow: the color of the sun in Arles, the color of happiness, the color of madness. Time dulled it down. London's National Gallery uses HP digital imaging technology and large-format color prints to examine the painting and guide conservation work. All to ensure van Gogh's yellow lives on, to mean whatever you think it means. www.hp.com/plus_nationalgallery

hp

= *everything is possible*

national gallery, london

The Odyssey of Ted and Kate

Sing, Muse, of the travels of Ted and Kate

upon the winedark sea. Of wily Ted,

broker of stocks, who renounced wingtips,

and white-armed Kate, who wore sunblock 40

and not much else. Tell of the lands they sailed

to on swift ships of many decks, and of

the laughing mammals who leap from the sea,

and the visit of Aphrodite and ensuing

warm sport, hinting they may soon expect an heir.

Sing, too, of the dawn with rosy fingers,

of the purpling dusk and diamond night, and

the keeneyed Captain, beloved of Poseidon.

Seven days they rode the waves and reached the shore

of their homeland, bearing gifts and tales and rolls

of undeveloped film. And their neighbors

saw their smooth bronzed limbs and felt envy

and their dog knew them not.

NORWEGIAN®
CRUISE LINE

It's

different

out

here.

Client: Hewlett-Packard
Agency: Goodby,
Silverstein & Partners
Year: 2002

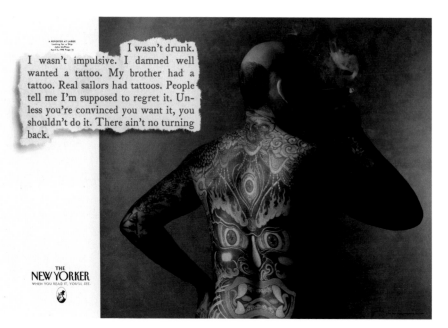

Client: The New Yorker
Agency: Goodby,
Berlin & Silverstein
Year: 1992

Jeremy Sinclair

In 1968, Jeremy Sinclair left Watford Art School with a diploma in Advertising Writing. His letter requesting an interview with Charles Saatchi read: I write for a job, I want to write for a living. Saatchi saw him and hired him on the back of one item in his portfolio, a "first person" ad for a slimming product. Headline: Two men offered me their seats on the bus. I needed them both.

After the creation of Saatchi & Saatchi Jeremy became the creative director in 1974, a post he held until 1986. He went on to various worldwide posts then left in 1995 to create M&C Saatchi, following the ejection of Maurice Saatchi by some American shareholders.

He is currently chairman of M&C Saatchi, which has 30 offices around the world, which, in contrast to the previous embodiment, have been fuelled by organic growth.

Words are Gods. They have the power to make people do things, because they carry ideas. So we must worship words. Cherish them, respect them, protect and polish them.

The most powerful of words are small ones. The most powerful of sentences are short ones.

"Even though a speech be a thousand words, but made up of senseless words, one word of sense is better, which if a man hears, he becomes quiet." Dhammapada, Chapter 8.

Opposite
Client: Conservative Party
Agency: Saatchi & Saatchi
Year: 1983

For Mrs Thatcher.
Mr Foot, the Labour leader, was standing on a leftist agenda.

"Like your manifesto, Comrade."

THE LABOUR PARTY MANIFESTO.

1983

THE COMMUNIST PARTY MANIFESTO.

1983

1. Withdrawal from the Common Market.
2. Massive increase in Nationalisation.
3. Cancel Trident, remove nuclear defences.
4. Cancel tenants' rights to buy their own council houses.
5. Oppose secret ballots for union members on selecting union leadership.
6. Abolish restraints on union closed-shops.
7. Abolish parents' rights to choose their children's school.
8. Oppose secret ballots for union members on strikes.
9. Abolish Immigration Act and British Nationality Act.
10. Exchange controls to be introduced.
11. Abolish Prevention of Terrorism Act.

1. Withdrawal from the Common Market.
2. Massive increase in Nationalisation.
3. Cancel Trident, remove nuclear defences.
4. Cancel tenants' rights to buy their own council houses.
5. Oppose secret ballots for union members on selecting union leadership.
6. Abolish restraints on union closed-shops.
7. Abolish parents' rights to choose their children's school.
8. Oppose secret ballots for union members on strikes.
9. Abolish Immigration Act and British Nationality Act.
10. Exchange controls to be introduced.
11. Abolish Prevention of Terrorism Act.

CONSERVATIVE ☒

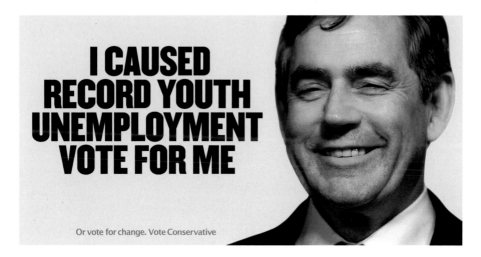

I CAUSED RECORD YOUTH UNEMPLOYMENT VOTE FOR ME

Or vote for change. Vote Conservative

Client: Conservative Party
Agency: M&C Saatchi
Art Director: Bill Gallacher
Year: 2010

30 years on and they
are still the agency's
favourite client.

Opposite top
Client: Conservative Party
Agency: M&C Saatchi
Year: 1997

This is the origin of the
Tony Blair Demon Eyes
poster. Highly prophetic
and highly ineffective.
Labour won by a mile.

Opposite bottom
Client: Conservative Party
Agency: Saatchi & Saatchi
Year: 1979

This was right after
Labour's winter of
discontent. It was cold
and gloomy, and we tried
to inject some cheer.
Another wonderful client
who took the agency's
advice seriously.

Opposite
Client: Health
Education Council
Agency: Cramer Saatchi
Year: 1969

If an ad breaks out into
the editorial columns,
it can become famous.
This is how *Time*
magazine reported
the pregnant man.

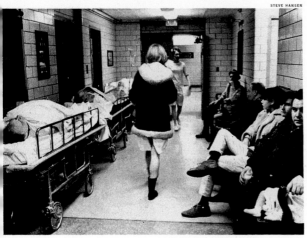

OUTSIDE EMERGENCY ROOM IN BOSTON CITY HOSPITAL

MEDICINE

The Crisis in Health Care

Medical care in the U.S. is more a collection of bits and pieces with overlapping duplication, great gaps, high costs and wasted effort than an integrated system in which needs and efforts are closely related.

—Health Manpower Commission, 1967

That somber conclusion is shared by the Senate Subcommittee on Executive Reorganization, which has spent the past two years assessing the state of medical care in the U.S. Under the direction of Chairman Abraham Ribicoff, the subcommittee listened to scores of doctors, hospital administrators and Government bureaucrats. Their testimony adds up to a dismal tale of extravagant inefficiency, of reliance on slogans rather than thoughtful, effective solutions to the pressing health problems of the nation. As a result, although the U.S. is the richest country in the world, it ranks 18th in infant mortality and 22nd in longevity.

Family Doctor. Such statistics strongly suggest that the system of private health care is on the verge of crisis. In a 500-page report to be released next month, the subcommittee notes that one reason the poor receive improper care —or none at all—is simply the growing shortage of doctors. According to the report, to provide all the physicians needed (an estimated 600,000) would cost the U.S. $1.2 billion a year until 1985. Meantime, the country has become dependent on an influx of foreign doctors, who account for 20% of the new physicians licensed every year.

The symptoms of the health-care shortage are ever more obvious. For the affluent it becomes harder to get an immediate appointment to see a doctor for anything short of an emergency. For the poor, the hospital emergency room has become a kind of "family doctor." Yet the Federal Government has spent enormous sums on health care. With passage of the Comprehensive Health Planning and Services Act in 1966, federal spending has soared from $5.9 billion to $16.6 billion in fiscal 1969, and the direction is ever upwards.

The fault, according to the subcommittee, is the lack of a national health policy to provide form and direction to federal health programs. Under the current setup, even HEW's Dr. Roger O. Egeberg, the nation's top health officer, has effective control over only 22% of his department's budget. To consolidate health programs, the subcommittee has called for a council of health advisers similar to the agencies now dealing with economic and environmental matters.

Empty Beds. Competition between different departments and agencies of Government makes for enormous waste, says the Ribicoff report. In Vallejo, Calif., for example, one hospital received a $607,000 grant under the Hill-Burton hospital-construction program. Meantime, another hospital received a $380,-000 loan from the Small Business Administration to expand its facilities. The result: so many beds that half of them are usually empty. In San Francisco, interservice rivalry between the Army and the Navy resulted in the construction of separate hospitals. The cost to the taxpayer was an extra $10 million in building costs and $8.2 million each year in operating expense.

More than anything, the report emphasizes the need for a review of the whole system as a prelude to a fresh approach to public health. Too often in the past, the federal remedy for any ill has been to appropriate more money. That cure is no longer effective. As Dr. James A. Shannon, former director of the National Institutes of Health, told the subcommittee: "It is clear that a simple extension of present activities, coupled with further patchwork approaches to critical needs now apparent, will provide no long-term solution."

Mr. Pregnant

This bizarre poster is part of a new campaign in Britain to reduce the number of illegitimate births, which have more than doubled in the past ten years. Dr. William Jones, director of the Health Education Council, hopes that copies of the poster, which are now on display in some 1,000 Family Planning Association clinics throughout Britain, will minimize male irresponsibility. As he puts it: "Men must become more concerned about the girl who can all too often be left quite literally holding the baby."

Would you be more careful if it was you that got pregnant?

Contraception is one of the facts of life.
Anyone married or single can get advice on contraception from the Family Planning Association.
Margaret Pyke House, 25-35 Mortimer Street, London W1 N 8BQ. Tel. 01-636 9135.

Two men were watching a mechanical excavator on a building site.

There are two ways to regard technological development. As a threat. Or as a promise.

Every invention from the wheel to the steam engine created the same dilemma.

"If it wasn't for that machine," said one,

But it's only by exploiting the promise of each that man has managed to improve his lot.

Computer technology has given man more time to create, and released him from the day-to-day tasks that limit his self fulfilment.

"twelve men with shovels could be doing that job."

We ourselves are very heavy users of this technology ranging from golf ball typewriters to ink-jet printers to small and large computers, so we're more aware than most of that age-old dilemma threat or promise.

"Yes," replied the other, "and if it wasn't for your twelve shovels, two hundred men with teaspoons could be doing that job."

Yet during 27 years in the UK our workforce has increased from six to 15,000. And during those 27 years not a single person has been laid off, not a single day has been lost through strikes.

Throughout Britain, electronic technology has shortened queues. Streamlined efficiency. Boosted exports.

And kept British products competitive in an international market.

To treat technology as a threat would halt progress. As a promise it makes tomorrow look a lot brighter.

IBM

IBM United Kingdom Limited P.O. Box 41. North Harbour Portsmouth Hampshire PO6 3AU

Client: IBM
Agency: Saatchi & Saatchi
Year: 1977

Opposite
Client: Health
Education Council
Agency: Saatchi & Saatchi
Year: 1971

Long, long ago computers were seen as a threat to employment. Colin Bebrouth's unique art direction.

Written by an ex-smoker. Bill Atherton was the art director and we tried to give it what we thought was an "American" feel.

"I gave up smoking by eating prunes."

Once you decide to give up smoking, you hear of all sorts of methods to help you. There's prunes, dummy cigarettes, chewing gum, sweets and even hypnosis.

These aids have helped countless smokers give up. Yet countless more have tried them and failed.

Why?

The simple truth is that there is no guaranteed painless method of giving up cigarettes. The longer a person has smoked, the more his body cries out for its supply of nicotine and tobacco smoke. And when this supply is suddenly cut off, the body is bound to react.

The first few days are inevitably going to be very trying. So even the most bizarre gimmicks are useful if they help take your mind off the struggle that's going on inside your body.

Fortunately however, doctors have now discovered that there are several methods which will make it easier for any smoker to give up.

What kind of smoker are you?

First of all, it helps if you can decide what kind of smoker you are. There are six basic types. All smokers fall into one (or several) of these categories, and once you've discovered which apply to you, you can then plan your campaign of attack.

Crutch Smokers. These are the smokers who light up in moments of stress and worry. Whenever things go wrong they reach for their cigarettes. When a crutch smoker gives up, it's vital that he chooses the right moment. He must be as far as possible from strain and tension. So a good time is just before he goes on holiday or on a Friday night before a relaxing week-end.

Handling Smokers. They smoke because it gives them something to do with their hands. They like to play around with the packet and the cigarette lighter. These are people who have the greatest success with dummy cigarettes, but a pencil or a pipe can be just as effective. With handling smokers half the problem is finding something to do with their hands for the first few days. After that they find it easy.

Habit Smokers. Habit smokers smoke automatically. They're hardly conscious of the fact that they are smoking. For them there is no substitute, no easy way out. Yet remarkably they're often the most successful at giving up. Because once they've made the initial break they adapt quickly to the new routine. They fall into the habit of not smoking.

Relaxation Smokers. They feel they can't relax without a cigarette. After a meal, with a coffee or a cup of tea, they love to light up. The solution is obvious. For a few days they should avoid the situation when they need to smoke. Drink something else in place of coffee (or tea). And instead of sitting about after a meal, get up and do something. There's nothing more fatal than just sitting waiting for the old pangs to come back.

Craving Smokers. A craving smoker is psychologically addicted to tobacco. The craving for the next cigarette begins the moment he puts the last one out. His problem is mental, because he believes he can't live without cigarettes. The solution is determination—all a craving smoker has to do is decide that he really wants to give up—and the rest, for him, is comparatively easy.

Stimulation Smokers. They smoke to give themselves a perk. They feel that a cigarette picks them up. When a stimulation smoker gives up he usually looks for a substitute which will have a similar effect on his nervous system, such as coffee, tea, spicy foods or alcohol. Unfortunately, these substitutes trigger off the desire for a cigarette, and so they should be avoided, if possible.

Plans of action to help you stop smoking.

How one goes about stopping is entirely up to the individual.

Some smokers prefer to give up without any fuss. They don't follow a plan, They don't tell anyone. They just quietly go about giving up. With this approach, you'll only have yourself to betray.

But it does require plenty of will power. Most smokers find it easier to follow a plan.

Plan 1. Decide two or three weeks in advance that you're going to quit on a certain date. Then gradually reduce your smoking over the three weeks. And then stop for good.

Plan 2. Start by cutting out the most enjoyable cigarettes of the day. The one after dinner, the one during the tea break at work. This may seem like the hardest way to give up. But if you can stop smoking these 'key' cigarettes, the rest will soon become meaningless.

Plan 3. You cut out the first cigarette of the day. Then the second. Then the third. Each day going a little longer without a cigarette.

Until eventually you're down to one or two a day. Then try and cut that one out. But if you find you just can't survive without it, allow yourself one, (and only one) cigarette after each meal.

But be warned. It is far harder to cut down than to give up completely. Because a person who has the occasional cigarette is always liable to think, "one more won't make any difference."

So he has another.

And another.

And another.

How to make sure you don't start smoking again.

Once you've given up cigarettes, there are going to be many temptations to start again. Friends will offer them to you — you'll begin to notice the enticing advertisements — you'll think of a thousand excuses why you should have 'just one'.

There are many smokers who once gave up, but are now smoking again just because they thought it would be safe to have the occasional cigarette. And it seems such a pity to go to all that effort giving up, only to start again.

There are, however, a few ways which will help you resist the temptations.

1. Give up with a friend. You'll be able to encourage and give each other moral support. And of course the less you see people smoke, the easier it'll be for you to give up.

2. Travel in non-smoking compartments of trains and buses.

3. Change your routine for a few days so that you avoid the situations when you really enjoyed or needed a cigarette.

4. Announce that you've given it up. Tell your family and friends that you've stopped smoking. They'll help see you over the worst time. And it'll also make it harder for you to go back on your word.

5. If you're absolutely desperate for a smoke, switch to a pipe or cigars—they are far less dangerous.

Finally, be prepared for a struggle. It probably took quite some time before you smoked as heavily as you do now. It may take just as long for you to give up. But even if you've smoked heavily for years, it's still worth making the effort, because from the day you stop, you reduce your chances of getting lung cancer or any of the diseases which are caused and aggravated by cigarette smoking.

If you don't smoke, or if you've already given up, please cut this out and give it to a friend who hasn't yet managed to stop.

The Health Education Council
©Health Education Council, Middlesex House, Ealing Road, Wembley, Middlesex, HA0 1HH.

Indra
Sinha

Indra Sinha was twenty years in advertising, all in London. His longest single spell was at Collett Dickenson Pearce, where for seven years he had the pleasure of partnering Neil Godfrey, then perhaps the most acclaimed art director in the world.

In 1995, having grown disgusted with advertising, he burned away his portfolios, threw away his awards and left CDP to write. Since then he has published three books, Internet memoir *The Cybergypsies* in 1999, *The Death of Mr Love* in 2002, and *Animal's People* in 2007.

In 1994, after a visit from a Bhopali man who had heard of the Amnesty advertising, he started the Bhopal Medical Appeal and for the next 16 years was a literary activist. He quit in July 2010 to focus on his novels.

A few weeks ago, having all but given up on this piece, I rang Neil French to find out if he had done his, and caught him picnicking on a beach in Mallorca. He was about to fill one of those wine glasses, which when flicked go ting for a very long time.

My problem, I said, was that the ads I'd written since the original *Copy Book* were about the vilest aspects of human nature. They'd make grim reading. Besides which they hadn't worked.

"Of course they worked, silly old bear," said Frenchie. "Brought in pots of money, didn't they?"

True. The Bhopal fundraising ads had paid for themselves off-the-page. With the surplus we were able to open a free clinic in the city and run it for fourteen years.

"Bit of a poke in the eye for idiots who say nobody reads long copy."

"People give money, but the problems don't go away."

"Did you think you could write them away."

"Evidently."

"I see your problem," he said. "Well, you'll just have to write something funny."

What seems funny, with hindsight, is the hubris of my piece in the first *Copy Book*:

"As a writer, your words go out into the world to millions of people and change things. It's a big responsibility. If all you care about are awards and money, you are playing for the smallest available stakes. Me? Because I know how powerful words are, I want to play for the highest stakes. I want to help shape the future."

I've spent the last sixteen years trying, and mostly failing, to live up to these words. The profession of writing has led me from advertising to be an activist, journalist, artist, novelist and screenwriter. I've been up for several awards, albeit none for advertising, and can report that being a finalist and not winning is just as galling as it ever was. I've discovered that the struggles of the writer and the artist are not different from those of the activist or the revolutionary. Anyone inspired, crazy, pompous or naive enough to want to shape the future soon finds themself straining against the inertia of the universe, and if they can't budge it with words they have to find another way.

Yet words work and things do move. I knew this from my Amnesty work, to the extent that I wagered £12,000 of my own money that the first ever ad for the Bhopalis, a double-page spread in *The Guardian*, would turn a profit. It did, and out of the surplus we bought a building and started a free clinic that has now treated 30,000 people. The secret was to trust not in writing but storytelling. Storytelling is not the same as writing, it is only superficially about things like plot, character and narrative. At the deepest level it is entirely about the reader. Stories change things by enabling people to realise for themselves that they are powerful and can do much in the world, and, crucially, that they want to do it.

There are many ways to tell stories. The best ones tell themselves. In 1998, I ran an advertising competition in India, challenging creatives to make me feel the anguish of people who had suffered for years without justice. The brief, *Torture Me*, was a poem made from fragments of speech heard and overheard in Bhopal. Individual voices wove the tale of a whole city. In time the piece found a life of its own and became known as *The Survivors' Poem*. It would have had no power had I invented it.

To write is one thing, but to write something that triggers earthquakes and wakes tigers, this is the problem. In July 2002, when the Indian government tried to undermine the criminal case against Union Carbide, three friends went on indefinite hunger strike. They were camped on a Delhi pavement in temperatures of 117°F. We were terrified they'd die. Lacking other ideas I decided to email all my friends and ask them to pass on my message hoping that sooner or later it would reach someone who'd know what to do. Nothing I could write was strong enough. Anger and anguish sounded equally shrill. Running through my mind were the lines of the *Survivors' Poem*: "My heart bursts my ribs with useless anger. Make me weep." When the email was finally written, the poem lay hidden among its words:

"When grief turns to anger, when your rage is as useless as your tears, when those in power become blind, deaf and dumb in your presence, when the rest of the world has forgotten you, what are you to do?" ("An Urgent Appeal to My Friends", 2002)

The message circled the world three times in a week and was widely published in magazines and websites, but luckily the outcome did not depend on my eloquence. The judge gave the politicians a roasting, the Bhopalis celebrated and we all breathed again.

In June 2010, in the same criminal case, eight Indian defendants were fined £17,000. Not each. Total. If shared out equally as compensation for 26 years of living inside the *Survivors' Poem* each gas victim would get 3 pence. The prime accused, Union Carbide Corporation was not in court. For 18 years it had been ignoring the court's summons, and the Indian government had not pursued it. Now it issued a statement rejoicing that justice had been done. The Indian news magazine *Tehelka* asked me to comment.

"It's 7.20 in the morning in a rainy south-west France. The sun, which a few days ago was too hot to bear, has left us. On the balcony above the river is a slug, pearly nude, shaped like a dog's dick. I drop it into the river and smoke a cigarette. I am seriously tired. I was supposed to have written this piece yesterday, but couldn't find a way. Got to bed at 3.30 am, and lay, unable to sleep. How many words have I written about Bhopal? Over the last sixteen years, it must be hundreds of thousands. Fifteen hundred more needed by 10:30, three hours away, but where to begin this long story of suffering, greed and betrayal? With what words? And anyway, what is the use of words if in the end the powerful can do as they please?"
("The Evening Language of the Poor", *Tehelka*, 2010)

I really didn't want to write that piece. It raised questions I would rather not face.

Speech and writing are our most civilised tools for social and political action. This is why we cherish free speech and democracy, why we have parliaments, debates, laws, a universal declaration of human rights, and courts to hear evidence and arguments. But when free speech is stifled, laws are emasculated, justice is denied and writers censored or bullied into silence, what then? What happens when words fail?

In 2008, Vickie and I had dinner in Delhi with my old classmate Pradip Krishen, and his wife Arundhati Roy. We talked about Pradip's much-praised book *Trees of Delhi* and about Arundhati's work with the anti-dam campaign which after years of struggle was unable to prevent hundreds of thousands of tribal people being forced off their land. We talked about central India, where tribals are brutalised and driven out so their forests can be handed over to mining corporations and steel-makers, and where the failure of laws, media and politicians to protect people has bred a full-scale Maoist insurrection.

"I am angry," Arundhati said. "So angry."

In a 2009 piece, *Walking With the Comrades*, Arundhati talked about the weeks she spent in the jungle with the Maoists. There came a moment when the guerillas slipped off the safety catches on their AK47s.

"Do you know what to do if we come under fire?" one asked.

"Yes. Immediately declare an indefinite hunger strike."

When I read this I laughed and laughed. But how it hurt.

Laughter is like fire. It cleans. This piece, like the ads I've written about human rights and the poor, has a rather solemn, even pious tone. I really don't like it and I apologise. When, in my novel *Animal's People*, I treated the same cruel subjects the words crumbled to black comic dust because the speech of the poor is full of laughter. We laugh when we recognise truth. We laugh when there is nothing else we can do.

Next spread
Client: Metropolitan Police
Agency: Collett
Dickenson Pearce
Year. 1989

My introduction to writing
on important social issues.

One of the most beautiful novels I have read is John Berger's
A to X. In it he says:

"*To tell the truth? Words tortured until they give themselves up
to their polar opposites: Democracy, Freedom, Progress, when
returned to their cells, are incoherent. And then there are other
words, Imperialism, Capitalism, Slavery, which are refused entry,
are turned back at every frontier point, and their confiscated
papers given to impostors such as Globalisation, Free Market,
Natural Order.*

*Solution: the evening language of the poor. With this some truths
can be told and held.*"

It's important that we hear and hold these truths, because
for writers who have lost hope in justice but won't give in
to despair, the job now is to find words powerful enough
to stop bullets.

COULD YOU TURN

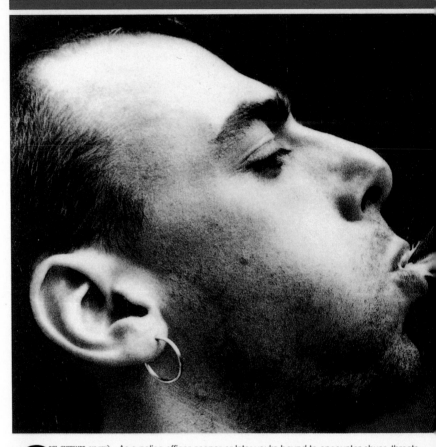

As a police officer, sooner or later you're bound to encounter abuse, threats, provocation, even physical violence. Be careful how you respond. Lose your temper and you could lose your job. **Photograph by Don McCullin**

COOL CUSTOMER, are you? Okay, let's see how far you can get before you blow your stack.

You are walking down a street. Some youths start jeering at you: "'Ello, 'ello, 'ello." Smile. You've heard it all before, every name a copper can be called: rozzer, old bill, pig, fuzz, peeler, flatfoot, the filth. And some less complimentary. Shrug it off.

You're out in the patrol car when you see a car without lights weaving through the traffic. You flash your headlights at him to stop. Instead, he accelerates away.

Siren on. Ahead your target, still without lights, narrowly misses a woman on a pedestrian crossing and then goes the wrong way round a roundabout, while a youth leaning out of the passenger window showers you with empty beer cans and two-finger salutes.

The car skids round another corner

and slides into a brick wall, but the youths inside are out and running. You chase, abandoning your car with its engine still on and door left wide open. As you grab the driver, he mouths obscenities at you.

"You can't go on the attack, whatever the provocation."

Still in control of your temper? Okay, try this.

A demonstration is turning into a riot. You're bussed in, nervous and not sure what to expect. It's frightening. The crowd, in ugly mood, surges against the frail police line.

Suddenly a lone voice calls your number "EF203, EF203." The others take

it up. "EF203, EF203." They're all staring at you, trying to psyche you out. Why you?

It gets worse. Bottles arc down and burst in showers of flame. Stones and half bricks drop out of the air and threaten to brain you. You cannot leave the line.

At last the crowd starts drifting away. As the tension ebbs, you see a man step forward and deliberately stub out his cigarette on the flank of a police horse.

This all sounds a bit melodramatic, but we've made none of it up. Each of the details we've described really happened.

How would you have reacted?

Strangely, people often find that in a real emergency they stay calm. But stress builds up in the body like static and can earth itself without warning.

Three days after a riot like the one

above you may arrest a well dressed drunk. "Look here," he drawls, "do you realise who you're talking to?" And jabs you in the chest.

Careful. This trivial annoyance may become the lightning rod for all that pent up stress and rage.

If, in any of the situations we have described above, you were to lose your temper, you might also lose your job.

It doesn't seem fair, does it? But then being a police officer is no ordinary job. As someone sworn to uphold the law, you of all people cannot break it.

And the law says that you may use no more than reasonable force. You can't go on the attack. No matter what the provocation.

So what should you do? Should you say: "Are you going to come quietly or do

HE OTHER CHEEK?

I have to use earplugs?" In fact, a bit of humour can often defuse a potentially ugly situation. As can tact, restraint and good common sense.

Of course, it's a strain being on best behaviour 24 hours a day. Never switching off. With the very highest standards to set and live up to. Sometimes, all that bottled up stress can make us difficult to live with.

An officer on motorway patrol raced to an accident. A car was on fire. The heat was ferocious. He had to watch, helpless, as a child the same age as his own daughter burned to death before his eyes.

When he got home, his wife produced supper. Without a word, he picked up his plate of food and flung it through the window. Until then he had kept control of his emotions. But that night of all nights he could not face a cooked meal.

As a police officer you will inevitably endure your share of unpleasantness and you'll have to evolve your own way of dealing with it.

But why are we dwelling on these traumatic subjects? Isn't this supposed to be a recruitment advertisement? Are we trying to put you off?

Actually, yes.

If you're put off by an advertisement, you'd never be able to cope with the reality.

"It gets worse. Bottles arc down and burst in showers of flame."

And we need people who can cope. People who are tough, tender, sensitive, strong and disciplined, all at the same time. They aren't easy to find. At present we take only one in five applicants. We'd rather look at fewer, better candidates.

Seeing you've got this far, we'll now admit that a career in the Met isn't all grief. Few jobs are as rewarding.

Ask the much loved Streatham home beat officer who, helmet under arm, cigar stuck firmly in mouth in flagrant disregard of regulations, can tell you the name of every child in his manor.

Ask the constable who, while patiently unravelling the intricacies of gang warfare in, of all places, Southall, has been invited to six Indian weddings in the last year.

Ask the sergeant who now runs what is virtually a Bengali advice centre in Whitechapel.

We can offer 28,000 more examples. If you don't believe us, stop any police officer in the street and ask.

When you've learned what they get out of the job, ask how they got in.

They'll tell you about our twenty week basic training course at Hendon. And life on the beat at one of London's 187 police stations where, under the tutelage of a sergeant, you will learn the art of handling people. And yourself.

Right now, your next step is to fill in and post the coupon below.

We're looking for mature, fit people aged between 18½ and 45, especially from the ethnic minorities. You should be at least 172cms tall if you're a man, 162cms if you're a woman.

Ideally, you'll have some 'O' level passes or their equivalents, but we value your personal qualities more.

To find out more please telephone: 01-725 4492 (Ansaphone: 01-725 4575) or fill in the coupon or write to: The Recruiting Officer, The Metropolitan Police Selection Centre, Department MD 960, Freepost, London W2 1BR.

Name

Address

Postcode   Age

Opposite
Novel: *Animal's People*
Publisher: Simon &
Schuster
Year: 2007

Next spread
Client: Amnesty
International
Agency: Collett
Dickenson Pearce
Year: 1990

Pages 486–487
Client: Campaign for
Justice in Bhopal
Agency: Freelance
Year: 2010

Impotent anger was
resolved in the novel
Animal's People by
laughing at tragedy
and refusing to take
it seriously.

Working for Amnesty
taught me the power,
and futility, of anger.

A personal response to
Dow's "Human Element"
campaign, which for me
embodies all that is worst
about advertising.

filled with such hatred, I think my skin will burst. Wicked are they beyond all limits, didn't I see the proof myself last night in the gardens of Jehannum? An animal isn't subject to the laws of men, I will slit their eyeballs, I will rip out their tongues with red hot pliers, I will shit in their mouths. Blood's shaking my heart, I'm giddy with rage. Then it's just as quickly gone, leaving me limp, body's like a goatskin filled with grief.

Nisha is speaking. 'Zafar my love, when grief and pain turn into anger, when rage is as useless as our tears, when those in power become blind, deaf and dumb in our presence and the world's forgotten us, what then should we do? You tell us to put away anger, choke back our bitterness, and be patient, in the hope that justice will one day win? We have already been waiting twenty years. And when the government that is supposed to protect us manipulates the law against us, of what use then is the law? Must we still obey it, while our opponents twist it to whatever they please? It's no longer anger, Zafar, but despair that whispers, if the law is useless, does it matter if we go outside it? What else is left?'

After this there is a long silence. No one is saying anything. No one can speak. At last comes Zafar's voice, sounding weary.

'Nothing is left.'

'And then?'

'What else? We fight. We carry on. We don't give up.'

'People do give up,' says Nisha. 'They give up when they've nothing left to give.' A private battle's still going on between them, something that must have started long before this day.

'There is always something left to give,' says Zafar.

'Zafar, my love, there's nothing left.'

Then Zafar says something beautiful. *Jahaañ jaan hai, jahaan hai.* While we have life, we have the world. These words send thrills up and down my crooked back, they make me want to weep. 'Wah wah,' I say, before I can stop myself.

'Who's there? Who's out there?'

So I am brought into the room.

"When our children were dying you did nothing to help. Now God help your children."

Iraqi Kurdish refugee

The Kurdish district of Garmyan in the mountains of north-eastern Iraq used to be a pretty place.

There were wheatfields and apricot orchards. The gardens grew melons and pomegranates and grapes. Most houses had a cow tethered outside.

One April morning in 1988, the mountainsides echoed to the drone of Iraqi bombers and the flat thud of chemical bombs.

A white cloud drifted among the apricot blossom. Whoever breathed it, died.

Later that day, a group of Kurdish guerrillas came across a procession of people, blistered and burned, stumbling silently from a stricken village.

Azad Abdulla was one of the guerrillas. "Can you imagine," he asks, "what it's like to die this way? If it's cyanide you get dizzy and choke. If it's mustard gas your skin blisters and your lungs begin to bleed and you drown in your own blood."

Abdulla laughed when we showed him a leaflet which tells Americans how to survive a chemical attack.

(It's reproduced here.)

light they would go and look for them. They thought it was night. They did not realise that they were blind.

Almost to the day (on April 12th 1988), Junior Foreign Office Minister David Mellor was forecasting that British industry would soon find "a large market in Iraq."

Was he unaware that Saddam Hussein was systematically gassing Iraq's Kurdish minority? Hardly.

Only three weeks earlier, more than 5,000 men, women and children had died horribly in an Iraqi poison gas attack on the Kurdish town of Halabja. The atrocity received worldwide TV and newspaper coverage.

"Bodies lie in the dirt streets or sprawled in rooms and courtyards of the deserted villas, preserved at the moment of death in a modern version of the disaster that struck Pompeii. A father died in the dust trying to protect his child from the white clouds of cyanide vapour. A mother lies

by side. In a cellar a family crouches together." (Washington Times, March 23rd 1988.)

The world was shocked. But not shocked enough to do anything effective. While the USA condemned Iraq's use of chemical weapons, calls for sterner action were resisted.

According to James Adams, Defence Correspondent of the Sunday Times, such western impotence must have acted as an incentive to President Saddam Hussein.

The world's inaction is a subject about which we at Amnesty International find it difficult to remain polite.

For years we have been exposing atrocities committed by the Iraqi government. Nothing effective has ever been done.

On 8th September 1988, five months after Halabja, Amnesty appealed directly to the United Nations Security Council to stop the

(After expressions of concern from another UN body in August 1990, we are still awaiting effective action.)

Saddam Hussein's annexation of

You, Margaret Thatcher, did nothing effective. You, George Bush, did nothing effective. You – yes you – reading this advertisement, did nothing effective.

Right now you have a choice. Get offended, or get involved.

This advertisement is an appeal for

```
TYPES OF GAS

A.  MUSTARD GAS
    -  TOXIC IRRITANT - BLISTERS ON SKIN,
       INFLAMMATIONS, ETC.
    -  MAKES YOUR LUNGS BLEED, SLOW DEATH.
    -  WATER SOLUBLE, WET TOWEL ON HEAD, STAY
       IN SHOWER.
    -  LASTS 1 TO 2 HOURS

B.  CYANIDE
    -  HIGHLY HEMOTOXIC.
    -  NO EXTERNAL INFLAMMATION, ETC.  WORKS
       INSIDE.
    -  LOSS OF CO-ORDINATION, DIZZINESS, DIFFICULTY
       BREATHING, PAIN.
    -  WATER SOLUBLE - SAME AS ABOVE.
    -  LASTS UP TO ONE HOUR

C.  NERVE GAS (VARIOUS TYPES)
    -  NEWROTOXIC
    -  QUICK ACTING.
    -  LOSS OF MOTOR CONTROL, SHAKING, BLURRED
       VISION, ETC.
    -  BEST FILTERED VIA ACTIVATED CHARCOAL
    -  WET CLOTH MASK MAY HELP.
    -  DISPERSES QUICKLY, LASTS 30 MIN MAX.

GOOD LUCK.
```

running shower.

But the Kurdish villagers had no such luxuries.

Instead, they had to evolve their own crude methods of coping with poison gas attacks.

They would retreat into a cave after having lit a fire at its mouth. They would climb to the tops of mountains. They would wet turbans and wrap them round their faces.

On that April morning there had been no time to take even these crude measures.

Azad Abdulla and his companions found a small boy and girl clinging to each other. While running away through a wheat field they had come under attack from an Iraqi helicopter and become separated from their parents. The parents had died but the children did not know this.

They kept saying that when it grew

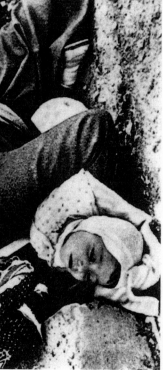

cradling her baby alongside a minibus that lies sideways across the road, hit while trying to flee. Yards away, a mother, father and daughter lie side

```
PREVENTIVE MEASURES:    CHEMICAL WARFARE

A.  YOU ARE OUTSIDE
    YOU WILL DIE.  DO NOTHING.

B.  YOU ARE INSIDE
    1) SEAL ALL AIR LEAKS, DRYER VENT, BATHROOM CEILING
       VENT, PET DOOR.
    2) TURN OFF A/C.  IT WILL ATOMIZE/CIRCULATE ANY GAS
       WHICH ENTERS.
    3) LOOK OUT YOUR WINDOWS:
       -- BIRDS DROPPING FROM TREES
       -- CATS/DOGS/PEOPLE DROPPING, CHOKING, ETC.
       -- CARS CRASHING
       -- GENERAL CHAOS
       -- VISIBLE FOG/MIST IN AIR
       ALL THESE ARE SYMPTOMS, WHEN YOU SEE THEM:
       -- BARRICADE DOORS/WINDOWS, LET NOBODY IN OR
          OUT OF THE HOUSE
       -- YOU CANNOT MAKE IT TO YOUR CAR, DON'T
          EVEN TRY.
    4) DRESS TO THE HILT, LONG SLEEVES, PANTS, SOCKS,
       GLOVES, SCARF, HAT. COVER YOUR ENTIRE HEAD WITH A WET TOWEL OR
       BLANKET.
```

massacre of Kurdish civilians by Iraq. Nothing effective was done.

A year after Halabja, we published a report detailing how an eyewitness saw a baby seized as a hostage and deliberately deprived of milk to force its parents to divulge information.

How children as young as 5 years old had been tortured in front of their families.

We revealed that at least thirty different forms of torture were in use in Iraqi prisons, ranging from beatings to burning, electric shocks and mutilation. Torturers had gouged out the eyes of their victims, cut off their noses, ears, breasts and penises, and axed limbs. Objects were inserted into the vaginas of young women, causing the hymen to break. Some of these methods had been used on children.

The report failed to move the United Nations Commission on Human Rights which, days after its publication, voted not to investigate human rights violations in Iraq.

Kuwait seems to have taken many people by surprise. Why?

Why be surprised by the savagery of the Iraqi regime that daily tortures and kills Kuwaiti citizens?

Why be surprised that westerners trapped by the invasion are now helpless hostages?

Why be surprised that it is now young Britons who face the chemical weapons that wiped out thousands of defenceless Kurdish villagers?

Yes, we told you so. In '80, '81, '82, '83, '84, '85, '86, '87, '88 and '89. And you did nothing effective to help.

now little Amnesty can do for the people trapped in Iraq and Kuwait, be they Kuwaitis, Westerners, Asians or the 4 million Iraqi Kurds who are also living in fear.

So why should you join us?

Because we failed with Iraq. Failed to make any impact on Saddam Hussein. Failed to stir the United Nations into doing anything effective. Failed to reach enough ordinary people, like you, who were willing to channel their outrage into constructive action.

God knows how many lives this failure will yet cost.

We have got to make it impossible in future for governments to ignore the genocide of helpless women and children. It must become morally unacceptable for governments to look at photographs of dead children from places like Halabja and then carry on 'business as usual' with their murderers.

That's why you should join us and, if you can afford it, make a donation to our campaign funds. (Small donations gratefully received. business-people please think big.)

'We were screaming till we could not speak' says Azad Abdulla, 'and yet no-one listened.' It's you he's talking to. If you can hear what he's saying, clip the coupon.

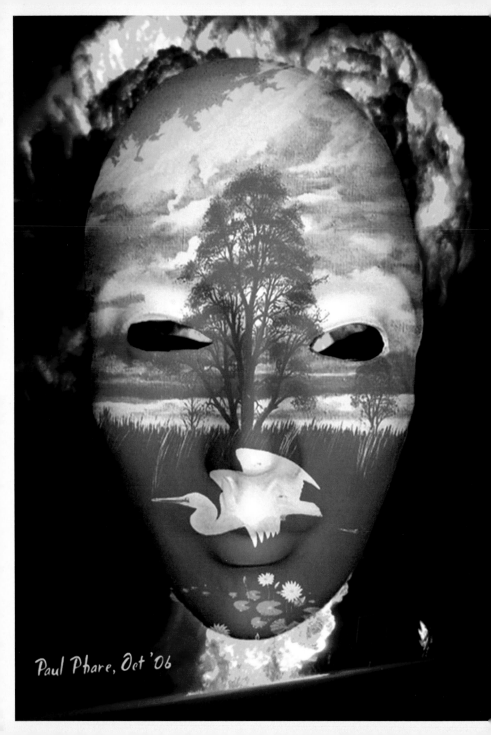

Paul Phare, Oct '06

A glimpse behind
the masks of Dow

Dow's 'Human Element' advertising campaign uses stunning photography and film to portray itself as a caring and benevolent company, but behind the beautiful masks is a world of horror, suffering and pain. This series of images is my personal response to Dow's campaign.

Dow made napalm for the Vietnam war. A US army person said, 'We sure are pleased with those backroom boys at Dow. The original product wasn't so hot - if the gooks were quick they could scrape it off. So the boys started adding polystyrene - now it sticks like shit to a blanket. But if the gooks jumped under water it stopped burning, so they started adding Willie Peter (white phosphorus) so's to make it burn better. And just one drop is enough, it'll keep burning right down to the bone so they die anyway from phosphorus poisoning.' A most inhuman element.

WWW.THETRUTHABOUTDOW.ORG

John Stingley

John Stingley's early career included stints at BBDO Minneapolis and Martin/Williams Minneapolis.

He next began a nearly eight-year stay at Fallon McElligott where he created advertising for a number of the agency's blue-chip clients including Porsche. He moved to Chiat\Day Los Angeles as creative director to relaunch the Nissan Infiniti brand.

He then moved east to New York and became a creative director at Ammirati & Puris and then a senior partner/creative director at Ogilvy & Mather, before starting his own company, The Observatory. Designed to go beyond traditional branding and creative solutions, The Observatory concept is to bring together elite creative talent from various disciplines and backgrounds in order to use all the unique communication avenues available today.

I like to say that my work has spanned the gamut from Spam to Porsche. The ultimate expression of range, almost anyone would agree.

As with acting, range is the most important characteristic for an advertising writer if one is to be prolific. This is assuming raw talent. But many writers with raw talent have created one or two good campaigns for products that are near and dear to them, then disappeared.

In many ways, then, creating advertising actually is the same discipline as acting. You must start by mentally discarding your own identity. You have to become the people you are communicating with. Internalise their interests, joys, fears, tastes, even biases. Often it means mentally and emotionally becoming someone you would never in a million years be like yourself.

I think that's why virtually every great advertising creative I've met is a student of humanity; interested in every trend or personality type or culture they've ever been exposed to. They are fascinated by the "human condition". They are incessant people-watchers. And while they often get a reputation for being spoiled prima donnas who refuse to bend or compromise, that is usually because they are defending this very need for uniqueness; the need to break through the homogeneity of modern life and speak in a powerful and distinct way to one pocket of humanity, creating a powerful and distinct identity for a brand by doing so.

This need is often shunned or even resisted by clients who want to be everything to everybody. After all, it's the nature of the corporate world to try and fit in. In a Porsche commercial, I once likened the committee thinking of corporations to a flock of small birds, huddling in a tree "seeking safety in numbers".

This leads to another key aspect of the creative process. Just as you must "become" your prospect in order to create a message that will be meaningful to them, you must "become" your client if you expect to sell them on the idea. This is the process many creatives fail at. They feel cheap if they attempt to "play the corporate game". In reality, your client is a consumer just like those for whom you created the advertising. You must understand their beliefs, fears and prejudices. This doesn't mean that you become political; it simply means that just as you must learn to speak the language of your prospect, you must learn to speak the language of your client to make them understand your thinking. Of course, you can't do great advertising for a bad client. Some companies are so overwrought with fear and the desire for safety that they will never buy a truly breakthrough way of presenting their product. At the same time, a lot of the greatest advertising ever written is collecting dust in file cabinets because the creatives didn't think through how to communicate the idea to their client in a fashion that would overcome any reservations they might have.

This is what makes advertising so tricky to practise, yet at the same time so rewarding. Advertising is a bridge between the worlds of art and business. It must entertain, intrigue and emotionally move people if you are going to get their attention, yet it must fulfil very basic marketing needs. Those creatives who learn how to cross back and forth between those two worlds are the ones who not only create good work but see it produced.

With these basic tenets in mind for preparing to create great advertising and preparing to sell it, some of the caveats or practices I have found valuable would be:

— Pay careful attention to your first ideas. They are formed with the same innocence, naiveté and lack of jadedness that consumers have when first exposed to your advertising. There is value in that innocence and simplicity.

— On the other hand, don't stop too soon. Even if the essence of your first ideas is correct, explore every possible expression of that essence. Write every headline 100 different ways. Advertising is art, and like poetry, every comma will affect the balance of meaning.

— Understand what the perceptions of your product are now. The current attitude of the consumer is the starting-point, and the desired attitude is the finish line. Often, clients are reticent to admit what the current attitude towards them is. You have to make them understand. You can't start a race in the middle.

— Once you have placed yourself in the mind-set of the consumer, relax and be human. Don't be afraid to think cynical thoughts or joke about the product as you work. I've found that a lot of great ideas started as jokes which, when explored, could be turned around to make a powerful, positive statement. Ideas that start this way have an honesty the consumer appreciates.

— Don't just accept cultural change, embrace it and try to understand what leads to it. Advertising is a living chronicle of the evolution of society.

— Resist developing a style. You're trying to speak with people on their own terms.

The basic motivations of people never really change. That's why Shakespeare is still relevant today. Human history pretty much boils down to the influence of love, hate, sex, greed, hunger and insecurity. If you want to write great advertising, always go back to the basics.

———

UPDATE: Since the original edition of this book, society has hurtled forward. Changes that used to take a decade now take a year… or less. The most obvious factor has been the Internet, which has given new meaning to the term "small world". People everywhere are connected to each other. Instantly. Nothing can be hidden from the public for long. Not by companies, or governments.

Without question it has changed the advertising and branding business forever. Still, I am amazed at the people in our business who see it as the end. In fact, it just opens incredible new opportunities. Anything can be a medium. At The Observatory, we developed a launch for a client where the whole thing was built around a piece of installation art… the concept of which supported the brand message. The work and reputation of the artist also supported that message. A website became the "gathering place" for supporters… then we used a teaser campaign of traditional and guerrilla media to create buzz and draw people to the website. Events were developed which would allow people to become involved in the art installation and actually sign pieces of it.

Agencies don't tend to think this way. They had better learn to.

I like to refer to The Observatory as a creative skunkworks, where anything that involves creative content can be pursued. We're developing everything from documentaries to new website concepts.

So, as technology keeps changing the way people live almost daily, are there any tenets going forward that will help in developing great brands and communications?

The few that come to mind:

— Honesty, which has always led to the most powerful advertising, is more important than ever. People today can smell manipulation a mile away. They've seen it all.

— Open your mind. The big idea that represents the brand is still the foundation, but be equally as creative in how you deliver it. Anything can be a medium.

— And yet, don't get caught up in the technology. Don't do something just because you can. Figure out where and how your prospects live, then find the best tools out there today to connect with them.

— Make everything work together. Too many websites, email campaigns, etc. seem to have nothing to do with the overall brand communication. What a waste.

— Help your clients understand the need to be socially responsible. Caring about more than profits is going to be more and more expected of companies. Nearly 90% of people now call themselves conscious consumers, and they're making that known with their pocketbooks.

Opposite
Client: Prince
Spaghetti Sauce
Agency: Fallon
McElligott Rice
Year: 1986

Pages 494–497
Client: Porsche Cars
of North America
Agency: Fallon McElligott
Year: 1991

I guess the simple message is, don't resist change. Have fun with it. Let it work for you. But at the same time, never let it get in the way of the basics. People themselves never really change. That is humanity's sad truth… but it is also humanity's charm. And it is what will keep this business going as long as civilisation does.

Original.   Chunky.

When we make Prince Spaghetti Sauce, we give you a choice. Because no two people have quite the same taste.

There are some things in life that simply defy explanation to those who have not shared the experience. Such has always been our dilemma at Porsche.

In 1948, in the image of his own dream, Professor F. Porsche created a sports car so responsive and with such an individualistic personality it was almost alive; an extension of the driver's own thoughts and feelings; childlike in its unbridled spirit. For two generations we have sought to explain the sensation. And have always found ourselves saying, simply, you have to try it.

The 1991 Porsche 911 Carrera 4 is part of the current generation in this legendary, mystical family.

To test-drive the Carrera 4 is to discover a relationship between yourself and a car we can but feebly try to express here. Race-bred components are intricately matched to make it seem almost as if it were an extension of your own limbs.

It is this tactile sense of direct contact and control that has been the hallmark of every Porsche. Today, the Carrera 4 uses electronically controlled all-wheel drive to bring the feeling to an unprecedented peak.

Combining sensors and a sophisticated computer, the Carrera 4 monitors traction at each wheel with every revolution. Upon detecting any spin, within 25 thousandths of a second it directs power to the wheels having

It's like
You can't understan

more grip, correcting slip usually before the driver is even aware of it. Not only does it put more of the car's incredible potential to the ground, but it makes it more useable and predictable.

The all-wheel drive system works together with a new suspension, including a self-correcting design in the rear, to make cornering a startling display of synergy between car and driver.

Every facet of the car contributes to this character. Porsche engineers, for example, say the ideal brakes should make it feel as if you are squeezing the brake discs between your fingertips. Engage the massive, internally vented ABS disc brakes in the Carrera 4, and you'll sense time momentarily freeze as you are hauled to a rock-solid, straight-line standstill.

The fact is, it's ludicrous of us to try and explain the experience further.

In over 40 years, we have yet to find a way to do so. All we can say is, if you are the type who looks for joy and stimulation where others see only one of life's necessities, you will no doubt visit your authorized Porsche dealer for a test-drive. Then we'll be able to talk.

hildren.
until you've had one.

It's what happens when eng
but have to drive on twist

The new Porsche 968. It is the latest vision to come down from Porsche's legendary development center, perched high on a hill overlooking the ancient village of Weissach. And, like each and every Porsche which has rolled down this hill before it, it is a dichotomy.

On one hand, it possesses racebred components and performance historically found in only a smattering of exotic sports cars. Yet, Professor Porsche has always insisted that no car which bore his name be an impractical toy, but rather, durable, everyday transportation.

From the earliest days, while other sports car owners would truck their cars to weekend races, Porsche owners would drive their cars hundreds of miles, win the race, then drive home and to work on Monday. It was this melding of performance and function that set Porsche apart and created a mystique. A melding unduplicated by any other car to this day. And a melding which makes the 968 the inheritor of a unique place in the automotive world.

Like its forebears the 968 is, at once, futuristic yet classic. Keeping the best of what has come before; combining it with forward-thinking technology and design.

Brimming with the results of 15 new patents, the 968 is a study in what is now possible. Realizing a sports car today must

Porsche 968

eers work in an ivory tower
arrow roads to get there.

take resources, the environment and daily function into account, the 968 breaks new ground. Throughout the car, features that improve performance are designed to simultaneously improve efficiency.

Employing our patented new Porsche VarioCam,™ fuel combustion is made far more precise and thorough. This improves throttle response, power and torque, while at the same time dramatically lowering emissions.*

A stunning new catalytic converter uses thin, rare metal inner walls, speeding air flow for more power while also reducing emissions. Porsche's renowned transaxle platform with near-perfect 50-50 weight balance has been further buttressed for the added performance. Yet detail changes have actually increased comfort. And in the belief that performance must be mated with equivalent safety, only Porsche makes both driver and passenger front airbags standard on every model.

As a Porsche engineer will tell you, "If you only make a car for a few years, you are always starting over." This is why a new Porsche comes along far more seldom than typical cars. And evolves out of all those which came before. It's also why we can't begin to describe all the developments in the 968 in the space we have here.

Call 1-800-252-4444 for more information, or to arrange a personal viewing at your authorized Porsche dealership. The 968 may have been born in an ivory tower. But it's built to live in the real world.

ext evolution.

Luke Sullivan

Luke Sullivan is an acclaimed author and copywriter with a 32-year track record. His CV includes ten years at Fallon, five at The Martin Agency, and ten at GSD&M in Austin. He has more than 20 medals to his credit in the One Show.

A self-described "ad geek", Luke Sullivan is the author of the best-selling book *Hey Whipple, Squeeze This: A Guide to Creating Great Advertising*. The book was ranked by Advertising Age readers at #5 on the list of top 10 media and marketing books of all time.

Luke is now chair of the advertising department at the Savannah College of Art and Design. He reports that he "enjoys the indoors" and likes to spend a lot of his time there.

In praise of the humble print ad.

It is no longer as fashionable as it once was to be able to write a great print ad. A print ad, well, it just isn't as cool as it once was.

A print ad is not interactive and it doesn't link to other print ads. To create a print ad, you don't have to go to LA or Cape Town. It usually ends its short life under a puppy, and print ads are almost never featured on YouTube. Yet in its bare two dimensions, the humble print ad contains all the challenges of the entire creative process.

In fact, when I am looking for talent to hire, I find the most telling pieces in their portfolios are the print ads.

There's nowhere to hide in a print ad. The idea is right there on the surface or it isn't. There's no music to tell me how to feel; no loading bar to tell me the clever bit is about to happen.

You are reading a book that is still devoted (I presume) to print ads. If this edition is anything like the last, it is fairly bursting with good advice from great writers on their creative process. So I'll limit my remarks today to just this: If you are a student or just starting out in this business, I encourage you to learn (before you learn *anything* else) how to write a great print ad.

It is the molecular building block of the advertising universe.

Where does Calvin Klein stand on the use of fur?

Whether trapped or ranched, every year millions of animals, including minks and beavers, are gassed, electrocuted, or stomped to death by the fur industry for fashion's sake. Join us and help send the message to Calvin Klein that fur is not a fabric. Call People for the Ethical Treatment of Animals at 301-770-PETA, or write P.O. Box 42516, Washington, DC 20015.

PeTA

Client: Lee jeans
Agency: Fallon McElligott
Art Director: Arty Tan
Year: 1991

A trade ad for Lee jeans
with no headline and no
logo. Still my favorite, even
after all these years.

Previous page
Client: PETA
Agency: Fallon McElligott
Art Director: Joe Paprocki
Year: 1993

I love Paul Fishlock's ad:
"Here's a dead dog.
Where's my award?"
He had a point. So we
used a fox.

Next spread
Client: Successful Farming
Agency: The Martin
Agency
Art Director: Cabell Harris
Year: 1985

Trade ad for a magazine
called *Successful Farming*.
Fairly counter-intuitive
strategy, telling ad buyers
its readers were broke.

WARNING

This changing booth may be monitored by store personnel to prevent theft, particularly theft of Lee jeans, the #1 brand of women, something that would really cheese off our store buyers, especially now that Lee has lowered their wholesale prices and the store stands to rake in some serious profit.

FOR 4 MONTHS THE WEATHER MAKES DURING THE OTHER 8,

UT OF THE YEAR,
ARMING IMPOSSIBLE.
E GOVERNMENT DOES.

Imagine what it would be like if the weather kept you from buying media for four months out of every year.

Then imagine that during the other eight, your hands were tied. Tied while trade deficits, tight money, and foreign policy dictated how you'd buy your media.

Essentially, that's what running a farm is like these days.

Given all that, wouldn't you look for the best advice you could find? Sure you would.

That's why so many farmers read Successful Farming® every month. Successful Farming ties together the total farm operation. Not with long-winded feature articles, but with concise, informative how-to articles on contemporary management practices.

They also read the ads as proved by the high Chilton readership scores. Which is great for our advertisers, considering that our magazine reaches the high-income farmers responsible for 85% of all production expenses in America.

Which is why if you have a product that can help today's farmers make a better living off the land, there's no better place to tell them about it than Successful Farming.

For more information, contact your nearest Successful Farm-ing sales executive. Or call Gil Spears, collect, at 515-284-3118. Successful Farming. Meredith Corporation, Locust at Seventeenth. Des Moines, Iowa 50336.

Hey, fathead. Do you find most advertising insulting?

Ring around the collar? The Doublemint twins? Clearly there's room in the field of advertising for some intelligent and creative thinkers. And the best way to break into it is with a smart portfolio. After 8 semesters, you'll have a good book and a good shot at getting into a field that's both creatively and financially rewarding.

ArtCenter

Classes begin spring, summer and fall. Call 818-584-5035. Or write to Admissions, Art Center College of Design, 1700 Lida St., Pasadena, CA, 91103.

Client: ArtCenter
Agency: Fallon McElligott
Art Director: Joe Paprocki
Year: 1994

Ad promoting ArtCenter's advertising program. Having no budget can force you to solve a problem using only words.

Opposite
Client: ArtCenter
Agency: Fallon McElligott
Year: 1994

Ad promoting ArtCenter's advertising program. Photographer Rick Dublin originally shot the picture for another client. We just asked to borrow the image for ours.

Next spread
Client: Mercury Marine
Agency: Fallon McElligott
Art Director: Bobby Appleby
Year: 1997

We found this guy a couple of hours before the shoot, working at a diner. He was way better than the actor we'd already cast for the shot.

Get paid to think up stuff like this.

DOESN'T SMOKE ANYMORE. DRINKS

Direct fuel injection gives the new OptiMax™ 45% better fuel-efficiency. It's n

5% LESS. THE ENGINE, WE MEAN.

ust a new engine. It's a new level. For information, call 1-800-MERCURY.

Tom Thomas

Tom Thomas started working on the client side writing copy for a toilets manufacturer, so no matter how bad agency life got, he would forever be able to remember worse.

He later worked at Scali, McCabe, Sloves; Young & Rubicam; Needham, Harper & Steers; and Ammirati & Puris. (Three of these agencies no longer exist, and the fourth is now unrecognisable.) In 1985, he started Angotti, Thomas, Hedge, which went from zero to over $100 million in billings in seven years. (It too no longer exists.) He has won many awards, including 27 One Show Pencils, and served as vice president of the One Club.

From all this he has drawn one obvious conclusion: people and agencies follow story arcs that often end badly. But certain best practices outlive them, and for good reasons, some of which he has outlined here.

Except for the client, the agency and the copywriter's significant other, no one is under any obligation to read anyone's ad (and don't be too sure about the significant other, either).

So it's not surprising that much advertising is driven by this modest insight, which is true as far as it goes. The problem is that it doesn't go far enough. The hurdle every ad faces isn't simply getting noticed but getting believed. An ad enters a reader's life like a sullen, shifty-eyed suspect in a police line-up, and there's no presumption of innocence to protect it. The presumption is more likely to be that it's lying, and it will be led off in handcuffs unless it can prove otherwise.

What can an ad do to overcome that bias? Some thoughts:

1. Demonstrate greater insight into the needs of the audience.

People who better understand your needs (a category that includes spouses and shrinks) are seen as better able to meet them. The same for ads. *This ad knows me*, the reader feels, *I can trust it a little bit*. That helps dispel the wariness that buyers feel towards sellers, who often can't be trusted even a little bit. An ad for Xerox information retrieval systems used an obscure provision of Murphy's Law to show an understanding of the problem its target audience faced. It pictured someone in an office with a phone planted in his ear, hearing the bad news: "We've tracked down the information you've been looking for, sir. It's definitely lost."

2. Since facts are more believable than claims, it's better to express claims as facts.

In advertising, *claim* is often a euphemism for *lie*. Many of these euphemised lies are specially constructed to wiggle past lawyers and network censors. You can't say your peanut butter has more peanuts, not without a notarised peanut count, but you can say someone will be a better mother if she serves it. At your arraignment all you have to do is plead Puffery. All charges are dropped. Puffery forgives everything. To lawyers and censors, it's okay to lie as long as you lie on a grand enough scale. To everyone else, a lie is still a lie, and it's almost always transparent. That's why, instead of just asserting that BMW was a good investment, a BMW ad used the car's high resale value to prove the point. And it did so, not by comparing the car to other cars but to other investments people in that target audience might make: "Last year a car outperformed 318 stocks on the New York Stock Exchange."

3. Give the reader permission to believe.

Despite universal cynicism towards salesmen in general and ads in particular, there's a part of us that really wants to believe we'll have more and better sex if we use a certain aftershave or hair conditioner. Unfortunately that part is patrolled by a beefy armed guard who can easily wrestle inanities like this to the ground. What our beefy armed guard needs is enough supporting logic to accept your premise and not look like an idiot. DDB's advertising for Avis didn't just say Avis tried harder; it said when you're only number two you have to — or else.

4. Make it illogical for the reader not to believe.

A corollary to point three. There's a line from Coleridge that goes: "Nothing can permanently please which does not contain within itself the reason why it is so, and not otherwise." The Avis premise, evoking a world where little fish swim faster or get swallowed by bigger fish, met that standard. So did a Volkswagen billboard that showed the car's hood opened onto its rear, air-cooled engine. "No radiator problems. No radiator," read the irrefutable headline.

5. Be the smartest choice in your category.

This notion crops up on every other creative brief these days. It's your basic, all-purpose, 21st-century strategy, although it's lying about its age; advertisers were using it when buyers paid in seashells. It works because everyone wants to be seen as having done something intelligent when he buys a product, or at least not having done something dumb, buyer's remorse being timeless and universal. That's why the Saab 9000 was positioned as "The sports sedan for people who inherited brains instead of wealth."

6. Create an aspiration to buy.

If you have a pulse, you have aspirations. And if a product embodies your aspirations, its advertising doesn't need to be a salesman any more. It can be an alluring inner voice whispering encouragement to act on those urges. For Wild Turkey, the premium entry in the bourbon category, that meant reminding its audience that anything less was foolish economy and self-denial: "There are less expensive bourbons. There are also thinner steaks and smaller cars."

In short, an ad is, by definition, a half-truth; it only argues the case *for* the product. The case *against* will cheerfully be provided by the competition, and will be helped along by the healthy cynicism a reader brings to every ad. Which means if he only believes half of what you say your half-truth is reduced to something like a quarter-truth, and you've come perilously close to the point where it's not worth bothering any more.

If there's a simple principle that sums all this up — and there isn't, but here goes anyway — it's that people who write ads should assume readers are at least as bright as they are. This has the advantage of being true much, maybe most, of the time. It also makes for honest writers — and credible ads.

Client: Wild Turkey
Bourbon
Agency: Angotti,
Thomas, Hedge
Year: 1987

LAST YEAR, A CAR OUT-PERFORMED 318 STOCKS ON THE NEW YORK STOCK EXCHANGE.

If you'd bought a new BMW 320i in the beginning of 1980, and sold it at the end, your investment would have retained 92.9% of its original value.
If you'd done the same with any of 318 NYSE stocks, you'd have done less well.
And you'd have forfeited an important daily dividend:
The unfluctuating joy of driving one of the world's great performance sedans.

THE ULTIMATE DRIVING MACHINE.
BMW MUNICH GERMANY

*Based on average retail price according to January 1981 NADA Used Car Guide. Your selling price may vary according to the condition of your car and whether you sell it privately or to a dealer. © 1981 BMW of North America, Inc. The BMW trademark and logo are registered trademarks of Bayerische Motoren Werke, A.G.

Client: BMW of North America
Agency: Ammirati & Puris
Year: 1981

Opposite
Client: Xerox
Agency: Needham, Harper & Steers
Year: 1977

Next spread
Client: Saab Cars USA
Agency: Angotti, Thomas, Hedge
Year: 1991

XEROX® is a trademark of XEROX CORPORATION.

"We've tracked down the information you've been looking for, sir. It's definitely lost."

Of all the pieces of information that might get lost, the one that does will probably be the one you need.

Of all the times it might turn up missing, the time it does will be the worst possible time.

These Axioms of Business Life are brought to you by Xerox. For the purpose of adding our own:

Of all the ways to deal with the problem of lost information, the best is to prevent it from getting lost in the first place.

Which is why we offer electronic typing systems that let you store and retrieve documents as they're typed.

Computer services that let you retrieve information with the efficiency of a computer, but without having to own the computer.

Even telecopier transceivers that let you send copies of documents cross-country without ever having the original leave the office.

At Xerox, our interest in all this is simple. Our business is helping businesses manage information.

Which brings us to our final axiom: You have to find it before you can manage it.

There are basically two ways to approach the purchase of a sports sedan. You can spend your way into one, or you can think your way there.

For those who'd rather think than spend, there's the Saab 9000S.

The 9000S is the sports sedan that brings something rare to the category: a complete car.

First, it's a driver's car, engineered for those who take driving seriously

The Saab 900 Series:
From $18,295 to $33,295.*

The Saab 9000 Series:
From $22,895 to $33,995.*

For more information,
call 1-800-582-SAAB.

and do it well. It's propelled by the largest engine Saab ever built and a highly tactile steering system.

But unlike some driver's cars, the 9000S doesn't shortchange passengers. It's the only import roomy enough to be rated a "Large" car by the EPA.

Nor does it yield to a station wagon in its practicality. Fold down the split rear seats, and there's enough cargo space (56.5 cubic feet) to fit a six-

THE SPORTS SEDAN FOR PEOPLE WHO INHERITED BRAINS INSTEAD OF WEALTH.

foot sofa, with a hatchback for easy loading.

In fact, you could buy a 9000S for its utility alone, but then you'd have to ignore its full complement of standard amenities. Including leather upholstery, electric sunroof, heated seats, a driver's-side air bag and anti-lock brakes.

All this comes in a car that, according to studies by the Highway Loss Data Institute (HLDI), ranks among the safest cars in its class. And is backed by one of the longest warranties

in its class: 6 years or 80,000 miles.**

No $26,995* sports sedan can offer all that.

So if you've in fact inherited brains instead of wealth, the best place to spend that inheritance is at your Saab dealer, where the 9000S awaits your test drive.

SAAB

WE DON'T MAKE COMPROMISES. WE MAKE SAABS.™

Dave Trott

Dave Trott was born in London, got a degree from Pratt Institute in New York, then trained mainly at Carl Ally on Madison Avenue. He came back to London in 1970 and got a job at BMP where he worked with John Webster.

In 1980 he started Gold Greenlees Trott. Campaign voted GGT "Agency of the Year" and New York's *Advertising Age* voted it "Most Creative Agency in the World". GGT did campaigns like "Aristonandonandon", "You Can Break A Brolly But You Can't Knacker A Knirps", "Does You Does Or Does You Don't Take Access", Lurpak Butterman and Holsten Pils.

He's proudest of the work he's done on Anti Third World Debt advertising, with people like Gordon Smith and Paul Arden. They've produced and run dozens of ads absolutely free, with no client. Films that have been seen around the world, such as "Toilet", "Concentration Camp" and "Naked Shit".

I was always taught, 5% of people who turn to your page read the headline.

And 5% of the people who read the headline, read the copy.

If that's true, the copy is 5% of 5% of the ad.

In which case, who are we writing the copy for?

Opposite
Client: Victory-V
Agency: BMP
Year: 1977

Next spread
Client: Pepsi
Agency: BMP
Year: 1976

Lipsmackinth
acetastinmoti
buzzincooltal
fastlivinevergi

irstquenchin
vatingood
inhighwalkin
vincoolfizzin...

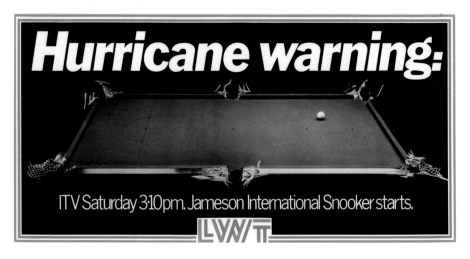

Client: LWT
Agency: GGT
Years: 1985–1988

Client: Toshiba
Agency: GGT
Year: 1986

Mary Wear

With a degree in English and Philosophy and an almost completed copywriting course, Mary Wear started on no salary at FCB in 1984.

She went on to work at Gold Greenlees Trott, Saatchi & Saatchi and AMV before going freelance and moving to the country with far more children and animals than is strictly sensible.

She has won lots of awards on fun things like London Transport, British Airways, Yellow Pages, Famous Grouse, Tampax, Walkers Crisps and Maltesers. And lots more on serious things like road safety, the RSPCA and anti-smoking.

Her best moment was hearing Nelson Mandela asking the world to Make Poverty History after he was released from jail.

Because she'd written the line, not because he'd been released.

Although it was great about the jail thing too.

Some (until now) unwritten rules I set myself:

1. Know when to shut up. The best copywriting isn't always in the lines. It's also between them.

2. Know there's always a fresh way to tell an old, old story. Stand-up comedians are brilliant at this, taking the most mundane subject — life — and retelling it in ways that make us laugh, wonder and think.

3. Know your target audience. Not intellectually, but intuitively. Think like them, empathise with them, identify with them. Because at some level, the reader needs to like the writer.

4. Know that we are all creative creatures. Everyone enjoys the quirks and whimsy of creativity. You don't have to logic people into a corner, you can charm them into wanting to come out and play.

5. Clive James said that humour is common sense dancing. Following the great advertising tradition of "borrowing" from someone much cleverer, I would say that copywriting is persuasion dancing. So if it doesn't dance, go back and do it again until it does.

Opposite
Client: London Transport
Agency: FCB
Year: 1986

Three words. Always been my favourite number for a line.

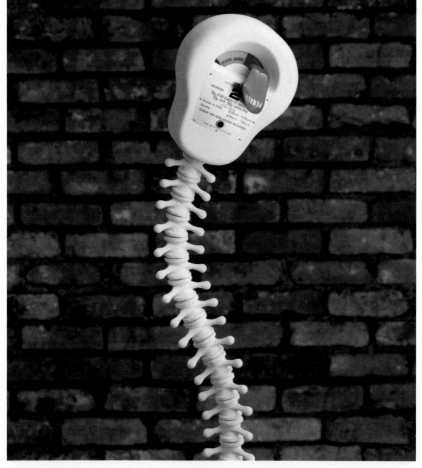

STARVE A METER.

UNDERGROUND

Client: Richard Curtis
Agency: AMV
Year: 2005

OK, technically not an ad.
But it was a phrase that
became known world-
wide, was quoted by
world leaders, led a truly
noble movement and was
only three words. What's
not to love?

Next spread
Client: Health Education
Authority
Agency: AMV BBDO
Year: 1998

My favourite poster
campaign. On the tube
every day, I saw women
stopping to read them.
At rush hour. Now, that
is a thrill.

**Clinically proven
to give you
grottier looking skin.**
There's certainly one
product that guarantees
fast, effective results
when it comes to skincare.
Every cigarette contains
special active ingredients
called "toxins" that
constrict blood vessels,
starve your skin of oxygen
and remove the lingering
traces of a healthy
complexion. In fact, the
only thing glowing
about your face will be
the cigarette end.
Quitline 0800 002200

Worried about dark
shadows?
Unhealthy complexion?
Fading looks?
On a pack a day
you certainly should be.
We'd like to reassure you
that you're just being
paranoid. Your skin, despite
the 4000 toxins in
every cigarette you smoke,
is still dewy and radiant.
Your eyes, despite the
poisonous effect of smoke,
are still clear and bright.
We'd like to reassure you,
but we can't.
Be afraid. Be very afraid.
Quitline 0800 002200

Client: Tampax
Agency: AMV BBDO
Year: 1996

Lots of copy aimed at
13–15 year olds. You don't
have to patronise to talk
to 13-year-old girls. You
can actually have a laugh.

Dan
Wieden

Dan Wieden grew up in Portland and worked briefly in public relations before trying his hand at copywriting.

In 1982 he was working at a local agency with his partner David Kennedy on a regional sneaker account. When the agency-client relationship began to sour, they moved to open their own shop, taking the upstart company Nike with them. Soon after, their only client introduced himself, announcing, "I'm Phil Knight. And I don't believe in advertising." So Dan and David set about making some of the greatest advertising that "doesn't believe in advertising" ever made.

Wieden+Kennedy has since grown to be a global brand in its own right, working on projects as varied as branding international companies, producing sports documentaries and releasing some of Japan's best music through W+K Tokyo Lab.

I find most personal thoughts on ad writing complete and utter drivel. I'm talking about my thoughts, not some luminary's. And so my advice to those of more tender years would be precisely the advice I now give myself on this issue: if you can't write something startling don't write anything at all.

Client: Nike
Agency: Wieden+Kennedy
Year: 1994

Next spread
Client: Nike
Agency: Wieden+Kennedy
Year: 1998

Most heroes are anonymous.

Beaverton, Oregon

JUST

DO IT.

About
D&AD

For 56 years D&AD has stimulated, celebrated and enabled creative excellence in design and advertising, in the firm belief that great work always creates better outcomes. As a not-for-profit organisation, D&AD puts all its surpluses back into the creative community, helping new talent prosper and campaigning for a fairer, more diverse, more sustainable industry.

D&AD was founded as British Design & Art Direction in 1962 by a group of London-based designers and art directors including David Bailey, Terence Donovan, Alan Fletcher and Colin Forbes. They were dedicated to celebrating creative communication, rewarding its practitioners, and raising standards across the industry. D&AD continues that tradition through its awards, festival, education and professional development programmes. Today, D&AD Pencils are coveted the world over as the pinnacle of many creative careers.

Over 200 of the industry's most talented individuals meet in London each year to judge the best global work in advertising and design at the D&AD Awards, followed by three days of creative inspiration at D&AD Festival. Entries are judged by nearly 30 specialist juries ranging from Writing for Advertising to Graphic Design, Film Advertising to Experiential and Media to Digital Design.

D&AD has awarded excellence in the craft of copywriting since the late '60s. The first D&AD Black Pencil for copywriting was awarded in 1971 to Charles Saatchi for the long copy ad, 'Why your first cigarette made you feel giddy', for the Health Education Council. In 2009, the second Black Pencil for copywriting was awarded to Dan Sterling and Sarah Silverman for 'The Great Schlep', the viral film for the Jewish Council for Education & Research, viewed by millions in the lead-up to the 2008 US Presidential Election. In 2013, the third Black Pencil for copywriting was awarded to the UK Government Digital Service and HM Government for the Gov.uk website.

The D&AD New Blood Awards, which identify the best new graduating talent each year, have set copywriting briefs with international brands.

Looking ahead, D&AD remains committed to recognising and stimulating brilliant writing across an increasingly diverse range of media available via emerging technologies, not forgetting, of course, the ever-powerful printed word.

Credits

D&AD would like to thank all the copywriters who so generously contributed to this book. We are also indebted to The History of Advertising Trust, for providing access to their remarkable archive of creative work.

Editorial Committee
Alfredo Marcantonio
Tim Riley
Jana Labaki

Commissioning Author
Alastair Crompton

Editorial Manager
Jana Labaki

Design
Paul Belford
Rick Banks

Project Managers
Sue Evans
Natalie Wetherell

Editorial Assistance
Ed Carter
Peter Coles
Beatriz Hernández

TASCHEN
Editor in Charge
Julius Wiedemann

Editorial Coordination,
Design & Layout
Daniel Siciliano Brêtas

Lithography Manager
Stefan Klatte

Proofreading
Chris Allen
John Daniel Bolton

Editors' note

In a book about copy, legibility is key. We've made *The Copy Book* smaller in size, so you can keep it with you to dip into whenever you need inspiration. So that this change in size doesn't affect legibility, every effort has been made to track down the original proofs or high-quality digital versions of contributors' work, and in some cases the orientation of the ads has been changed. However, some of the ads from previous editions would have been reproduced at such a small size that they would not have been legible. We regret that therefore we have had to omit them from this edition.

100 Illustrators

Illustration Now!
Portraits

Illustration Now!
Fashion

100 Manga Artists

Fritz Kahn.
Infographics Pioneer

Logo Design

Logo Design.
Global Brands

Bodoni. Manual of
Typography

The Package Design
Book

D&AD.
The Copy Book

The Golden Age of
DC Comics

Bookworm's delight:
never bore, always excite!

TASCHEN
Bibliotheca Universalis

Tiki Pop

Mid-Century Ads

1000 Tattoos

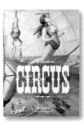

The Circus.
1870s–1950s

Menu Design
in America

1000 Pin-Up Girls

1000 Record Covers

Funk & Soul Covers

Jazz Covers

Extraordinary
Records

Steinweiss

20th Century Fashion

20th Century Travel

20th Century
Classic Cars

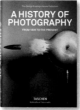
A History of
Photography

20th Century
Photography

100 Interiors Around
the World

Interiors Now!

Burton Holmes.
Travelogues

The Polaroid Book

Photo Icons

Living in Morocco

Living in Bali

Living in Mexico

Living in Provence

Living in Tuscany

The Grand Tour

Case Study Houses

Tree Houses

Scandinavian Design

Industrial Design A–Z

domus 1950s

domus 1960s

Design of the
20th Century

1000 Chairs

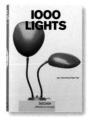
1000 Lights

2194

2195

2196

StickerNation.Net

2198

Swallow

2199

ZWERFVUIL
BLIKSEMSNEL IN DE BAK!

2200

2202

2203

2204

2206

EDITION
52

2207

2208

Sure signs

Diverse logos from around the world

A good logo can glamorize just about anything. Now available in our popular *Bibliotheca Universalis* series, this sweeping compendium gathers diverse brand markers from around the world to explore the irrepressible power of graphic representation. Organized into chapters by theme, the catalog explores how text, image, and ideas distil into a logo across events, fashion, media, music, and retailers. Featuring work from both star names and lesser-known mavericks, this is an excellent reference for students and professionals in design and marketing, as well as for anyone interested in the visuals and philosophy behind brand identity.

"An excellent visual reference..."
— *Curve Magazine*, Sydney

Logo Design
Julius Wiedemann
664 pages
TRILINGUAL EDITION IN:
ENGLISH / DEUTSCH / FRANÇAIS